HowExpert Forensic Psychology

The Ultimate Handbook for Understanding Criminal Behavior, Legal Processes, and Psychological Assessments

HowExpert

For more tips related to this topic, visit HowExpert.com/forensicpsychology.

Recommended Resources

- HowExpert.com – How To Guides on All Topics from A to Z by Everyday Experts.
- HowExpert.com/free – Free HowExpert Email Newsletter.
- HowExpert.com/books – HowExpert Books
- HowExpert.com/courses – HowExpert Courses
- HowExpert.com/clothing – HowExpert Clothing
- HowExpert.com/membership – HowExpert Membership Site
- HowExpert.com/affiliates – HowExpert Affiliate Program
- HowExpert.com/jobs – HowExpert Jobs
- HowExpert.com/writers – Write About Your #1 Passion/Knowledge/Expertise & Become a HowExpert Author.
- HowExpert.com/resources – Additional HowExpert Recommended Resources
- YouTube.com/HowExpert – Subscribe to HowExpert YouTube.
- Instagram.com/HowExpert – Follow HowExpert on Instagram.
- Facebook.com/HowExpert – Follow HowExpert on Facebook.
- TikTok.com/@HowExpert – Follow HowExpert on TikTok.

Publisher's Foreword

Dear HowExpert Reader,

HowExpert publishes quick 'how to' guides on all topics from A to Z by everyday experts.

At HowExpert, our mission is to discover, empower, and maximize everyday people's talents to ultimately make a positive impact in the world for all topics from A to Z…one everyday expert at a time!

HowExpert guides are written by everyday people just like you and me, who have a passion, knowledge, and expertise for a specific topic.

We take great pride in selecting everyday experts who have a passion, real-life experience in a topic, and excellent writing skills to teach you about the topic you are also passionate about and eager to learn.

We hope you get a lot of value from our HowExpert guides, and it can make a positive impact on your life in some way. All of our readers, including you, help us continue living our mission of positively impacting the world for all spheres of influences from A to Z.

If you enjoyed one of our HowExpert guides, then please take a moment to send us your feedback from wherever you got this book.

Thank you, and I wish you all the best in all aspects of life.

To your success,

Byungjoon "BJ" Min   민병준
Founder & Publisher of HowExpert
HowExpert.com

PS…If you are also interested in becoming a HowExpert author, then please visit our website at HowExpert.com/writers. Thank you & again, all the best! John 3:16

Table of Contents

Book Overview

HowExpert Guide to Forensic Psychology: The Ultimate Handbook for Understanding Criminal Behavior, Legal Processes, and Psychological Assessments

If you're eager to unravel the mysteries of the criminal mind and understand how psychology influences the justice system, then "HowExpert Guide to Forensic Psychology" is the essential resource you?ve been searching for. Whether you're an aspiring forensic psychologist, a criminology student, or simply fascinated by the psychological dynamics of crime, this book offers an in-depth and accessible exploration of the mind behind criminal behavior and the vital role psychology plays in law enforcement and the courts.

- Chapter 1: Introduction - Trace the evolution of forensic psychology, from its historical roots to its critical role in today?s legal landscape, setting the stage for your journey into this fascinating field.

- Chapter 2: Theories and Frameworks in Forensic Psychology - Dive into the foundational theories that explain criminal behavior, integrating insights from biology, psychology, and sociology to provide a well-rounded understanding of what drives criminal actions.

- Chapter 3: The Criminal Mind - Explore the psychological profiles of criminals, focusing on complex disorders such as psychopathy and sociopathy, and uncovering the motivations that lead to criminal behavior.

- Chapter 4: Juvenile and Developmental Forensic Psychology - Examine the unique factors that influence juvenile delinquency, including developmental psychology and environmental influences that shape young offenders.

- Chapter 5: Legal Processes and Forensic Psychology - Gain a deep understanding of how forensic psychologists contribute to the criminal justice system, from providing expert testimony to shaping legal outcomes with psychological insights.

- Chapter 6: Psychological Assessments and Legal Implications - Learn the critical techniques of psychological assessments, mastering the skills needed to conduct risk evaluations, competency assessments, and insanity defense evaluations with accuracy and precision.

- Chapter 7: Victimology and Trauma Response - Understand the psychological impact of crime on victims, exploring effective strategies for providing psychological support and addressing trauma.

- Chapter 8: Forensic Psychology in Law Enforcement and Corrections - Discover the vital contributions of forensic psychology to law enforcement, including criminal profiling, interrogation techniques, and the application of psychology in correctional settings.

- Chapter 9: Ethical and Legal Issues in Forensic Psychology - Navigate the complex ethical and legal challenges inherent in forensic psychology, ensuring you adhere to the highest professional standards in practice.

- Chapter 10: Research and Future Trends in Forensic Psychology - Stay at the forefront of the field by exploring cutting-edge research methodologies and emerging trends that are poised to shape the future of forensic psychology.

- Chapter 11: Building a Career in Forensic Psychology - Get practical advice on how to build a successful career in forensic psychology, from educational pathways to specialization opportunities and real-world career tips.

- Chapter 12: Case Studies and Real-World Applications - Apply your knowledge to real-life scenarios with detailed case studies that showcase the practical applications of forensic psychology in high-profile cases.

- Chapter 13: Conclusion - Reflect on the essential insights gained throughout the book and prepare for the challenges and opportunities that await you in the dynamic field of forensic psychology.

Packed with interactive exercises, in-depth case studies, and expert guidance, "HowExpert Guide to Forensic Psychology" goes beyond traditional textbooks. It?s your comprehensive toolkit for mastering the ever-evolving field of forensic psychology. Whether you're starting your journey or advancing your expertise, this guide equips you with the knowledge, skills, and confidence to excel.

HowExpert publishes how to guides on all topics from A to Z. Visit HowExpert.com to learn more.

Chapter 1: Introduction

Forensic psychology is a dynamic and multifaceted field that lies at the intersection of psychology and the legal system. As we embark on this journey through the world of forensic psychology, this chapter sets the stage by providing a comprehensive overview of the field's core concepts, historical development, and the critical roles played by forensic psychologists. Whether you're an aspiring forensic psychologist, a student, or simply curious about the psychological aspects of crime and justice, this chapter will equip you with the foundational knowledge needed to delve deeper into the complexities of forensic psychology.

1.1 What is Forensic Psychology?

Forensic psychology is a complex and multifaceted field that merges the principles of psychology with the intricacies of the legal system. It acts as a bridge between understanding human behavior and applying this knowledge in legal contexts. This section explores the fundamental aspects of forensic psychology, focusing on its definition, scope, roles, and the significant impact it has on both individuals and society.

1. Definition and Scope of Forensic Psychology

A. Defining Forensic Psychology

- Application to Legal System: Forensic psychology is broadly defined as the application of psychological theories, methods, and practices within the legal system. It involves using psychological expertise to assist in understanding legal issues, particularly the behavior of individuals in legal contexts.

- Range of Activities: The field encompasses a wide variety of activities, including assessing individuals involved in legal proceedings and applying psychological research to inform legal policies and practices.

B. Scope of Forensic Psychology

- Criminal and Civil Law: The scope of forensic psychology is vast, covering both criminal and civil law. In criminal law, forensic psychologists may evaluate defendants' mental states to determine competency to stand trial, provide expert testimony, or develop criminal profiles for investigations. In civil law, they may work on cases involving child custody disputes, personal injury claims, or workplace discrimination, assessing the psychological impact on individuals and informing legal decisions.

- Correctional Psychology: The field extends into correctional psychology, where psychologists work in prisons and rehabilitation centers to assess and treat inmates, develop rehabilitation programs, and evaluate the risk of reoffending.

2. Roles of Forensic Psychologists

A. Expert Witness and Legal Consultant

- Courtroom Testimony: One of the most visible roles of forensic psychologists is serving as expert witnesses in court, providing testimony on psychological issues such as a defendant's mental state, future dangerousness, or witness credibility.

- Legal Consultation: As legal consultants, forensic psychologists advise attorneys on the psychological aspects of their cases, helping to shape legal strategies and prepare witnesses for testimony, thus influencing both criminal and civil case outcomes.

B. Psychological Assessment and Evaluation

- Competency and Insanity Assessments: Forensic psychologists conduct assessments that include evaluating competency to stand trial, insanity defenses, and the potential risk of reoffending. These assessments are comprehensive, involving interviews, psychological testing, and review of relevant records, and require a deep understanding of both clinical and legal standards.

- Impact Evaluations: They also assess the psychological impact of traumatic events, providing courts with essential information for sentencing and rehabilitation decisions.

C. Research and Policy Development

- Influencing Legal Policy: Forensic psychologists contribute to the development of research and policy within the legal system. They conduct studies that explore the relationship between psychology and law, such as examining jury decision-making or the effectiveness of rehabilitation programs.

- Developing Best Practices: Their research informs the development of policies and practices within the legal system, contributing to more effective and humane approaches to justice, such as reforms in police lineups to reduce wrongful convictions.

3. *Impact of Forensic Psychology on Society*

A. Advancing Legal Understanding

- Integration of Psychology in Law: Forensic psychology plays a critical role in advancing the legal system's understanding of human behavior by integrating psychological knowledge into legal processes. This integration leads to more informed legal decisions and promotes justice that considers mental health and behavior.

- Therapeutic Jurisprudence: The field contributes to therapeutic jurisprudence, an approach that emphasizes rehabilitation over punishment, reflecting a more compassionate and effective legal system.

B. Protecting the Rights of Individuals

- Advocacy for Vulnerable Populations: Forensic psychologists play a vital role in protecting individuals' rights within the legal system, especially for vulnerable populations such as those with mental illnesses, children, or victims of trauma. Their work ensures that justice is served fairly and equitably.

- Ethical Legal Practices: By providing insights into mental health and behavior, forensic psychologists help ensure that legal processes uphold ethical standards, respecting the rights and dignity of all individuals involved.

C. Ethical Challenges and Responsibilities

- Navigating Ethical Dilemmas: Forensic psychologists face significant ethical challenges, such as maintaining objectivity, ensuring confidentiality, and balancing legal demands with psychological ethics. These challenges require a strong commitment to professional integrity.

- Maintaining Field Credibility: Their ability to navigate ethical issues effectively is crucial to maintaining the credibility and trustworthiness of the field, ensuring that forensic psychology continues to contribute positively to the legal system.

Forensic psychology is a field that intertwines the complexities of human behavior with the demands of the legal system. This section has outlined the essential aspects of the field, highlighting the roles forensic psychologists play in shaping legal decisions and protecting individual rights. As you progress through this book, you'll explore the specialized applications of forensic psychology, building on the foundational knowledge presented here.

1.2 History and Evolution of Forensic Psychology

The history and evolution of forensic psychology provide a fascinating exploration of how psychological science has progressively intertwined with the legal system. This section delves into the origins, significant milestones, and modern advancements that have shaped forensic psychology into the critical discipline it is today.

1. The Foundations of Forensic Psychology

A. The Birth of Experimental Psychology and Its Legal Implications

- Emergence of Experimental Psychology: The late 19th century marked the beginning of psychology as a formal scientific discipline, with pioneers like Wilhelm Wundt establishing the first psychology laboratory in 1879. This era focused on understanding human perception, cognition, and behavior through rigorous experimentation.

- Early Legal Applications: Early applications of psychology to legal matters were seen in the work of James McKeen Cattell, who conducted experiments on eyewitness accuracy. His findings revealed significant inaccuracies in eyewitness testimony, challenging the reliability of this form of evidence, which was heavily relied upon in legal proceedings.

B. Hugo Münsterberg and the Formalization of Forensic Psychology

- Introduction to Legal Arenas: Hugo Münsterberg, often regarded as the father of forensic psychology, was instrumental in introducing psychological concepts into the legal arena. His seminal work, "On the Witness Stand" (1908), emphasized the importance of psychological expertise in assessing the reliability of witness testimony, detecting deception, and understanding the psychological underpinnings of criminal behavior.

- Controversial Impact: Münsterberg's advocacy for the application of psychology in legal contexts was met with both support and controversy. His work sparked debates on the credibility of psychological insights in legal settings, laying the groundwork for the formal recognition of forensic psychology as a distinct field.

C. Early Ethical Debates and Challenges

- Ethical Challenges: The initial integration of psychology into the legal system brought about significant ethical challenges. Early forensic psychologists grappled with maintaining objectivity in a field that often demanded adversarial positions.

- Need for Ethical Standards: The need for ethical standards became apparent as psychologists navigated issues such as confidentiality, the potential for bias, and the ethical implications of their testimony in court.

2. The Expansion of Forensic Psychology in the 20th Century

A. The Influence of Legal Realism and Behavioral Sciences

- Rise of Legal Realism: The early to mid-20th century saw the rise of legal realism, a movement that emphasized the importance of understanding the law as a social process. This perspective aligned well with the goals of forensic psychology, which sought to apply behavioral science to legal problems.

- Public Attention through Landmark Cases: Landmark cases, such as the Leopold and Loeb trial in 1924, brought forensic psychology to public attention. Psychological analysis of the defendants' mental states played a crucial role in shaping legal strategies and outcomes, influencing public perceptions of criminal responsibility.

B. Development of Psychological Assessment Tools

- Introduction of Standardized Tools: The mid-20th century witnessed the development of standardized psychological assessment tools, such as the Minnesota Multiphasic Personality Inventory (MMPI), which became essential in evaluating defendants' mental states. These tools provided a more scientific basis for assessments related to competency, insanity defenses, and risk of reoffending.

- Specialization and Formalization: As the field matured, forensic psychologists began to specialize in the creation and validation of these tools, ensuring they met both psychological and legal standards. This period also saw the establishment of forensic psychology as a recognized specialty within psychology, with formal training programs and certifications emerging.

C. The Role of Forensic Psychology in Shaping Legal Precedents

- Influence on Legal Cases: Forensic psychologists played a critical role in several landmark legal cases that set important precedents for the field. One such case was Jenkins v. United States (1962), where the court ruled that psychologists could serve as expert witnesses in legal cases. This decision significantly expanded the role of psychologists in the courtroom, allowing their expertise to influence a wide range of legal issues.

- Increased Demand and Influence: The growing influence of forensic psychology in the legal system led to an increased demand for psychological evaluations and testimony in criminal and civil cases, cementing the field's importance in modern jurisprudence.

3. Modern Forensic Psychology

A. Integration with the Legal System

- Full Integration into Legal Processes: Today, forensic psychology is fully integrated into the legal system, with forensic psychologists contributing to criminal investigations, court proceedings, and correctional programs. Their work spans from providing expert testimony in high-profile cases to conducting risk assessments for parole boards.

- Advancements in Research and Technology: The field continues to evolve with advancements in research and technology, which enhance the accuracy and effectiveness of psychological assessments used in legal contexts. These developments have solidified the role of forensic psychologists as essential contributors to the pursuit of justice.

B. Global Perspectives and Cultural Considerations

- International Expansion: Forensic psychology has expanded internationally, with different countries adopting unique approaches to integrating psychological expertise into their legal systems. Comparative studies reveal how cultural norms, legal traditions, and societal values shape the practice of forensic psychology around the world.

- Navigating Multicultural Environments: Understanding these global perspectives is crucial for forensic psychologists working in multicultural environments, where they must navigate diverse legal systems and cultural expectations.

C. Ethical and Professional Standards in Modern Practice

- Heightened Ethical Responsibilities: The rapid growth of forensic psychology has brought with it heightened ethical responsibilities. Modern forensic psychologists must adhere to stringent ethical guidelines, balancing the demands of the legal system with the ethical obligations of their profession.

- Maintaining Credibility and Integrity: Issues such as maintaining objectivity, avoiding conflicts of interest, and ensuring the confidentiality of sensitive information are paramount. These ethical considerations are central to the credibility and integrity of forensic psychology as a discipline.

Forensic psychology has undergone a remarkable evolution, from its early roots in experimental psychology to its current status as a vital component of the legal system. The field's growth has been shaped by significant legal cases, advancements in psychological assessment, and ongoing ethical challenges. Understanding this history is essential for appreciating the complexities of modern forensic psychology and the critical role it plays in advancing justice. As we move forward in this book, we will build on this historical foundation to explore the specialized applications and emerging trends within forensic psychology.

1.3 The Role of Forensic Psychologists

Forensic psychologists play a critical role at the intersection of psychology and law, where their expertise influences a wide range of legal outcomes. Their responsibilities are diverse, extending beyond the courtroom and into various areas of the criminal justice system. This section explores the key roles that forensic psychologists fulfill, the specialized skills required for these roles, and the significant impact they have on both individuals and the legal process as a whole.

1. Expert Witness and Legal Consultant

A. Expert Testimony in Court

- Primary Role in Legal Proceedings: One of the primary roles of forensic psychologists is serving as expert witnesses in legal proceedings. They provide scientifically grounded insights into psychological issues central to legal cases, including assessments of a defendant's mental state at the time of the crime, evaluations of competency to stand trial, and risk assessments regarding future dangerousness.

- Impact on Court Decisions: The testimony of forensic psychologists often holds considerable weight in court, helping judges and juries understand complex psychological concepts. Their input can be decisive in cases involving the insanity defense, child custody disputes, or the credibility of witness testimony.

B. Consultation with Legal Teams

- Shaping Case Strategies: Forensic psychologists frequently serve as consultants to legal teams, providing expertise to help shape case strategies. They assist attorneys in understanding the psychological elements of a case, such as the motivations of a defendant or the psychological impact of a crime on a victim.

- Jury Selection and Witness Preparation: In this role, forensic psychologists might also participate in jury selection, advising on psychological profiles that could favor or hinder a case. Their consultation can extend to preparing witnesses, ensuring they are mentally ready for the rigors of cross-examination.

2. Psychological Assessment and Evaluation

A. Competency and Insanity Evaluations

- Determining Competency: A significant part of a forensic psychologist's role involves conducting psychological assessments to determine a defendant's competency to stand trial. These evaluations are critical for ensuring that defendants understand the charges against them and can participate meaningfully in their defense.

- Evaluating Insanity Claims: Forensic psychologists are tasked with evaluating claims of insanity, assessing whether a defendant could understand the nature of their actions or distinguish right from wrong at the time of the offense. These evaluations require a deep understanding of both psychological disorders and legal standards.

B. Risk Assessments and Sentencing Recommendations

- Assessing Reoffending Risk: Forensic psychologists conduct risk assessments to determine the likelihood of a defendant reoffending. These assessments are used by courts to inform sentencing decisions, parole hearings, and decisions about the placement of individuals in correctional facilities.

- Influence on Sentencing: The recommendations provided by forensic psychologists can influence whether an individual is sentenced to incarceration, mandated to receive psychological treatment, or placed under probation. Their assessments help balance the need for public safety with the potential for rehabilitation.

C. Evaluations in Civil Cases

- Assessing Psychological Damages: In civil law, forensic psychologists are often called upon to evaluate psychological damages in cases involving personal injury, workplace harassment, or medical malpractice. These assessments help courts determine the extent of emotional or psychological harm, influencing compensation awards.

- Child Custody Evaluations: Forensic psychologists may also be involved in child custody evaluations, where they assess the mental health of parents and the best interests of the child. Their evaluations are critical in guiding court decisions that affect the welfare of children in custody disputes.

3. Research, Education, and Policy Development

A. Conducting Research to Inform Legal Practices

- Research on Legal Issues: Forensic psychologists are deeply involved in research that informs legal practices. Their studies may focus on topics such as the reliability of eyewitness testimony, the effectiveness of different interrogation techniques, or the psychological impact of incarceration.

- Practical Implications: This research not only advances the field of forensic psychology but also has practical implications for improving legal processes and outcomes. For example, research on cognitive biases in juries can lead to reforms in how jury instructions are given or how evidence is presented in court.

B. Teaching and Training Future Forensic Psychologists

- Academic Roles: Many forensic psychologists work in academic settings, where they teach and train the next generation of professionals. They provide specialized education on the intersection of psychology and law, covering topics such as criminal behavior, legal standards for mental health evaluations, and ethical issues in forensic practice.

- Preparation for Complexities of the Field: These educational roles are essential for ensuring that future forensic psychologists are well-prepared to navigate the complexities of the legal system and make meaningful contributions to the field.

C. Influencing Policy and Legal Reform

- Policy Development: Forensic psychologists often contribute to the development of policies that impact the legal system. Their expertise is sought in areas such as criminal justice reform, mental health law, and correctional practices.

- Shaping Laws and Regulations: By participating in policy discussions and advisory committees, forensic psychologists help shape laws and regulations that are informed by psychological science, ensuring that legal practices are both effective and humane.

Forensic psychologists are indispensable to the legal system, where their expertise informs critical decisions and shapes the administration of justice. From providing expert testimony in court to conducting comprehensive psychological evaluations, their work has far-reaching implications for individuals and society. As we continue to explore the field of forensic psychology, it becomes clear that these professionals not only advance our understanding of human behavior but also contribute to a legal system that is more just, informed, and equitable.

1.4 Self-Reflection on Interest in Forensic Psychology

Forensic psychology is a field that captivates many due to its unique blend of psychological expertise and legal application. As you explore this discipline, it's important to engage in self-reflection to better understand your interest in forensic psychology and what draws you to this challenging and impactful field. This section will guide you through a reflective process, helping you assess your motivations, skills, and aspirations within the context of forensic psychology.

1. Understanding Your Motivations

A. Identifying the Roots of Your Interest

- Initial Spark of Interest: Begin by considering what initially sparked your interest in forensic psychology. Was it a fascination with criminal behavior, a desire to understand the psychological factors that influence legal outcomes, or perhaps an interest in the ethical complexities of the field?

- Influence of Experiences: Reflect on any experiences, such as coursework, media, or personal encounters, that may have shaped your desire to pursue forensic psychology. Understanding the origins of your interest can provide insight into what aspects of the field resonate most with you.

B. Evaluating Your Passion for the Field

- Commitment to the Profession: Forensic psychology is a demanding profession that requires a deep commitment to both psychology and the legal system. Reflect on how passionate you feel about the work forensic psychologists do. Are you driven by a desire to contribute to justice, support vulnerable populations, or advance psychological research within legal contexts?

- Alignment with Field Realities: Consider how your passion aligns with the realities of the field. Forensic psychologists often work in high-stakes environments, where their assessments and testimony can have significant legal consequences. It's important to assess whether you feel energized by these challenges or if they might lead to stress or burnout.

2. Assessing Your Skills and Aptitudes

A. Analytical and Critical Thinking Skills

- Complex Analysis and Evaluation: Forensic psychology requires strong analytical and critical thinking skills. Reflect on your ability to analyze complex information, evaluate evidence, and draw conclusions based on psychological principles. Are you comfortable with the level of scrutiny and precision required in forensic assessments?

- Research and Data Analysis: Consider your aptitude for research and data analysis, as these are key components of forensic psychology. Being able to critically evaluate research findings and apply them to real-world legal situations is essential in this field.

B. Communication and Interpersonal Skills

- Effective Communication: Effective communication is vital for forensic psychologists, especially when presenting findings in court or consulting with legal professionals. Reflect on your ability to communicate complex psychological concepts clearly and persuasively, both in writing and verbally.

- Interpersonal Relationships: Interpersonal skills are equally important, as forensic psychologists often work with individuals who are in distress or involved in adversarial legal situations. Consider your ability to build rapport, maintain objectivity, and navigate sensitive topics with empathy and professionalism.

C. Ethical Judgment and Integrity

- Ethical Decision-Making: Forensic psychology demands a high level of ethical judgment and integrity. Reflect on your comfort level with making ethical decisions, especially in situations where legal and psychological considerations may conflict.

- Responsibility in Testimony: Consider how you would handle the responsibility of providing testimony that could significantly impact someone's life. Are you prepared to maintain objectivity and uphold ethical standards, even in the face of external pressures?

3. Exploring Career Goals and Aspirations

A. Defining Your Career Path in Forensic Psychology

- Career Objectives: Reflect on what you hope to achieve in your career as a forensic psychologist. Are you interested in working directly with legal cases as an expert witness, focusing on research and policy development, or perhaps teaching and training future forensic psychologists?

- Preferred Work Environments: Consider the settings in which you see yourself working. Forensic psychologists can be found in a variety of environments, including courts, prisons, academic institutions, and private practice. Reflect on which of these settings aligns best with your career aspirations and personal values.

B. Long-Term Impact and Contribution

- Desire for Long-Term Impact: Think about the long-term impact you wish to have in the field of forensic psychology. Are you driven by a desire to contribute to legal reforms, improve the accuracy of psychological assessments, or advocate for mental health awareness within the legal system?

- Legacy in the Field: Reflect on how you can use your skills and interests to make a meaningful contribution to the field. Whether through advancing research, shaping policy, or directly influencing legal outcomes, consider the legacy you want to leave as a forensic psychologist.

4. Preparing for the Journey Ahead

A. Continuing Education and Skill Development

- Commitment to Lifelong Learning: Forensic psychology is a dynamic and evolving field that requires ongoing education and skill development. Reflect on your willingness to engage in continuous learning, whether through advanced degrees, certifications, or professional development opportunities.

- Identifying Skill Gaps: Consider the areas where you might need to strengthen your skills, such as in legal knowledge, psychological assessment techniques, or ethical decision-making. Developing a plan for your education and professional growth will help you prepare for the challenges and opportunities in forensic psychology.

B. Building a Support Network

- Importance of Support Networks: A career in forensic psychology can be demanding, and having a strong support network is crucial. Reflect on the people in your life who can provide support, whether they are mentors, colleagues, or loved ones who understand the unique challenges of the field.

- Seeking Professional Connections: Consider how you will seek out professional connections and mentors who can guide you as you navigate your career. Building relationships within the forensic psychology community can provide valuable insights, opportunities, and support throughout your career.

Self-reflection is a critical component of your journey into forensic psychology. By taking the time to assess your motivations, skills, and aspirations, you can ensure that your path in this field is aligned with your passions and strengths. This reflection will not only prepare you for the challenges ahead but also help you make informed decisions that lead to a fulfilling and impactful career in forensic psychology. As you continue through this book, use the insights gained from this self-reflection to guide your exploration of the field and your professional development.

Chapter 1 Review

Chapter 1 introduced the foundational aspects of forensic psychology, providing a comprehensive overview of what the field entails, its historical evolution, the roles of forensic psychologists, and the importance of self-reflection for those considering a career in this specialized area. Below is a summary of the key points covered in this chapter.

1.1 What is Forensic Psychology?

- Definition and Scope: Forensic psychology was defined as the application of psychological principles and methods to the legal system. The scope of the field is broad, encompassing both criminal and civil law, as well as areas such as correctional psychology and policy development.

- Roles and Responsibilities: Forensic psychologists are involved in a wide range of activities, including providing expert testimony, conducting psychological assessments, and consulting with legal professionals. Their work is crucial in informing legal decisions and ensuring that psychological insights are integrated into the legal process.

1.2 History and Evolution of Forensic Psychology

- Foundational Beginnings: The chapter traced the origins of forensic psychology back to the late 19th century, highlighting the contributions of early pioneers like Wilhelm Wundt and Hugo Münsterberg. These early developments laid the groundwork for the integration of psychological expertise into legal contexts.

- 20th Century Expansion: The field expanded significantly during the 20th century, with the development of standardized psychological assessment tools and the increasing recognition of psychologists as expert witnesses in legal cases. Key legal precedents and ethical challenges were also explored, emphasizing the growing importance of forensic psychology in modern legal systems.

1.3 The Role of Forensic Psychologists

- Expert Witness and Legal Consultant: Forensic psychologists play a vital role as expert witnesses, providing testimony on psychological matters that are central to legal cases. They also serve as consultants to legal teams, offering insights that shape case strategies and influence outcomes.

- Psychological Assessment and Evaluation: The chapter detailed the various assessments conducted by forensic psychologists, including competency evaluations, risk assessments, and evaluations in civil cases. These assessments are crucial in guiding legal decisions and ensuring that psychological considerations are properly addressed.

- Research, Education, and Policy Development: Forensic psychologists contribute to the field through research, teaching, and policy development. Their research informs legal practices, while their teaching ensures that future professionals are well-prepared. They also play a role in shaping policies that impact the legal system.

1.4 Self-Reflection on Interest in Forensic Psychology

- Understanding Motivations: The importance of self-reflection was emphasized, encouraging readers to consider their motivations for pursuing a career in forensic psychology. This section explored how personal experiences and interests might align with the demands of the field.

- Assessing Skills and Aptitudes: Readers were guided to evaluate their own skills, including analytical thinking, communication, and ethical judgment, all of which are crucial for success in forensic psychology.

- Exploring Career Goals: The chapter encouraged readers to think about their long-term career goals and the impact they wish to have in the field. Whether interested in direct casework, research, or policy, understanding one's aspirations is key to a fulfilling career.

- Preparation and Support: The chapter concluded with advice on continuing education, skill development, and the importance of building a support network to navigate the challenges of a career in forensic psychology.

Chapter 1 provided a detailed introduction to forensic psychology, laying the groundwork for deeper exploration in subsequent chapters. By understanding the history, roles, and responsibilities of forensic psychologists, and engaging in self-reflection, readers are well-equipped to dive into the more specialized areas of the field that will be covered in the rest of the book.

Chapter 2: Theories and Frameworks in Forensic Psychology

Understanding the theories and frameworks that underpin forensic psychology is essential for grasping the complexities of criminal behavior. This chapter delves into the biological, psychological, social, and environmental factors that contribute to criminal behavior, exploring how these elements interact to shape individual actions. It also examines integrated frameworks that bring these theories together, providing a comprehensive approach to understanding crime. The chapter concludes with a case study that applies multiple theories to a real-world scenario and a self-assessment quiz to reinforce key concepts.

2.1 Biological and Psychological Theories of Criminal Behavior

Understanding the roots of criminal behavior requires a deep dive into both biological and psychological perspectives. These theories provide critical insights into how innate factors, mental processes, and individual characteristics contribute to criminal behavior. This section explores the key biological and psychological theories that have shaped our understanding of why individuals commit crimes.

1. Biological Theories of Criminal Behavior

A. Genetic Influences on Criminal Behavior

- Role of Genetics: Biological theories often begin with the premise that genetic factors play a significant role in predisposing individuals to criminal behavior. Research in behavioral genetics has identified certain genes associated with aggressive and antisocial behavior, such as the MAOA gene, sometimes referred to as the "warrior gene," which is linked to an increased likelihood of violent behavior.

- Evidence from Twin and Adoption Studies: Twin and adoption studies provide further evidence for the genetic basis of criminal behavior. These studies compare the similarities in criminal behavior between individuals with varying degrees of genetic relatedness, such as identical versus fraternal twins or biological versus adopted children, suggesting that genetics can account for a portion of the variance in criminal behavior.

B. Neurological and Brain Structure Abnormalities

- Impact of Brain Abnormalities: Neurological research has shown that certain brain abnormalities are associated with criminal behavior. Impairments in the prefrontal cortex, responsible for decision-making, impulse control, and social behavior, have been linked to increased aggression and antisocial behavior, potentially leading to a higher risk of criminal activity.

- Role of the Amygdala: The amygdala, involved in emotional processing, has also been implicated in criminal behavior. Abnormalities in the amygdala can result in difficulties processing emotions such as fear and empathy, making individuals less responsive to the emotional consequences of their actions and more likely to engage in criminal acts.

C. Biochemical Factors and Neurotransmitter Imbalances

- Influence of Neurotransmitters: Biochemical factors, including imbalances in neurotransmitters such as serotonin, dopamine, and norepinephrine, have been studied in relation to criminal behavior. For example, low levels of serotonin are associated with impulsivity and aggression, both risk factors for criminal behavior.

- Hormonal Influences: Hormonal influences, particularly testosterone, have been linked to criminal behavior. Higher levels of testosterone are associated with increased aggression and a propensity for violent behavior, suggesting a hormonal role in predisposing individuals to certain types of crime.

2. Psychological Theories of Criminal Behavior

A. Psychoanalytic Theories

- Unresolved Internal Conflicts: Psychoanalytic theories, originating from Sigmund Freud, suggest that criminal behavior can be understood as an expression of unresolved internal conflicts, often rooted in childhood experiences. For example, unresolved Oedipal conflicts or an overactive id may lead to impulsive, criminal behavior as individuals seek to satisfy unconscious desires.

- Role of the Unconscious Mind: These theories emphasize the influence of the unconscious mind in behavior. Criminal acts may manifest as repressed emotions or desires that surface destructively, with defense mechanisms like projection or displacement playing a role in how individuals justify or rationalize their actions.

B. Behavioral and Social Learning Theories

- Behavior as a Learned Response: Behavioral theories, rooted in the work of B.F. Skinner, suggest that criminal behavior is learned through interactions with the environment. Behaviors reinforced through rewards or the avoidance of punishment are more likely to be repeated, implying that criminal behavior is a learned response rather than an innate predisposition.

- Role of Observation and Imitation: Social learning theory, developed by Albert Bandura, expands on behavioral theories by emphasizing the role of observation and imitation in learning criminal behavior. Bandura's Bobo doll experiment demonstrated that individuals, particularly children, are likely to imitate aggressive behavior modeled by others, suggesting that criminal behavior can be learned by observing others, especially if such behavior appears rewarded or goes unpunished.

C. Cognitive Theories

- Distorted Thinking Patterns: Cognitive theories focus on the thought processes underlying criminal behavior, suggesting that individuals who engage in criminal acts often exhibit distorted thinking patterns, such as justifying their actions, minimizing harm, or blaming others. These cognitive distortions allow individuals to engage in criminal acts without significant guilt or remorse.

- Cognitive-Behavioral Interventions: Cognitive-behavioral approaches aim to address these distorted thinking patterns by reshaping the cognitive processes that contribute to criminal behavior. Through cognitive-behavioral therapy (CBT), individuals are encouraged to recognize and challenge justifications for illegal actions, reducing the likelihood of reoffending.

3. The Interaction Between Biological and Psychological Factors

A. The Biopsychosocial Model

- Integration of Multiple Factors: The biopsychosocial model integrates biological, psychological, and social factors to provide a comprehensive understanding of criminal behavior. This model recognizes that while biological predispositions may exist, they interact with psychological traits and environmental influences to shape behavior. For example, an individual with a genetic predisposition to aggression may only exhibit criminal behavior if they also experience adverse environmental conditions or psychological stressors.

- Complexity of Criminal Behavior: This model emphasizes the complexity of criminal behavior, suggesting that no single factor is sufficient to explain why an individual commits a crime. Instead, it is the interaction between multiple factors that creates the conditions for criminal behavior to occur.

B. Case Examples and Research Findings

- Research on Interacting Factors: Research supports the interaction between biological and psychological factors in predicting criminal behavior. For instance, studies have shown that individuals with both a genetic predisposition to aggression and a history of childhood trauma are at a higher risk of engaging in violent crime than those with only one of these risk factors.

- Importance of Multidisciplinary Approaches: Case examples, such as individuals with a history of traumatic brain injury who later engage in criminal acts, highlight how biological impairments can interact with psychological and social factors to influence behavior. These cases illustrate the need for a multidisciplinary approach in forensic psychology, considering both biological and psychological assessments to understand and address criminal behavior.

Understanding the biological and psychological theories of criminal behavior provides a foundation for analyzing why individuals commit crimes. These theories offer insights into the complex interplay of genetics, brain function, mental processes, and environmental influences that contribute to criminal actions. As we continue to explore the various frameworks within forensic psychology, it becomes clear that a multifaceted approach is essential for a comprehensive understanding of criminal behavior.

2.2 Social and Environmental Influences on Crime

Crime is not only the result of individual psychological or biological factors but is also deeply influenced by the social and environmental contexts in which individuals live. This section examines the sociological and environmental theories that explain how external factors such as social structures, cultural norms, and physical environments contribute to criminal behavior.

1. Sociological Theories of Crime

A. Strain Theory

- Disconnect Between Goals and Means: Strain theory, developed by Robert K. Merton, posits that crime arises when individuals experience a disconnect between societal goals and the means available to achieve them. In societies where wealth, success, and social status are highly valued, individuals who lack the legitimate means to achieve these goals may turn to crime as an alternative. This strain between aspirations and reality creates pressure that can lead to deviant behavior.

- Modes of Adaptation: Merton identified five modes of adaptation to strain: conformity, innovation, ritualism, retreatism, and rebellion. "Innovation" is most commonly associated with criminal behavior, as it involves using illegitimate means, such as theft or fraud, to achieve societal goals.

B. Social Disorganization Theory

- Impact of Social Instability: Social disorganization theory, first articulated by Shaw and McKay, suggests that crime is more likely to occur in communities experiencing social instability, such as high rates of poverty, residential mobility, and ethnic diversity. These conditions weaken the social fabric of a community, reducing the ability of residents to exert informal social control and maintain order.

- Collective Efficacy: The theory emphasizes the importance of community structures and relationships in preventing crime. In socially disorganized neighborhoods, residents may have less collective efficacy—the shared belief in a community's ability to maintain order and achieve common goals—which leads to higher crime rates. This theory is often used to explain why crime rates are higher in urban areas with concentrated poverty.

C. Differential Association Theory

- Learning Through Social Interactions: Differential association theory, proposed by Edwin H. Sutherland, argues that criminal behavior is learned through interactions with others. Individuals are more likely to engage in criminal behavior if they associate with others who condone or participate in crime. The theory suggests that criminal behavior is not inherent but is learned through communication and socialization.

- Principles of Learning Criminal Behavior: Sutherland identified nine key principles of differential association, including the idea that criminal behavior is learned in interaction with others and that the learning process involves techniques of committing crimes as well as the motivations and rationalizations for such behavior. The frequency, duration, intensity, and priority of associations with others who engage in criminal behavior are critical factors in determining whether an individual will adopt similar behaviors.

2. Environmental Influences on Crime

A. Environmental Criminology

- Crime and the Physical Environment: Environmental criminology focuses on the relationship between crime and the physical environment. It examines how the spatial and temporal distribution of crime is influenced by factors such as the design of urban spaces, the availability of targets, and the presence or absence of guardians. This field of study highlights the importance of "crime opportunities"—situations where potential offenders find it easier to commit crimes due to environmental factors.

- Crime Pattern Theory: The theory of "crime pattern theory" suggests that criminals follow predictable patterns in their movements and that crimes often occur in places that are familiar to the offender. This has led to the development of crime prevention strategies that focus on altering the environment to reduce opportunities for crime, such as improving street lighting, increasing surveillance, and designing public spaces to be more defensible.

B. Routine Activities Theory

- Convergence of Key Elements: Routine activities theory, developed by Lawrence Cohen and Marcus Felson, posits that crime occurs when three elements converge: a motivated offender, a suitable target, and the absence of a capable guardian. Changes in daily routines and social patterns can influence crime rates by affecting the availability of targets and the presence of guardians.

- Examples of Routine Activities: For example, increases in the number of women working outside the home in the latter half of the 20th century led to more homes being left unoccupied during the day, providing more opportunities for burglary. Similarly, the proliferation of portable electronics has created more "suitable targets" for theft. Routine activities theory emphasizes that crime can be prevented by altering routine activities to reduce opportunities for crime, such as by increasing guardianship through neighborhood watch programs or the use of security systems.

C. Broken Windows Theory

- Signs of Disorder Leading to Crime: Broken windows theory, proposed by James Q. Wilson and George Kelling, suggests that visible signs of disorder and neglect, such as broken windows, graffiti, and litter, can lead to an increase in crime. The theory posits that these signs of disorder signal to potential offenders that the area is poorly monitored and that deviant behavior is tolerated, leading to more serious crimes.

- Influence on Law Enforcement: This theory has been influential in shaping law enforcement strategies, particularly in urban areas. Policies such as "zero tolerance" policing, where even minor offenses are strictly enforced, are based on the idea that maintaining order and addressing minor signs of disorder can prevent more serious crimes from occurring. However, broken windows theory has also been criticized for contributing to aggressive policing tactics that disproportionately affect marginalized communities.

3. The Role of Socialization and Culture

A. Social Learning Theory

- Learning by Observation and Imitation: Social learning theory, developed by Albert Bandura, emphasizes the role of observation and imitation in the learning of criminal behavior. Individuals learn to engage in criminal behavior by observing others, particularly those they admire or perceive as successful. This learning process is reinforced by the rewards or lack of punishment associated with criminal behavior.

- Influence of Media: Bandura's theory also highlights the role of media in shaping behavior. Exposure to violent or criminal behavior in media, such as television, movies, or video games, can desensitize individuals to violence and increase the likelihood of imitation, particularly if the behavior is portrayed as glamorous or without consequence.

B. The Influence of Subcultures

- Adopting Subcultural Norms: Subcultural theories suggest that crime can result from individuals adopting the values and norms of a particular subculture that condones or encourages criminal behavior. These subcultures often emerge in response to social strain or marginalization, offering alternative ways to achieve success or gain status when mainstream avenues are blocked.

- Example of Gang Culture: For example, in some gang cultures, criminal behavior such as violence, drug dealing, or theft is not only accepted but is also a means of gaining respect and power. Members of these subcultures may reject mainstream societal values and instead adhere to a different set of rules and expectations that justify or even glorify criminal behavior.

C. Cultural Transmission of Crime

- Passing Down Criminal Behaviors: Cultural transmission theory posits that criminal behavior is passed down from one generation to the next within a particular community or group. This transmission occurs through socialization processes, where children learn criminal behaviors, values, and techniques from older individuals in their community, often within the family or peer group.

- Breaking the Cycle: This theory emphasizes the importance of intergenerational influences on crime, suggesting that efforts to reduce crime must address the cultural and social contexts that perpetuate criminal behavior across generations. Interventions might include community-based programs that focus on breaking the cycle of crime by providing positive role models and opportunities for youth in high-crime areas.

4. Integrating Social and Environmental Theories

A. The Interaction of Social and Environmental Factors

- Combined Influence on Crime: Social and environmental factors do not operate in isolation; rather, they interact to create conditions that are conducive to crime. For example, a socially disorganized neighborhood (social factor) might also have poorly designed public spaces that lack natural surveillance (environmental factor), leading to higher crime rates.

- Comprehensive Understanding of Crime: Integrating social and environmental theories provides a more comprehensive understanding of criminal behavior. By considering how social structures and environmental conditions influence each other, forensic psychologists can better assess the root causes of crime and develop more effective prevention strategies.

B. Case Studies and Applications

- Illustrative Case Studies: Case studies that examine specific neighborhoods or communities can illustrate how social and environmental factors combine to influence crime rates. For example, research on urban areas with high crime rates often reveals a combination of social disorganization, lack of economic opportunities, and environmental factors such as poorly lit streets and abandoned buildings.

- Crime Prevention Programs: Applications of these integrated theories are seen in crime prevention programs that address both social and environmental factors, such as community policing initiatives that aim to strengthen community ties while also improving the physical environment through better lighting, public art projects, and the maintenance of public spaces.

Understanding the social and environmental influences on crime is crucial for developing comprehensive strategies to prevent and reduce criminal behavior. These theories highlight the importance of considering the broader context in which individuals live, as crime is often a product of the interaction between people and their environments. By addressing both social and environmental factors, forensic psychologists and law enforcement agencies can work together to create safer communities and reduce the incidence of crime.

2.3 Integrated Frameworks for Understanding Criminal Behavior

To fully grasp the complexity of criminal behavior, it is essential to integrate various theoretical perspectives that consider biological, psychological, social, and environmental factors. Integrated frameworks offer a comprehensive approach to understanding how these different factors interact to influence criminal actions. This section explores key integrated frameworks that have been developed to provide a more holistic understanding of criminal behavior.

1. The Biopsychosocial Model

A. Overview of the Biopsychosocial Model

- Interdisciplinary Framework: The biopsychosocial model is an interdisciplinary framework that combines biological, psychological, and social factors to explain human behavior, including criminality. It suggests that no single factor is solely responsible for criminal behavior; instead, it is the result of the interaction between various influences.

- Relevance to Forensic Psychology: This model is particularly valuable in forensic psychology because it acknowledges the complexity of human behavior and the need to consider multiple dimensions when assessing individuals involved in the legal system.

B. Biological Components

- Genetic and Neurological Factors: The biological aspect of the biopsychosocial model includes genetic predispositions, neurological conditions, and biochemical imbalances that may increase the likelihood of criminal behavior. For example, an individual with a genetic predisposition to aggression may be more prone to violent behavior, especially when combined with other risk factors.

- Physical Health and Behavior: This component also considers the impact of physical health, brain injuries, and other medical conditions that can influence behavior. Understanding these biological factors is crucial for forensic psychologists when evaluating defendants or providing expert testimony in court.

C. Psychological Components

- Mental Processes and Disorders: The psychological aspect focuses on individual mental processes, personality traits, and emotional states that contribute to criminal behavior. This includes cognitive distortions, impulsivity, and personality disorders such as antisocial personality disorder.

- Role of Psychological Assessments: Psychological assessments are key tools in this area, helping to identify underlying mental health issues that may contribute to criminal behavior. Forensic psychologists use these assessments to inform legal decisions, such as determining competency to stand trial or assessing the risk of reoffending.

D. Social Components

- Influence of Environmental Factors: The social aspect of the biopsychosocial model examines the influence of environmental factors, such as family dynamics, socioeconomic status, peer groups, and cultural norms. Social conditions, like poverty, lack of education, and exposure to violence, can create a context in which criminal behavior is more likely to occur.

- Socialization and Learning: This component also considers the role of socialization and learning, where individuals may adopt criminal behaviors through their interactions with others, particularly in communities where crime is prevalent.

E. Interactions Between Components

- Complex Interactions: The biopsychosocial model emphasizes that these components do not operate independently but interact with each other in complex ways. For example, an individual with a genetic predisposition to impulsivity (biological) may be more likely to commit a crime if they also experience social stressors like unemployment (social) and have poor coping skills (psychological).

- Comprehensive Analysis: Understanding these interactions allows forensic psychologists to provide a more comprehensive analysis of criminal behavior, taking into account the full range of factors that may contribute to an individual's actions.

2. Ecological Systems Theory

A. Overview of Ecological Systems Theory

- Framework for Environmental Influence: Developed by Urie Bronfenbrenner, ecological systems theory provides a framework for understanding how different levels of environmental influence affect behavior. This theory is particularly useful in forensic psychology for examining how various environmental contexts contribute to criminal behavior over time.

- Structure of the Theory: The theory is structured around multiple systems that range from the immediate environment (microsystem) to broader societal influences (macrosystem). Each system interacts with the others to shape an individual's behavior.

B. The Microsystem

- Immediate Environments: The microsystem includes the immediate environments that an individual interacts with daily, such as family, school, and peer groups. These environments have a direct impact on behavior, and disruptions or dysfunctions within the microsystem, such as family conflict or negative peer influences, can increase the likelihood of criminal behavior.

- Impact of Dysfunctional Environments: For example, children who grow up in abusive households may develop behavioral problems that lead to criminal activity, especially if they lack positive role models or support systems.

C. The Mesosystem

- Interactions Between Microsystems: The mesosystem refers to the interactions between different microsystems, such as the relationship between a child's home environment and their school experience. Conflicts or inconsistencies between these environments can contribute to stress and maladaptive behavior.

- Influence on Behavior: In the context of crime, a child who experiences harsh discipline at home and bullying at school may develop aggressive behaviors that manifest in delinquency or criminal acts.

D. The Exosystem

- Indirect Influences: The exosystem includes the broader social systems that indirectly influence an individual's life, such as parental workplace conditions, community resources, and media exposure. While the individual may not interact directly with these systems, they can still have a significant impact on behavior.

- Examples of Indirect Influence: For example, economic downturns that lead to parental job loss can create financial stress in the household, which may increase the likelihood of criminal behavior in children due to the resulting instability and lack of supervision.

E. The Macrosystem

- Cultural and Societal Context: The macrosystem encompasses the larger cultural and societal context in which an individual lives, including cultural values, laws, and economic systems. These factors shape the norms and expectations that influence behavior at all other levels.

- Impact of Societal Factors: Cultural attitudes towards crime, societal inequality, and systemic discrimination are all aspects of the macrosystem that can contribute to higher crime rates in certain populations. Forensic psychologists must consider these broader societal influences when assessing criminal behavior.

F. The Chronosystem

- Influence of Time: The chronosystem adds the dimension of time to ecological systems theory, considering how changes over time—such as developmental stages, historical events, or changes in family structure—affect behavior. This is particularly relevant in understanding the long-term effects of early life experiences on criminal behavior.

- Long-Term Impact of Experiences: For example, a traumatic event in childhood may have a delayed impact, contributing to criminal behavior in adolescence or adulthood. Understanding these temporal dynamics is crucial for forensic psychologists working with individuals who have experienced significant life changes.

3. The Interactionist Approach

A. The Principle of Interactionism

- Dynamic Interaction: The interactionist approach emphasizes the dynamic interaction between individual characteristics and environmental factors in shaping behavior. Rather than viewing criminal behavior as the result of static traits or isolated environmental influences, this approach considers how ongoing interactions between a person and their environment contribute to criminal actions.

- Understanding Susceptibility to Crime: This perspective is particularly valuable for understanding how certain individuals may be more susceptible to criminal behavior due to their unique combination of personal and environmental factors.

B. Situational Action Theory

- Criminal Behavior as an Interaction: Situational Action Theory (SAT), developed by Per-Olof H. Wikström, is an example of an interactionist framework that examines how personal traits and situational contexts interact to influence criminal behavior. SAT posits that criminal behavior occurs when an individual's propensity to commit crime intersects with criminogenic situations— environments or situations that promote criminal behavior.

- Role of Internal and External Factors: According to SAT, both individual factors (such as moral values and self-control) and situational factors (such as peer pressure or lack of supervision) are necessary for criminal behavior to occur.

This theory highlights the importance of both internal and external factors in understanding crime.

C. Implications for Forensic Psychology

- Comprehensive Forensic Assessments: The interactionist approach underscores the need for forensic psychologists to consider both the individual and their environment when assessing criminal behavior. This includes understanding how personal vulnerabilities, such as impulsivity or aggressive tendencies, are activated or mitigated by environmental conditions.

- Informing Legal Strategies: Forensic assessments that incorporate an interactionist perspective are better equipped to identify the full range of factors contributing to criminal behavior, which can inform more effective interventions and legal strategies.

4. Integrating Frameworks in Practice

A. Applying Integrated Frameworks to Case Analysis

- Comprehensive Case Analysis: Integrated frameworks like the biopsychosocial model, ecological systems theory, and the interactionist approach are invaluable tools for forensic psychologists. They allow for a comprehensive analysis of criminal behavior by considering multiple levels of influence.

- Example of Juvenile Offender: For example, in assessing a juvenile offender, a forensic psychologist might use the biopsychosocial model to evaluate genetic predispositions, mental health status, and family dynamics, while also applying ecological systems theory to understand the broader social and environmental context in which the individual operates.

B. Benefits of an Integrated Approach

- Holistic Understanding: The primary benefit of using integrated frameworks is that they provide a more holistic understanding of criminal behavior, which can lead to more accurate assessments and more effective interventions. By considering the interplay between biological, psychological, social, and environmental factors, forensic psychologists can develop more nuanced and tailored approaches to prevention and treatment.

- Effective Communication in Legal Settings: Integrated frameworks also enhance the ability of forensic psychologists to communicate their findings in legal settings, as they offer a comprehensive explanation that accounts for the complexity of human behavior. This can be particularly persuasive in court, where understanding the full context of an individual's actions is crucial for fair and informed decision-making.

Integrated frameworks are essential for understanding the multifaceted nature of criminal behavior. By combining insights from biology, psychology, sociology, and environmental studies, these frameworks provide a comprehensive approach to analyzing why individuals commit crimes. Forensic psychologists who utilize these frameworks are better equipped to assess criminal behavior, develop effective interventions, and contribute to the legal process in a meaningful way. As we continue to explore forensic psychology, the importance of integrating multiple perspectives will become increasingly clear, offering a deeper and more complete understanding of the causes of crime.

2.4 Case Study: Multi-Theoretical Analysis

To illustrate how various theories and frameworks can be applied to understand criminal behavior, this section presents a detailed case study involving a fictional individual. By analyzing the case from multiple theoretical perspectives— biological, psychological, social, and environmental—we can gain a comprehensive understanding of the factors that contributed to the individual's criminal actions.

1. Case Background

A. Overview of the Individual

- Name: John Doe

- Age: 28

- Criminal History: John has a history of violent offenses, including assault and armed robbery. He is currently serving a prison sentence for a series of armed robberies that he committed over a two-year period. John's criminal behavior began in his late teens and escalated in severity over time.

- Personal Background: John was raised in a low-income neighborhood characterized by high crime rates and social instability. His father was frequently absent due to incarceration, and his mother struggled with substance abuse. John dropped out of high school at age 16 and became involved with a local gang, which provided him with a sense of belonging and protection.

2. Biological Perspective

A. Genetic Predispositions

- Family History and Aggression: From a biological perspective, it is possible that John has a genetic predisposition to aggressive and impulsive behavior. His family history reveals a pattern of criminal behavior among male relatives, suggesting a potential genetic link. Additionally, John's father's criminal behavior and his absence due to incarceration may have influenced John's genetic predispositions, possibly exacerbating his tendencies toward aggression.

B. Neurological Factors

- Impact of Traumatic Brain Injury: John may also have neurological abnormalities that contribute to his criminal behavior. During his teenage years, John suffered a traumatic brain injury (TBI) from a physical altercation, which may have damaged his prefrontal cortex. This region of the brain is critical for impulse control, decision-making, and social behavior. Damage to the prefrontal cortex could have impaired John's ability to regulate his emotions and behavior, leading to increased aggression and poor decision-making.

C. Biochemical Imbalances

- Serotonin and Impulse Control: John's behavioral issues may also be linked to biochemical imbalances. For example, low levels of serotonin, which is associated with mood regulation and impulse control, could contribute to his aggressive tendencies. If John's environment further exacerbated these imbalances—such as through substance abuse or chronic stress—it could have amplified his predisposition to criminal behavior.

3. Psychological Perspective

A. Personality Traits and Disorders

- Antisocial Personality Disorder: From a psychological perspective, John exhibits traits consistent with antisocial personality disorder (ASPD). Symptoms of ASPD include a disregard for the rights of others, impulsivity, and a lack of remorse for one's actions. John's history of violent behavior, his involvement in gang activities, and his repeated offenses suggest that he may meet the criteria for this disorder.

- Intervention Needs: Understanding John's potential ASPD diagnosis is crucial for assessing his risk of reoffending and for developing appropriate intervention strategies. Psychological interventions, such as cognitive-behavioral therapy (CBT), may help address his distorted thinking patterns and reduce his impulsive behavior.

B. Cognitive Distortions

- Rationalizing Criminal Behavior: John likely experiences cognitive distortions that justify his criminal behavior. He may rationalize his actions by blaming society for his circumstances, minimizing the harm he causes to others, or believing that he is entitled to take what he wants by force. These distorted thought patterns allow him to engage in criminal behavior without experiencing significant guilt or remorse.

- Corrective Approaches: Addressing these cognitive distortions through therapeutic interventions could help John develop healthier ways of thinking and reduce his propensity for criminal behavior. Cognitive-behavioral approaches that challenge these distortions could be particularly effective in helping John reassess his beliefs and attitudes.

C. Emotional Regulation and Impulse Control

- Challenges in Emotional Management: John's criminal behavior may also be linked to difficulties with emotional regulation and impulse control. His traumatic upbringing, combined with potential neurological impairments, likely contributed to his inability to manage anger and frustration in non-violent ways. This lack of emotional regulation may have driven him to engage in criminal acts as a means of coping with or expressing his emotions.

- Therapeutic Interventions: Therapeutic interventions focused on improving emotional regulation and impulse control could be beneficial for John. Techniques such as anger management training and mindfulness practices may help him develop healthier coping mechanisms and reduce his reliance on violence as an outlet.

4. Social and Environmental Perspective

A. Social Disorganization and Strain

- Impact of Community Environment: John's upbringing in a socially disorganized neighborhood played a significant role in shaping his criminal behavior. The lack of social cohesion, high crime rates, and economic deprivation in his community created an environment where criminal behavior was normalized and opportunities for legitimate success were limited. Strain theory suggests that John turned to crime as a way to achieve success and gain social status in the absence of legitimate means.

- Preventive Measures: Addressing the social and environmental conditions that contributed to John's criminal behavior is essential for preventing future offenses. Community-based interventions that improve social cohesion, provide economic opportunities, and offer support to at-risk youth could help reduce the likelihood of individuals like John turning to crime.

B. Influence of Peer Groups and Gang Involvement

- Role of Gang Membership: John's involvement in a gang provided him with a sense of identity, belonging, and protection, which he lacked in his family environment. Differential association theory suggests that John learned criminal behavior through his interactions with gang members, who modeled and reinforced these behaviors. The gang likely provided John with both the motivation and the means to engage in criminal activities, further entrenching him in a life of crime.

- Alternative Social Networks: Interventions aimed at reducing gang involvement and providing alternative social networks could be effective in helping individuals like John disengage from criminal behavior. Mentorship programs, job training, and educational opportunities could offer John a path away from the gang lifestyle and towards legitimate success.

C. Environmental Criminology and Routine Activities

- Crime-Facilitating Environment: Environmental factors, such as the availability of suitable targets and the absence of capable guardians, likely influenced John's criminal behavior. Routine activities theory suggests that John's criminal activities were facilitated by his environment, which offered numerous opportunities for crime with minimal risk of apprehension. The lack of effective policing and community oversight in his neighborhood may have allowed John to engage in criminal behavior with relative impunity.

- Environmental Crime Prevention: Crime prevention strategies that address environmental factors, such as improving neighborhood surveillance, increasing police presence, and implementing community watch programs, could help reduce the opportunities for crime and deter individuals like John from engaging in criminal behavior.

5. Integrated Analysis and Conclusion

A. Synthesis of Theoretical Perspectives

- Comprehensive Understanding: John Doe's criminal behavior is best understood through an integrated analysis that considers biological, psychological, social, and environmental factors. His genetic predispositions, neurological impairments, and biochemical imbalances interacted with his psychological traits, cognitive distortions, and emotional dysregulation to create a heightened risk for criminal behavior. These individual vulnerabilities were exacerbated by the social disorganization of his neighborhood, his involvement in a gang, and the criminogenic environment in which he lived.

- Multi-Level Interventions: A comprehensive approach to understanding and addressing John's criminal behavior requires interventions at multiple levels. Biological interventions may include medical treatment for any neurological or biochemical issues, while psychological interventions may focus on therapy for ASPD, cognitive distortions, and emotional regulation. Social and environmental interventions should aim to improve community conditions, reduce gang involvement, and limit opportunities for crime.

B. Practical Applications for Forensic Psychology

- Multi-Theoretical Approach: This case study demonstrates the importance of using a multi-theoretical approach in forensic psychology. By integrating various theoretical perspectives, forensic psychologists can provide a more complete and accurate assessment of individuals involved in the legal system. This approach allows for more tailored and effective interventions that address the full range of factors contributing to criminal behavior.

- Training and Practice Implications: Forensic psychologists should be trained to apply integrated frameworks in their assessments and interventions. This training should include a deep understanding of the various theories of criminal behavior and the ability to synthesize these perspectives into a cohesive analysis. By doing so, forensic psychologists can contribute to more effective legal outcomes and better support for individuals involved in the criminal justice system.

This multi-theoretical analysis of John Doe's case illustrates the complexity of criminal behavior and the need for a comprehensive approach in forensic psychology. By considering the interplay of biological, psychological, social, and environmental factors, forensic psychologists can develop more accurate assessments and interventions that address the root causes of crime. As we continue to explore forensic psychology, the importance of integrating multiple perspectives will remain a central theme, offering a deeper and more complete understanding of criminal behavior and how to address it effectively.

2.5 Self-Assessment Quiz: Understanding Theories

This self-assessment quiz is designed to reinforce your understanding of the theories and frameworks covered in Chapter 2. The questions will test your knowledge of biological, psychological, social, and environmental influences on criminal behavior, as well as your ability to apply integrated frameworks to analyze criminal cases. After completing the quiz, review the provided feedback to enhance your comprehension of the material.

1. Multiple Choice Questions

1. Which of the following is most closely associated with biological theories of criminal behavior?

A. Cognitive distortions

B. Social learning

C. Genetic predispositions

D. Cultural norms

Answer: C. Genetic predispositions

Explanation: Biological theories emphasize the role of genetic factors in predisposing individuals to criminal behavior, such as the influence of certain genes linked to aggression.

2. Strain theory suggests that criminal behavior is most likely to occur when:

A. An individual has a neurological impairment.

B. Social structures prevent access to legitimate means of achieving societal goals.

C. Individuals are exposed to violent media content.

D. There is an overactive amygdala in the brain.

Answer: B. Social structures prevent access to legitimate means of achieving societal goals.

Explanation: Strain theory posits that crime arises when there is a disconnect between societal goals and the means available to achieve them, leading individuals to seek alternative (often illegal) ways to succeed.

3. According to differential association theory, criminal behavior is:

A. Inherited genetically.

B. Learned through interactions with others.

C. Caused by hormonal imbalances.

D. A result of brain structure abnormalities.

Answer: B. Learned through interactions with others.

Explanation: Differential association theory argues that criminal behavior is learned through social interactions, particularly when individuals associate with others who engage in or condone criminal activity.

4. The biopsychosocial model integrates which of the following factors to explain criminal behavior?

A. Only biological and psychological factors

B. Only social and environmental factors

C. Biological, psychological, and social factors

D. Only cognitive and cultural factors

Answer: C. Biological, psychological, and social factors.

Explanation: The biopsychosocial model integrates biological, psychological, and social factors to provide a comprehensive understanding of criminal behavior.

5. Which theory emphasizes the role of environmental design in preventing crime?

A. Routine activities theory

B. Psychoanalytic theory

C. Social disorganization theory

D. Environmental criminology

Answer: D. Environmental criminology.

Explanation: Environmental criminology focuses on how the physical environment, such as urban design and the availability of crime opportunities, influences the occurrence of crime.

2. Application Questions

1. Scenario: A 22-year-old male named Alex has been convicted of multiple burglaries. He grew up in a low-income neighborhood with high crime rates and had frequent conflicts with his parents. His friends are also involved in criminal activities. Which theoretical perspectives would you consider most relevant in understanding Alex's behavior? Select all that apply and explain your reasoning.

Possible Answer:

- Social Disorganization Theory: Alex's environment, characterized by high crime rates and social instability, likely contributed to his criminal behavior. This theory suggests that socially disorganized neighborhoods increase the likelihood of crime due to weakened social controls.

- Differential Association Theory: Alex's association with friends who engage in criminal activities supports the idea that he may have learned and adopted criminal behaviors through his social interactions.

- Strain Theory: Growing up in a low-income neighborhood, Alex may have experienced strain due to the limited legitimate means available to achieve societal goals, leading him to engage in crime as an alternative.

2. Scenario: A forensic psychologist is assessing a defendant who exhibits aggressive behavior and has a history of traumatic brain injury (TBI). Which integrated framework would be most appropriate for understanding the defendant's behavior, and why?

Possible Answer:

- Biopsychosocial Model: This model would be most appropriate as it allows the forensic psychologist to consider the biological impact of the TBI, the psychological effects of potential cognitive impairments, and the social environment that may influence the defendant's behavior. The biopsychosocial model provides a comprehensive understanding by integrating these factors.

3. Reflection and Feedback

1. Reflect on how your understanding of different theories and frameworks can influence your approach to assessing criminal behavior in a forensic psychology setting. How might integrating multiple perspectives lead to more effective interventions?

Possible Reflection:

- Understanding different theories allows forensic psychologists to consider various factors that contribute to criminal behavior. By integrating multiple perspectives, such as combining biological predispositions with environmental influences, professionals can develop more tailored interventions that address the root causes of criminal behavior. For example, if a forensic psychologist considers both the neurological impairments and the social environment of an individual, they can recommend a treatment plan that includes both medical interventions and social support services, leading to more comprehensive and effective outcomes.

2. Review your answers and consider any gaps in your understanding. Are there any theories or concepts that you found particularly challenging? How might you strengthen your knowledge in these areas?

Possible Reflection:

- Upon reviewing the quiz, I found that I struggled with understanding the nuances of environmental criminology. To strengthen my knowledge, I plan to revisit the section on environmental influences and seek out additional resources, such as academic articles or case studies, that focus on how urban design and environmental factors impact crime rates. This will help me better understand how to apply this theory in real-world forensic settings.

This self-assessment quiz is designed to help you solidify your understanding of the theories and frameworks discussed in Chapter 2. By reflecting on your answers and seeking to fill any gaps in your knowledge, you can continue to build a strong foundation in forensic psychology that will serve you well in both academic and professional contexts.

Chapter 2 Review

Chapter 2 provided an in-depth exploration of the various theories and frameworks that help explain criminal behavior. By understanding these different perspectives, you can gain a comprehensive view of the factors that contribute to crime, ranging from biological and psychological influences to social and environmental contexts. Below is a summary of the key points covered in this chapter.

2.1 Biological and Psychological Theories of Criminal Behavior

- Biological Theories: These theories emphasize the role of genetic predispositions, neurological abnormalities, and biochemical imbalances in influencing criminal behavior. Factors such as genetic links to aggression, brain injuries affecting impulse control, and neurotransmitter imbalances were discussed as contributing elements.

- Psychological Theories: Psychological perspectives focus on individual mental processes, personality traits, and cognitive distortions. Theories such as psychoanalytic, behavioral, and cognitive approaches were explored, highlighting how internal psychological mechanisms can lead to criminal behavior. The interaction between biological and psychological factors was also emphasized, with the biopsychosocial model offering an integrated approach.

2.2 Social and Environmental Influences on Crime

- Sociological Theories: The chapter examined how social structures and cultural norms influence criminal behavior. Strain theory explained how individuals might turn to crime when legitimate means to achieve societal goals are blocked. Social disorganization theory highlighted the impact of community instability, while differential association theory focused on the learning of criminal behavior through social interactions.

- Environmental Influences: Environmental criminology and related theories such as routine activities theory and broken windows theory were discussed, emphasizing how the physical and social environments create opportunities for crime. The role of socialization, peer influence, and cultural transmission in shaping behavior was also explored.

2.3 Integrated Frameworks for Understanding Criminal Behavior

- Biopsychosocial Model: This integrated framework combines biological, psychological, and social factors to provide a comprehensive understanding of criminal behavior. The model underscores the importance of considering multiple influences and their interactions when assessing criminal behavior.

- Ecological Systems Theory: Developed by Urie Bronfenbrenner, this theory examines how different levels of environmental influence, from immediate settings like family to broader societal factors, shape behavior. The theory's levels—microsystem, mesosystem, exosystem, macrosystem, and chronosystem—offer a layered understanding of how individuals interact with their environments.

- Interactionist Approach: This perspective emphasizes the dynamic interplay between individual characteristics and environmental factors in shaping behavior. Situational Action Theory, an example of this approach, was discussed for its focus on the interaction between personal traits and situational contexts that lead to criminal behavior.

2.4 Case Study: Multi-Theoretical Analysis

- Application of Theories: The case study of John Doe illustrated how multiple theoretical perspectives can be applied to understand an individual's criminal behavior. Biological factors such as genetic predispositions and neurological impairments were considered alongside psychological traits like antisocial personality disorder and cognitive distortions. Social and environmental influences, including gang involvement and neighborhood conditions, were also analyzed.

- Integrated Analysis: The case study demonstrated the importance of using an integrated approach to analyze criminal behavior, combining insights from various theories to provide a comprehensive understanding of the individual's actions. The analysis highlighted the need for multifaceted interventions that address the full range of factors contributing to criminal behavior.

2.5 Self-Assessment Quiz: Understanding Theories

- Reinforcement of Key Concepts: The self-assessment quiz provided an opportunity to test your understanding of the theories and frameworks discussed in the chapter. Multiple choice and application questions helped reinforce key concepts, while reflection questions encouraged deeper thinking about how these theories can be applied in real-world forensic psychology settings.

- Feedback and Reflection: The quiz emphasized the importance of reviewing your understanding and identifying areas where further study may be needed. Reflecting on your answers and seeking to strengthen your knowledge in challenging areas is crucial for developing a solid foundation in forensic psychology.

Chapter 2 offered a comprehensive exploration of the theories and frameworks that explain criminal behavior. By examining biological, psychological, social, and environmental influences, as well as integrated approaches, you gained a deeper understanding of the complex factors that contribute to crime. The chapter emphasized the importance of considering multiple perspectives and using integrated frameworks to analyze criminal behavior, both in theoretical contexts and through practical applications like case studies. As you move forward in your study of forensic psychology, the insights gained in this chapter will provide a strong foundation for understanding and addressing criminal behavior in a holistic and effective manner.

Chapter 3: The Criminal Mind

Understanding the criminal mind is central to forensic psychology, as it involves analyzing the psychological factors that contribute to criminal behavior. This chapter delves into the complexities of psychopathy, sociopathy, and other mental disorders commonly associated with crime. It also explores the correlation between mental health and criminality, supported by case studies and psychological profiles. To reinforce learning, the chapter concludes with an interactive exercise and reflection questions.

3.1 Psychopathy, Sociopathy, and Other Disorders

Understanding the distinctions between psychopathy, sociopathy, and other related disorders is crucial in forensic psychology, as these conditions often play a significant role in criminal behavior. This section delves into the characteristics, diagnostic criteria, and implications of these disorders, providing a comprehensive overview of how they manifest and influence criminal actions.

1. Psychopathy

A. Definition and Characteristics

- Lack of Empathy and Manipulativeness: Psychopathy is characterized by a profound lack of empathy, superficial charm, manipulativeness, and a disregard for societal norms and the rights of others. Psychopaths are often highly intelligent, calculating, and capable of appearing normal or even charismatic to those around them.

- Deceitfulness and Impulsivity: Common traits include deceitfulness, impulsivity, and a failure to accept responsibility for one's actions. Psychopaths are typically goal-oriented, using others as means to an end, without consideration for the harm they cause. They may engage in criminal activities with a level of detachment that makes their behavior particularly dangerous.

B. Diagnostic Tools: The Psychopathy Checklist-Revised (PCL-R)

- Comprehensive Assessment: The Psychopathy Checklist-Revised (PCL-R), developed by Dr. Robert Hare, is the most widely used tool for diagnosing psychopathy. It consists of 20 items that measure traits and behaviors associated with psychopathy, such as glibness, grandiosity, pathological lying, lack of remorse, and parasitic lifestyle.

- Scoring and Application: Each item is scored on a scale from 0 to 2, with higher scores indicating stronger psychopathic traits. A score of 30 or above out of 40 is generally indicative of psychopathy. The PCL-R is used in various settings, including criminal justice, to assess the risk of reoffending and to inform decisions about sentencing and parole.

C. Neurological and Genetic Underpinnings

- Brain Abnormalities: Research suggests that psychopathy has a neurological basis, with abnormalities observed in brain regions responsible for emotional processing, such as the amygdala and prefrontal cortex. These areas are crucial for regulating emotions, making decisions, and understanding social cues.

- Genetic Factors: Genetic factors also play a role in the development of psychopathic traits. Studies involving twins and families have shown that psychopathy is heritable, with certain genetic markers associated with traits like impulsivity and lack of fear. However, environmental factors can influence the expression of these traits, indicating that both nature and nurture are involved in the development of psychopathy.

2. Sociopathy

A. Definition and Characteristics

- Emotional Volatility and Impulsivity: Sociopathy, often used interchangeably with antisocial personality disorder (ASPD), is characterized by a pervasive pattern of disregard for the rights of others, impulsivity, and a lack of remorse. Sociopaths are more prone to emotional outbursts and less capable of forming long-term plans compared to psychopaths. Their behavior is often erratic and driven by external circumstances.

- Attachment and Relationships: Unlike psychopaths, sociopaths may form attachments to specific individuals or groups, although these relationships are often dysfunctional. Sociopaths tend to be more volatile and prone to rage, leading to spontaneous and poorly planned criminal acts. Their behavior is typically reactive, rather than premeditated.

B. Environmental and Social Influences

- Impact of Environmental Factors: Sociopathy is believed to be more strongly influenced by environmental factors than psychopathy. Experiences such as childhood trauma, abuse, or chronic exposure to criminal behavior can contribute to the development of sociopathic traits. Sociopaths often come from unstable or violent backgrounds, which may shape their worldview and behavior.

- Interaction of Nature and Nurture: Unlike psychopathy, which is often considered innate, sociopathy is seen as a product of environmental factors interacting with underlying vulnerabilities. This distinction has important implications for treatment and rehabilitation, as sociopathic behavior may be more responsive to interventions that address social and environmental conditions.

C. Comparison with Psychopathy

- Differences in Behavior and Planning: While both psychopathy and sociopathy share some similarities, such as a disregard for the law and the rights of others, there are key differences. Psychopaths are generally more calculated, manipulative, and able to maintain a façade of normalcy. Sociopaths, on the other hand, are more likely to act impulsively and display erratic behavior, with less ability to form coherent long-term plans.

- Implications for Forensic Psychology: The distinction between these disorders is important in forensic settings, as it can influence the approach to risk assessment, treatment, and legal decisions. For example, sociopaths may be more prone to crimes of passion, while psychopaths are more likely to engage in premeditated and organized criminal activities.

3. Other Related Disorders

A. Antisocial Personality Disorder (ASPD)

- Broad Diagnosis: Antisocial Personality Disorder (ASPD) is a broader diagnosis that includes both psychopathy and sociopathy. Individuals with ASPD exhibit a long-term pattern of violating the rights of others, engaging in deceitful behavior, and acting impulsively. They often have a history of criminal behavior and struggle to conform to social norms.

- DSM-5 Criteria: ASPD is diagnosed based on criteria from the Diagnostic and Statistical Manual of Mental Disorders (DSM-5), which includes a range of behaviors such as repeated unlawful acts, deceitfulness, impulsivity, irritability, and a lack of remorse. While not all individuals with ASPD are psychopaths or sociopaths, these disorders fall within the broader category of ASPD.

B. Narcissistic Personality Disorder (NPD)

- Grandiosity and Lack of Empathy: Narcissistic Personality Disorder (NPD) is characterized by grandiosity, a need for admiration, and a lack of empathy. While not inherently linked to criminal behavior, individuals with NPD may engage in manipulative or exploitative actions to achieve their goals, which can sometimes result in criminal acts.

- Potential for Conflict with Law: Narcissists may use others to fulfill their own needs, often disregarding the harm they cause. In some cases, their sense of entitlement and belief in their superiority can lead to conflicts with the law, particularly in situations where they feel their self-image is threatened.

C. Borderline Personality Disorder (BPD)

- Emotional Instability and Impulsivity: Borderline Personality Disorder (BPD) is marked by instability in relationships, self-image, and emotions. Individuals with

BPD may engage in self-destructive behaviors, including impulsive and potentially criminal acts, as a way to cope with their intense emotions.

- Criminal Implications: While BPD is not as strongly associated with crime as ASPD or psychopathy, it can still play a role in criminal behavior, particularly when individuals are under significant stress or emotional turmoil. Forensic psychologists must consider the emotional volatility and impulsivity associated with BPD when assessing the risk of criminal behavior.

4. Implications for Forensic Psychology

A. Assessment and Diagnosis

- Role of Forensic Psychologists: Forensic psychologists play a crucial role in assessing and diagnosing these disorders, particularly in legal contexts where an individual's mental state is relevant to criminal proceedings. Accurate diagnosis is essential for informing decisions about sentencing, parole, and treatment.

- Diagnostic Tools: Tools like the PCL-R and structured clinical interviews are used to assess psychopathy, sociopathy, and related disorders. These assessments help determine the risk of reoffending and guide interventions aimed at reducing criminal behavior.

B. Treatment and Rehabilitation

- Challenges in Treatment: Treating individuals with psychopathy, sociopathy, and ASPD presents significant challenges, as these disorders are often resistant to traditional therapeutic approaches. However, interventions that focus on behavior modification, improving emotional regulation, and addressing environmental factors can be effective in some cases.

- Rehabilitation Approaches: Rehabilitation efforts may include cognitive-behavioral therapy (CBT), anger management programs, and social skills training. For sociopaths, addressing the environmental factors that contributed to their disorder, such as improving social support and reducing exposure to criminal influences, can be particularly beneficial.

C. Legal and Ethical Considerations

- Criminal Responsibility and Ethics: The presence of these disorders in criminal defendants raises important legal and ethical considerations. For example, the question of criminal responsibility is complicated when a defendant's behavior is influenced by a severe personality disorder. Courts must balance the need for public safety with the rights of individuals who may have diminished capacity due to their mental state.

- Ethical Challenges in Treatment: Ethical considerations also arise in the treatment of these individuals, particularly in cases where they may be resistant to change or manipulative in therapy. Forensic psychologists must navigate these challenges carefully, ensuring that interventions are both effective and respectful of the individual's rights.

Understanding psychopathy, sociopathy, and other related disorders is essential for forensic psychologists, as these conditions often play a significant role in criminal behavior. By accurately diagnosing and addressing these disorders, forensic psychologists can contribute to more effective interventions, risk assessments, and legal outcomes. This knowledge is crucial for understanding the complexities of the criminal mind and for developing strategies to reduce the risk of reoffending.

3.2 Mental Health and Crime Correlation

The relationship between mental health and criminal behavior is complex and multifaceted, involving a range of mental health disorders that can influence an individual's likelihood of engaging in criminal activity. This section explores the various ways in which mental health issues contribute to criminal behavior, the challenges faced by the criminal justice system in addressing these issues, and the implications for forensic psychology.

1. Prevalence of Mental Health Disorders Among Offenders

A. Higher Incidence in Criminal Populations

- Increased Prevalence: Mental health disorders are more prevalent among incarcerated individuals than in the general population. Significant proportions of prisoners suffer from disorders like depression, anxiety, bipolar disorder, schizophrenia, and personality disorders.

- Statistical Contrast: Studies estimate that up to 50% of inmates have some form of mental illness, with severe conditions like schizophrenia or major depressive disorder being particularly common, contrasting sharply with the lower prevalence of these disorders in the general population.

B. Co-occurring Disorders and Substance Abuse

- Dual Diagnosis: Many offenders with mental health disorders also struggle with co-occurring substance abuse problems, which can exacerbate symptoms and increase criminal behavior likelihood. Substance abuse can impair judgment or drive crimes to obtain drugs or alcohol.

- Complex Treatment Needs: The presence of co-occurring disorders complicates treatment and rehabilitation, requiring integrated care that addresses both mental health and substance abuse issues.

C. Challenges in Diagnosis and Reporting

- Barriers to Diagnosis: Diagnosing mental health disorders in criminal populations is challenging due to stigma, fear of retribution, or distrust in the system, leading to underreporting. The prison environment can also exacerbate or mask symptoms, making accurate diagnosis difficult.

- Underreporting Consequences: Many inmates do not receive the necessary treatment, leading to a cycle of reoffending and further mental health deterioration.

2. The Role of Mental Illness in Criminal Behavior

A. Direct and Indirect Contributions to Crime

- Direct Contributions: Severe mental illnesses like schizophrenia or bipolar disorder can lead to criminal behavior during psychosis or mania episodes. For instance, a person experiencing paranoid delusions may commit violence, believing they are defending themselves.

- Indirect Contributions: Mental health disorders may indirectly increase criminal behavior by impairing societal functioning. Conditions like depression or anxiety can lead to unemployment, social withdrawal, or homelessness, pushing individuals towards crime as a survival mechanism.

B. Violent vs. Non-Violent Crimes

- Correlation with Violence: Mental health disorders have a stronger correlation with violent crimes, particularly conditions involving psychosis. However, most individuals with mental health disorders are not violent and are more often victims rather than perpetrators.

- Non-Violent Offenses: Non-violent crimes like theft or drug offenses are also common among those with mental health issues, often driven by impaired judgment, desperation, or the need to support substance abuse habits.

C. The Complexity of Causation

- Multifaceted Causation: The causation between mental health and crime is complex, with mental illness often being one of many contributing factors, including social, economic, and environmental influences. For example, those with mental health disorders lacking social support or living in poverty are at higher risk.

- Systemic Considerations: The criminal justice system must consider the multifaceted nature of mental health and crime when assessing offenders and determining appropriate interventions.

3. Criminal Justice Responses to Mentally Ill Offenders

A. Mental Health Courts and Diversion Programs

- Specialized Courts: Many jurisdictions have established mental health courts and diversion programs to address the high prevalence of mental illness among offenders. These programs focus on treatment and rehabilitation rather than punitive measures.

- Program Success: Diversion programs, which include mental health treatment and support services, aim to reduce recidivism and improve outcomes for offenders. Success rates for these programs are generally higher than for traditional incarceration.

B. Challenges in Treatment and Rehabilitation

- Resource Limitations: Prisons and jails often lack the resources to provide adequate mental health care, leading to untreated or poorly managed conditions. This can result in worsening symptoms and a higher risk of reoffending.

- Comprehensive Care: Effective rehabilitation must address mental health care alongside social and environmental factors like homelessness, substance abuse, and healthcare access. Integrated treatment plans are essential for reducing recidivism among mentally ill offenders.

C. Ethical and Legal Considerations

- Criminal Responsibility: The intersection of mental health and criminal justice raises ethical and legal challenges, such as determining criminal responsibility when an offender's actions are influenced by severe mental illness. Courts must balance public safety with the rights of those with diminished capacity.

- Treatment Ethics: Ethical concerns also arise in the treatment of mentally ill offenders, particularly regarding involuntary treatment or the use of solitary confinement, which can exacerbate mental health issues. Forensic psychologists must ensure that their assessments and recommendations are ethical and legally sound.

4. Implications for Forensic Psychology

A. The Role of Forensic Psychologists

- Critical Assessments: Forensic psychologists play a crucial role in assessing, treating, and rehabilitating mentally ill offenders. This includes conducting mental health evaluations, providing expert testimony, and developing treatment plans tailored to each offender's needs.

- Legal Considerations: In cases involving mental illness, forensic psychologists assess the offender's mental state at the crime time, competency to stand trial, and reoffending risk, which are critical for informing legal decisions and ensuring appropriate care.

B. The Need for Integrated Approaches

- Holistic Treatment: Addressing mental health and crime correlation requires integrated approaches combining mental health care with criminal justice interventions. Forensic psychologists must collaborate with legal professionals, healthcare providers, and social services to develop comprehensive treatment plans.

- Co-occurring Disorders: Integrated approaches are especially important for offenders with co-occurring disorders, who require coordinated care addressing both mental health and substance abuse issues. Collaborative efforts can reduce reoffending and improve overall well-being.

C. Future Directions and Research

- Continued Research: Ongoing research is essential to better understand mental health and crime relationships and to develop more effective interventions for mentally ill offenders. Research areas include diagnostic tool development, mental health courts, diversion program effectiveness, and long-term treatment outcomes.

- Advocacy and Practice: Forensic psychologists must stay informed about the latest research and best practices to provide effective care. Continued advocacy for improved mental health services within the criminal justice system is essential for ensuring mentally ill individuals receive the support needed for healthy, law-abiding lives.

The correlation between mental health and crime is a critical area of study in forensic psychology, with significant implications for the criminal justice system. By understanding the complex relationship between mental illness and criminal behavior, forensic psychologists can develop more effective interventions that address the root causes of crime and promote the rehabilitation of mentally ill offenders. This knowledge is essential for creating a more just and humane criminal justice system that recognizes the importance of mental health in preventing and addressing crime.

3.3 Case Studies and Psychological Profiles

Case studies and psychological profiles provide valuable insights into the minds of criminals, allowing forensic psychologists to analyze the complex interplay of factors that contribute to criminal behavior. This section presents detailed case studies of individuals with disorders such as psychopathy, sociopathy, and other mental health conditions, highlighting how these disorders manifest in criminal actions. By examining these real-world examples, we can better understand the psychological, social, and environmental influences on criminal behavior.

1. Case Study: The Psychopathic Serial Killer

A. Background and Early Life

- Subject: James, a 35-year-old male, was convicted of multiple counts of murder over a decade. Raised in a middle-class family with no apparent history of abuse or neglect, James exhibited signs of emotional detachment and cruelty towards animals from a young age. Despite being intelligent and academically successful, he had few close relationships and often displayed superficial charm.

- Childhood Behavior: James's early behavior indicated psychopathy, characterized by manipulativeness, deceitfulness, and a lack of empathy. His academic success masked these traits, allowing his behavior to go largely unnoticed by those around him.

B. Criminal Behavior and Diagnosis

- Crimes: James meticulously planned and executed his crimes, showing high levels of organization and control. His victims were chosen at random, with no apparent motive other than the thrill of the act. His calm demeanor during the trial, even when discussing his crimes, highlighted his lack of remorse.

- Psychological Profile: James scored highly on the Psychopathy Checklist-Revised (PCL-R), particularly in areas related to callousness, lack of empathy, and manipulativeness. His psychological profile aligned closely with the classic traits of psychopathy.

- Implications for Forensic Psychology: James's case underscores the challenges in managing individuals with high levels of psychopathy, who are manipulative, lack remorse, and pose a high risk of reoffending. Early intervention and specialized assessment tools are crucial in identifying psychopathic traits before they escalate into severe criminal behavior.

2. Case Study: The Sociopathic Gang Leader

A. Background and Social Environment

- Subject: Marcus, a 28-year-old male, was a leader of a notorious street gang involved in drug trafficking, robbery, and violent crimes. Unlike James, Marcus grew up in a highly unstable environment, frequently exposed to violence, poverty, and substance abuse. He dropped out of school at a young age and was heavily influenced by older gang members who served as role models.

- Family Dynamics: Marcus's chaotic family life, with a frequently incarcerated father and an addicted mother, led him to seek belonging and identity within the gang. His aggressiveness and strategic thinking allowed him to rise quickly to a leadership position within the gang.

B. Criminal Behavior and Diagnosis

- Crimes: Marcus was involved in numerous violent incidents, including armed robberies and assaults. His crimes were often impulsive and reactive, driven by a need to assert dominance and maintain his status within the gang.

- Psychological Profile: Marcus was diagnosed with Antisocial Personality Disorder (ASPD), which aligns with sociopathic traits. His impulsivity, aggression, and lack of remorse were evident, but unlike psychopaths, Marcus formed strong attachments to his gang members, viewing them as his family.

- Implications for Forensic Psychology: Marcus's case illustrates the significant influence of environmental factors, such as family dynamics and socialization, in developing sociopathy. Effective interventions for individuals like Marcus must address both their psychological traits and the social context that contributes to their criminal behavior.

3. Case Study: The Mentally Ill Offender

A. Background and Mental Health History

- Subject: Sarah, a 32-year-old female, was convicted of a violent crime during a psychotic episode. Sarah had a history of untreated schizophrenia, exacerbated by substance abuse. She had been in and out of psychiatric hospitals but struggled to maintain consistent treatment due to homelessness and lack of social support.

- Mental Health Challenges: Sarah's schizophrenia manifested in auditory hallucinations and delusions, leading her to believe she was in danger. Her substance abuse, particularly methamphetamine use, worsened her symptoms and contributed to her erratic behavior.

B. Criminal Behavior and Diagnosis

- Crimes: During a psychotic episode, Sarah attacked a stranger she believed was plotting against her. The unprovoked attack was a direct result of her untreated mental illness, compounded by her substance abuse.

- Psychological Profile: A psychological assessment revealed that Sarah's criminal behavior was directly linked to her untreated schizophrenia. Her hallucinations and delusions drove her to commit the crime, with substance abuse further impairing her judgment.

- Implications for Forensic Psychology: Sarah's case emphasizes the critical need for adequate mental health care and support for individuals with severe mental illnesses. Her criminal behavior stemmed from untreated mental illness rather than inherent criminal tendencies, highlighting the importance of advocating for treatment and rehabilitation over punitive measures.

4. Integrating Psychological Profiles with Criminal Behavior

A. The Role of Psychological Profiles in Forensic Assessments

- Comprehensive Understanding: Psychological profiles are essential tools for forensic psychologists in understanding the motivations behind criminal behavior, assessing the risk of reoffending, and informing legal decisions such as sentencing and parole.

- Holistic Approach: Integrating psychological profiles with an understanding of an individual's background and environmental influences provides a holistic view of the factors contributing to criminal behavior, allowing for tailored interventions that address specific needs and risks.

B. Ethical Considerations in Profiling

- Avoiding Stigmatization: Psychological profiling must be used with caution to avoid stigmatization and ensure fair and unbiased assessments. Forensic psychologists must consider the ethical implications of their work, particularly in cases where profiles may influence legal outcomes.

- Balancing Public Safety and Compassion: The goal of profiling should be to provide an accurate and compassionate understanding of the individual, balancing their potential for change with the need for public safety.

C. Application in Legal Settings

- Informing Legal Decisions: Psychological profiles are often used in legal settings to inform decisions about competency to stand trial, criminal responsibility, and the appropriate level of intervention. Forensic psychologists must present their findings clearly and objectively, ensuring that assessments are evidence-based and aligned with legal standards.

- Advocacy for Alternatives: The use of psychological profiles can be instrumental in advocating for alternatives to incarceration, such as mental health treatment or diversion programs, particularly for individuals whose criminal behavior is linked to mental illness.

5. *Reflection on the Use of Case Studies in Forensic Psychology*

A. Educational Value of Case Studies

- Real-World Insights: Case studies offer invaluable educational insights for students and professionals in forensic psychology, demonstrating how various psychological disorders manifest in criminal behavior and showing the practical application of theoretical knowledge.

- Skill Development: Analyzing case studies helps forensic psychologists deepen their understanding of criminal behavior complexities, refine their assessment skills, and develop more effective interventions.

B. Limitations of Case Studies

- Unique Cases: While informative, case studies have limitations, as each case is unique, and findings may not be generalizable to all individuals with similar disorders. Forensic psychologists must be cautious in applying insights from case studies to broader populations, recognizing the significant role of individual differences and contextual factors.

- Extremes vs. Norms: Case studies often focus on extreme examples, which may not represent the experiences of most individuals with psychological disorders.

Forensic psychologists should use case studies as one tool among many, complementing them with broader research and evidence-based practices.

Through these case studies and psychological profiles, Chapter 3 has provided a deeper understanding of the criminal mind, exploring how disorders such as psychopathy, sociopathy, and schizophrenia contribute to criminal behavior. By integrating these insights into their work, forensic psychologists can more effectively assess and intervene with individuals involved in the criminal justice system, ultimately contributing to better outcomes for both offenders and society.

3.4 Interactive Exercise: Building a Criminal Profile

This interactive exercise is designed to help you apply the knowledge gained in this chapter by constructing a detailed criminal profile based on a hypothetical case scenario. This exercise will guide you through analyzing psychological, social, and environmental factors, leading to a comprehensive profile that integrates multiple theoretical perspectives.

1. Scenario Description

Case Overview

- Subject: Alex, a 29-year-old male, has been arrested for a series of armed robberies targeting small businesses. Alex has no prior criminal record, but witnesses reported that he exhibited erratic behavior during the crimes, including sudden outbursts of anger and excessive force. The robberies were carried out with a high level of planning, yet Alex's behavior during the crimes appeared impulsive and disorganized.

Background Information

- Family History: Alex was raised in a volatile household with a father who was frequently incarcerated and a mother who struggled with mental health issues. He experienced physical and emotional abuse as a child and often witnessed domestic violence.

- Education and Employment: Alex dropped out of high school at age 17 and has since held various low-wage jobs. He has a history of unemployment and financial instability, leading to significant stress and frustration. His work history is marked by conflicts with supervisors and colleagues.

- Social Environment: Alex has few close relationships and has struggled with social isolation. He recently became involved with a group of individuals who share his feelings of resentment towards society. This group has a history of minor criminal activities, though nothing as severe as armed robbery.

2. Step-by-Step Guide

Step 1: Gather Information

- Objective: Begin by thoroughly reviewing the scenario and background information provided. Identify key details related to Alex's psychological traits, family dynamics, social environment, and criminal behavior.

- Tasks:

  - Note any potential psychological disorders or traits that may influence Alex's behavior.

  - Consider the impact of Alex's upbringing, including any history of trauma or abuse.

  - Evaluate Alex's current social situation, including his relationships and involvement with the group.

  - Analyze the nature of the crimes, noting any patterns in behavior, planning, and execution.

Step 2: Analyze Psychological Factors

- Objective: Examine the psychological traits and potential disorders that may be influencing Alex's behavior. Consider how these factors might manifest in his criminal actions.

- Tasks:

  - Identify any signs of antisocial personality disorder (ASPD) or sociopathy, such as impulsivity, aggression, and lack of remorse.

  - Consider the possibility of post-traumatic stress disorder (PTSD) due to Alex's abusive childhood, which may contribute to his anger and erratic behavior.

  - Evaluate the role of cognitive distortions in justifying his criminal actions, such as blaming society for his situation.

Step 3: Assess Social and Environmental Influences

- Objective: Evaluate how social and environmental factors have shaped Alex's behavior. Focus on his family background, social relationships, and current living conditions.

- Tasks:

  - Analyze the impact of Alex's dysfunctional family environment, including the potential modeling of criminal behavior by his father and the lack of stable, supportive relationships.

  - Consider the influence of Alex's social isolation and involvement with a group that reinforces negative attitudes towards society. This group may have provided both the opportunity and encouragement for Alex's criminal behavior.

  - Assess the role of economic stressors and unemployment in driving Alex towards crime as a means of coping with financial instability and feelings of powerlessness.

Step 4: Integrate Findings and Build the Criminal Profile

- Objective: Combine your analysis of psychological, social, and environmental factors to develop a comprehensive criminal profile of Alex. This profile should reflect the interplay of these factors and how they have contributed to his criminal behavior.

- Tasks:

- Synthesize the information gathered to create a narrative that explains Alex's path to criminal behavior. Consider how his psychological traits, past experiences, and current circumstances have interacted to produce the behavior observed during the robberies.

- Identify potential triggers for Alex's erratic behavior during the crimes, such as unresolved trauma, feelings of anger and resentment, or influence from the group.

- Assess the risk of reoffending and any potential avenues for intervention, such as psychological treatment, social support, and economic assistance.

3. Reflection and Feedback

A. Reflection on the Profile

- Reflect on the process of building Alex's criminal profile. Consider the following questions:

  - How did integrating psychological, social, and environmental factors enhance your understanding of Alex's behavior?

  - Were there any challenges in interpreting the information provided, and how did you address them?

  - How might this profile inform decisions about Alex's treatment, sentencing, or potential for rehabilitation?

B. Comparison with a Sample Profile

- After completing your profile, compare it with a sample profile provided below. Note any similarities and differences in the analysis and conclusions drawn. Consider whether the sample profile offers any additional insights or perspectives that could enhance your understanding of the case.

Sample Profile Overview

- Psychological Factors: The sample profile identifies potential ASPD, with signs of impulsivity, lack of remorse, and aggression. It also considers the impact of

PTSD from Alex's abusive childhood, which may have contributed to his erratic behavior and anger during the crimes.

- Social and Environmental Influences: The sample profile highlights the influence of Alex's dysfunctional family environment and social isolation. It suggests that his involvement with the group may have provided both a sense of belonging and the means to commit the crimes, while economic stressors acted as a significant motivator.

- Risk Assessment and Recommendations: The sample profile assesses Alex as having a high risk of reoffending due to his unresolved psychological issues and current social environment. It recommends a combination of psychological treatment, economic support, and interventions aimed at breaking his ties with the group to reduce this risk.

C. Applying Insights to Future Cases

- Consider how the skills and insights gained from this exercise can be applied to future cases in forensic psychology. Reflect on the importance of a comprehensive, multi-faceted approach to understanding criminal behavior and how this approach can lead to more effective interventions.

This interactive exercise in building a criminal profile is designed to deepen your understanding of the factors that contribute to criminal behavior. By applying theoretical knowledge to a practical scenario, you can develop the skills necessary to analyze complex cases in forensic psychology and provide informed recommendations for treatment, intervention, and legal decisions.

3.5 Reflection Questions

These reflection questions are designed to help you critically engage with the concepts covered in this chapter. By considering these questions, you can deepen your understanding of the criminal mind and the role of forensic psychology in analyzing and addressing criminal behavior.

1. How do psychopathy and sociopathy differ in terms of their impact on criminal behavior, and why is it important for forensic psychologists to distinguish between these disorders?

- Consider the specific traits and behaviors associated with psychopathy and sociopathy. Reflect on how these differences might influence the planning, execution, and motivation behind criminal acts. Discuss the implications for risk assessment, treatment, and legal decisions.

2. In what ways do mental health disorders contribute to criminal behavior, and what challenges do these disorders pose for the criminal justice system?

- Explore the direct and indirect ways that mental health disorders can lead to criminal behavior. Reflect on the challenges of diagnosing, treating, and managing mentally ill offenders within the criminal justice system. Consider how forensic psychologists can help bridge the gap between mental health needs and criminal justice requirements.

3. How can case studies and psychological profiles enhance our understanding of criminal behavior, and what limitations should be considered when using these tools in forensic psychology?

- Reflect on the value of case studies and psychological profiles in providing detailed insights into the minds of criminals. Consider how these tools can inform assessments and interventions. Also, discuss the limitations of these tools, such as the potential for bias, lack of generalizability, and ethical considerations.

4. Reflect on the interactive exercise. How did the process of building a criminal profile deepen your understanding of the factors that contribute to criminal behavior? What challenges did you encounter, and how did you address them?

- Consider how the exercise allowed you to apply theoretical knowledge to a practical scenario. Reflect on the specific challenges you faced, such as interpreting complex information or integrating multiple factors. Discuss how this experience has prepared you for future work in forensic psychology.

5. How might the integration of psychological, social, and environmental factors lead to more effective interventions for individuals involved in the criminal justice system?

- Explore the importance of a holistic approach in forensic psychology. Reflect on how considering the interplay of various factors can lead to more tailored and effective interventions. Discuss how this approach can help reduce recidivism and improve outcomes for offenders.

6. What ethical considerations should forensic psychologists keep in mind when assessing and profiling individuals with disorders like psychopathy or sociopathy?

- Reflect on the ethical responsibilities of forensic psychologists, particularly when dealing with individuals who have disorders that may limit their capacity for empathy or remorse. Consider how to balance the need for public safety with the rights and dignity of the individual being assessed.

7. How do environmental factors, such as upbringing and socialization, interact with psychological traits to influence criminal behavior? Provide examples from the case studies in this chapter.

- Consider the role of environmental influences in shaping criminal behavior. Reflect on how factors like family dynamics, peer relationships, and socioeconomic status can interact with individual psychological traits to create a predisposition to crime. Use examples from the case studies to illustrate your points.

8. What role does early intervention play in preventing the development of criminal behavior in individuals with traits associated with psychopathy or sociopathy?

- Reflect on the potential impact of identifying and addressing problematic behaviors early in life. Consider how early intervention strategies could mitigate the risk of these individuals developing more severe antisocial behaviors and engaging in criminal activity.

These reflection questions are intended to encourage deep thinking about the material covered in Chapter 3. By engaging with these questions, you can enhance your understanding of the complexities of criminal behavior and the critical role that forensic psychology plays in assessing, understanding, and intervening with individuals involved in the criminal justice system.

Chapter 3 Review

Chapter 3 of this guide delves into the intricate workings of the criminal mind, exploring various psychological disorders, their correlation with criminal behavior, and the use of case studies and psychological profiles in forensic psychology. This review summarizes the key points and takeaways from each section of the chapter.

3.1 Psychopathy, Sociopathy, and Other Disorders

- Psychopathy: Characterized by a lack of empathy, superficial charm, manipulativeness, and often violent behavior, psychopathy is one of the most researched disorders in forensic psychology. Psychopaths tend to be highly organized, with crimes that are carefully planned and executed. Their emotional detachment and lack of remorse make them particularly dangerous and challenging to rehabilitate.

- Sociopathy: Sociopaths, while similar to psychopaths, tend to be more impulsive and erratic in their behavior. They often form attachments to specific groups or individuals, such as gang members, and their crimes are more likely to be disorganized and spontaneous. Sociopaths are shaped more by their environment, such as a dysfunctional upbringing or exposure to violence, making their behavior somewhat more malleable with intervention.

- Other Disorders: Disorders such as borderline personality disorder, narcissistic personality disorder, and schizophrenia can also play a role in criminal behavior. Understanding these disorders helps forensic psychologists assess the risk of future offenses and the potential for rehabilitation.

3.2 Mental Health and Crime Correlation

- Correlation Between Mental Health and Crime: Mental health disorders, particularly those that impair judgment, impulse control, and emotional regulation, are strongly correlated with criminal behavior. Conditions such as schizophrenia, bipolar disorder, and severe depression can lead individuals to commit crimes, often in the context of untreated symptoms or substance abuse.

- Challenges in the Criminal Justice System: The criminal justice system often struggles to accommodate individuals with severe mental illnesses. Forensic psychologists play a crucial role in identifying these conditions, advocating for appropriate treatment, and determining the competency of individuals to stand trial or their criminal responsibility at the time of the offense.

3.3 Case Studies and Psychological Profiles

- Case Study Analysis: Detailed case studies of individuals with disorders like psychopathy and sociopathy provide valuable insights into how these disorders manifest in criminal behavior. By examining the backgrounds, psychological assessments, and behaviors of these individuals, forensic psychologists can develop more accurate profiles and risk assessments.

- Psychological Profiles: Creating psychological profiles based on case studies helps forensic psychologists understand the motivations and potential future behaviors of criminals. These profiles are used in criminal investigations, risk assessments, and legal proceedings to provide a deeper understanding of criminal behavior and to inform decisions related to sentencing, treatment, and rehabilitation.

3.4 Interactive Exercise: Building a Criminal Profile

- Application of Knowledge: The interactive exercise in this chapter allowed readers to apply the knowledge gained by constructing a detailed criminal profile based on a hypothetical case. This exercise emphasized the importance of analyzing psychological, social, and environmental factors in developing a comprehensive understanding of criminal behavior.

- Reflection and Feedback: Reflecting on the process of building a criminal profile helps forensic psychologists refine their analytical skills, ensuring that their assessments are thorough, accurate, and informed by multiple perspectives. This practice is essential for developing effective interventions and contributing to the fair administration of justice.

3.5 Reflection Questions

- Critical Thinking: The reflection questions provided at the end of the chapter encourage readers to critically engage with the material, deepening their understanding of the criminal mind and the role of forensic psychology in analyzing and addressing criminal behavior.

- Application to Practice: These questions also challenge readers to consider how the insights gained from this chapter can be applied to real-world scenarios, enhancing their ability to assess, intervene, and support individuals involved in the criminal justice system.

Chapter 3 provides a comprehensive exploration of the criminal mind, emphasizing the importance of understanding psychological disorders, their correlation with criminal behavior, and the use of case studies and psychological profiles in forensic psychology. By integrating theory with practical exercises, this chapter equips readers with the tools and insights necessary to analyze and address the complexities of criminal behavior, contributing to more effective interventions and a deeper understanding of the psychological underpinnings of crime.

Chapter 4: Juvenile and Developmental Forensic Psychology

Juvenile and developmental forensic psychology focuses on understanding the unique factors that influence the behavior of young offenders and the most effective ways to assess, intervene, and rehabilitate them. This chapter delves into the causes of juvenile delinquency, various rehabilitation approaches, and the importance of developmental assessments in crafting effective interventions. Through case studies and practical exercises, you will gain insights into the challenges and opportunities in working with juvenile offenders.

4.1 Juvenile Delinquency: Causes and Assessments

Juvenile delinquency is a complex issue influenced by a myriad of factors that contribute to a young person's involvement in criminal behavior. Understanding these causes is essential for forensic psychologists and professionals working in juvenile justice to effectively assess and intervene. This section explores the primary causes of juvenile delinquency and the methods used to assess these factors.

1. Causes of Juvenile Delinquency

A. Family Dynamics

- Dysfunctional Family Environment: A significant cause of juvenile delinquency is a dysfunctional family environment. This includes situations where children experience neglect, physical or emotional abuse, or witness domestic violence. The lack of a supportive and stable home environment often leads to feelings of insecurity and low self-esteem, driving juveniles to seek acceptance and belonging through delinquent behavior.

- Parental Influence: Parents who engage in criminal behavior, substance abuse, or display poor parenting skills can significantly influence their children's likelihood of becoming delinquent. Inconsistent discipline, lack of supervision, and inadequate role models contribute to the development of antisocial behavior in youths.

B. Peer Influence

- Peer Pressure: Adolescence is a period where peer influence becomes particularly strong. Juveniles often feel pressure to conform to the behaviors and values of their peer groups, which can include engaging in criminal activities. This is especially true in environments where gang culture is prevalent, and membership in such groups is associated with a sense of identity and protection.

- Gang Involvement: Gangs offer a sense of belonging and identity for many youths who feel alienated from mainstream society. However, involvement in gang activities often leads to violent and criminal behavior, including drug trafficking, theft, and assault. The social rewards of gang involvement, such as status and recognition, can outweigh the perceived risks for many young people.

C. Socioeconomic Factors

- Poverty: Socioeconomic disadvantage is closely linked to juvenile delinquency. Youths from low-income families often experience limited access to education, extracurricular activities, and other resources that promote positive development. The stress and frustration of living in poverty can lead to feelings of hopelessness and a higher likelihood of turning to crime as a means of survival or achieving financial gain.

- Educational Disengagement: Poor academic performance, truancy, and a lack of engagement in school are significant predictors of juvenile delinquency. Educational institutions often fail to meet the needs of at-risk youths, leading to disengagement and eventual dropout. Without a positive academic environment, juveniles are more likely to associate with delinquent peers and engage in criminal activities.

D. Psychological Factors

- Mental Health Issues: Psychological factors, including mental health disorders, play a crucial role in juvenile delinquency. Conditions such as conduct disorder, attention-deficit/hyperactivity disorder (ADHD), and oppositional defiant disorder (ODD) can impair a juvenile's ability to control impulses, follow rules, and interact positively with others. These issues often go untreated, leading to an increased risk of criminal behavior.

- Emotional Regulation: Many juveniles struggle with managing emotions such as anger, frustration, and anxiety. Poor emotional regulation can result in aggressive and impulsive behaviors, which are often at the root of delinquent acts. These youths may turn to crime as a way to express their emotions or to cope with internal turmoil.

E. Environmental Factors

- Community Influence: The environment in which a juvenile grows up significantly impacts their likelihood of engaging in delinquent behavior. High-crime neighborhoods, exposure to violence, and lack of positive community resources create an environment where criminal behavior is normalized. Juveniles in these environments may view crime as a necessary means of survival or as a way to gain respect.

- Exposure to Violence: Continuous exposure to violence, whether in the home, school, or community, can desensitize juveniles to aggressive behavior and make them more likely to engage in criminal activities. The normalization of violence in their daily lives reduces the psychological barriers to committing violent acts.

2. Assessment Methods

A. Risk and Needs Assessments

- Purpose: Risk and needs assessments are tools used to evaluate the factors that contribute to a juvenile's delinquent behavior and to identify the most appropriate interventions. These assessments help professionals determine the likelihood of reoffending and the specific needs that must be addressed to reduce that risk.

- Common Tools: Some widely used assessment tools include the Youth Level of Service/Case Management Inventory (YLS/CMI) and the Structured Assessment of Violence Risk in Youth (SAVRY). These tools assess various domains, including family background, peer relationships, school performance, and mental health, to create a comprehensive profile of the juvenile.

- Application: The results of these assessments are used to develop individualized treatment plans that target the underlying causes of delinquency. For example, a juvenile with significant family issues may benefit from family therapy, while one with educational challenges might be referred to tutoring or vocational training programs.

B. Developmental Assessments

- Purpose: Developmental assessments focus on understanding how a juvenile's cognitive, emotional, and social development impacts their behavior. These assessments are essential for identifying any developmental delays or disorders that may contribute to delinquent behavior.

- Components: Developmental assessments typically include evaluations of intellectual functioning, emotional regulation, social skills, and moral development. These assessments help professionals understand how a juvenile's developmental stage influences their decision-making and behavior.

- Application: The information gathered from developmental assessments is used to tailor interventions to the juvenile's developmental needs. For example, a juvenile with delayed cognitive development might require special education services, while one with poor social skills might benefit from social skills training or peer group therapy.

C. Psychological Evaluations

- Purpose: Psychological evaluations are conducted to assess the mental health status of juvenile offenders. These evaluations are critical for identifying any underlying psychological disorders or emotional issues that may contribute to delinquent behavior.

- Components: A comprehensive psychological evaluation includes interviews with the juvenile, parents, and teachers, as well as standardized tests and questionnaires. These assessments measure aspects such as personality traits, emotional well-being, cognitive functioning, and behavior patterns.

- Application: The findings from psychological evaluations inform treatment plans that address the specific mental health needs of the juvenile. For instance, a juvenile diagnosed with conduct disorder might receive cognitive-behavioral therapy (CBT) to address negative thought patterns and improve behavior.

D. Challenges in Assessment

- Complexity of Juvenile Behavior: Assessing juvenile delinquency is challenging due to the complex interplay of factors that influence behavior. A single assessment tool may not capture all relevant information, necessitating a multi-method approach.

- Bias and Accuracy: There is a risk of bias in assessments, particularly if the tools used are not culturally sensitive or if the assessor has preconceived notions about the juvenile. Ensuring accuracy requires careful consideration of the juvenile's unique circumstances and the use of validated, reliable tools.

- Dynamic Nature of Development: Juvenile behavior is dynamic and can change rapidly in response to interventions or changes in their environment. Ongoing assessment and monitoring are necessary to adjust treatment plans as needed and to track progress over time.

Understanding the causes of juvenile delinquency and using effective assessment methods are crucial steps in developing interventions that can help young offenders turn their lives around. By identifying the root causes of delinquent behavior and addressing them through tailored treatment plans, forensic psychologists and juvenile justice professionals can reduce the likelihood of reoffending and support the healthy development of at-risk youths.

4.2 Rehabilitation Approaches for Juvenile Offenders

Rehabilitation is a central focus in juvenile justice, as it aims to address the root causes of delinquent behavior and help young offenders reintegrate into society as responsible and productive individuals. This section explores various approaches to rehabilitating juvenile offenders, emphasizing the importance of tailored interventions that consider the unique needs and circumstances of each youth.

1. Cognitive-Behavioral Therapy (CBT)

A. Overview

- Cognitive-Behavioral Therapy (CBT) is one of the most widely used and effective therapeutic approaches for juvenile offenders. It focuses on helping juveniles identify and change negative thought patterns and behaviors that contribute to their delinquent actions.

- Application: CBT programs for juveniles often include modules on anger management, social skills training, and problem-solving. These programs teach juveniles how to recognize and modify harmful thoughts, develop healthier ways of thinking, and make better decisions in challenging situations.

B. Techniques and Strategies

- Cognitive Restructuring: This technique involves helping juveniles challenge and change irrational or harmful thoughts that lead to negative behaviors. For example, a youth who believes that violence is the only way to solve conflicts may learn alternative strategies for managing disagreements.

- Behavioral Interventions: CBT incorporates behavioral techniques such as role-playing, exposure therapy, and reinforcement strategies to help juveniles practice new skills and behaviors in a safe environment. These interventions are designed to increase the likelihood of positive behaviors and reduce the occurrence of negative ones.

C. Effectiveness and Outcomes

- Reducing Recidivism: Research has shown that CBT is particularly effective in reducing recidivism among juvenile offenders. By addressing the cognitive and behavioral roots of delinquency, CBT helps youths develop the skills needed to avoid future criminal behavior.

- Long-Term Benefits: Juveniles who participate in CBT programs often experience long-term improvements in their emotional regulation, interpersonal relationships, and decision-making abilities. These benefits contribute to their successful reintegration into society and reduce the likelihood of reoffending.

2. Family-Based Interventions

A. Overview

- Family dynamics play a crucial role in the development and maintenance of delinquent behavior, making family-based interventions essential for rehabilitation. These interventions focus on improving communication, resolving conflicts, and strengthening family bonds to create a supportive environment for the juvenile.

B. Types of Family-Based Interventions

- Functional Family Therapy (FFT): FFT is a short-term, evidence-based intervention that targets the entire family system. It aims to improve family functioning by addressing negative communication patterns, enhancing problem-solving skills, and fostering a positive family environment.

- Multisystemic Therapy (MST): MST is an intensive, home-based intervention that involves the juvenile, their family, and other key systems such as school and community services. MST focuses on changing the factors in the youth's environment that contribute to delinquent behavior, such as peer influence, family conflict, and school performance.

- Parent Management Training (PMT): PMT teaches parents effective discipline techniques and strategies for managing their child's behavior. This intervention empowers parents to take an active role in their child's rehabilitation by providing them with the tools needed to guide their child's behavior in a positive direction.

C. Challenges and Considerations

- Engagement of Family Members: The success of family-based interventions often depends on the active participation of family members. Challenges may arise when parents or guardians are unwilling or unable to engage in the process due to their own issues, such as substance abuse or mental health problems.

- Cultural Sensitivity: Interventions must be culturally sensitive and tailored to the specific needs and values of the family. Practitioners must be aware of cultural differences in family dynamics, parenting styles, and attitudes toward mental health to ensure that interventions are effective and respectful.

D. Impact on Recidivism

- Positive Outcomes: Family-based interventions have been shown to significantly reduce recidivism rates among juvenile offenders. By addressing the underlying family issues that contribute to delinquent behavior, these interventions help create a more stable and supportive environment for the youth.

- Long-Term Effects: The benefits of family-based interventions often extend beyond the juvenile to improve overall family functioning. This holistic approach can lead to long-term positive changes in the family system, reducing the risk of future delinquency for the youth and other family members.

3. Educational and Vocational Programs

A. Overview

- Education and vocational training are critical components of rehabilitation for juvenile offenders. These programs provide youths with the skills and knowledge needed to pursue legitimate opportunities, build self-esteem, and prepare for a successful transition into adulthood.

B. Types of Educational and Vocational Programs

- Traditional Education: Programs that focus on completing high school or obtaining a GED are essential for juveniles who have fallen behind academically or dropped out of school. These programs often include tutoring, special education services, and individualized learning plans to meet the needs of each youth.

- Vocational Training: Vocational programs offer training in specific trades or skills, such as carpentry, automotive repair, or culinary arts. These programs provide practical, hands-on experience that can lead to employment opportunities after release. Vocational training also helps youths develop a sense of purpose and direction, reducing the likelihood of returning to criminal behavior.

- Life Skills Education: Life skills programs teach juveniles essential skills for independent living, such as financial management, communication, and problem-solving. These programs aim to equip youths with the tools they need to navigate adulthood successfully and avoid future involvement in the criminal justice system.

C. Impact on Recidivism

- Improved Academic and Employment Outcomes: Access to education and job training significantly reduces the likelihood of reoffending by providing juveniles with alternative paths to success. Youths who achieve educational and vocational goals are more likely to find stable employment, which is a key factor in reducing recidivism.

- Addressing Root Causes: Educational and vocational programs also address some of the root causes of delinquency, such as poverty, lack of opportunity, and social exclusion. By empowering juveniles with the skills and knowledge needed to succeed, these programs help break the cycle of crime and improve long-term outcomes.

4. Restorative Justice Programs

A. Overview

- Restorative justice is an approach to rehabilitation that focuses on repairing the harm caused by criminal behavior and restoring relationships between the offender, the victim, and the community. This approach emphasizes accountability, empathy, and the importance of making amends.

B. Types of Restorative Justice Programs

- Victim-Offender Mediation: In this program, the juvenile offender meets with the victim of their crime in a mediated setting to discuss the impact of the offense and explore ways to make amends. This process helps the offender understand the consequences of their actions and provides an opportunity for the victim to express their feelings and receive closure.

- Community Service: Community service programs require juveniles to perform meaningful work that benefits their community as a way of making amends for their crimes. These programs help offenders develop a sense of responsibility and connection to their community while contributing to their rehabilitation.

- Restorative Circles: Restorative circles bring together the offender, victim, and community members in a facilitated discussion to address the harm caused by the crime and find a collective path forward. This approach fosters dialogue, mutual understanding, and a shared commitment to healing and reintegration.

C. Benefits of Restorative Justice

- Empathy and Accountability: Restorative justice programs encourage juveniles to take responsibility for their actions and develop empathy for their victims. By actively participating in the process of making amends, offenders are more likely to internalize the lessons of their rehabilitation and avoid future criminal behavior.

- Reduction in Recidivism: Research has shown that restorative justice programs can lead to lower recidivism rates compared to traditional punitive approaches. By focusing on repairing harm and rebuilding relationships, these programs address the underlying issues that contribute to delinquent behavior and promote long-term positive change.

D. Challenges and Considerations

- Voluntary Participation: Restorative justice programs typically require the voluntary participation of both the offender and the victim. This can be challenging in cases where the victim is unwilling or unable to participate or where the offender is resistant to the process.

- Cultural Sensitivity: Like other interventions, restorative justice programs must be culturally sensitive and adaptable to the specific needs and values of the participants. Facilitators must be trained to navigate cultural differences and ensure that the process is respectful and inclusive.

5. Challenges in Juvenile Rehabilitation

A. Resistance to Change

- Juvenile offenders may resist rehabilitation efforts due to a lack of motivation, fear of change, or deep-seated distrust of authority figures. Overcoming this resistance requires building rapport, fostering trust, and providing consistent support throughout the rehabilitation process.

B. Resource Limitations

- Many juvenile rehabilitation programs face challenges related to funding, staffing, and access to resources. These limitations can affect the quality and availability of services, making it difficult to meet the needs of all juvenile offenders.

C. Coordination Among Agencies

- Effective rehabilitation often requires collaboration between multiple agencies, including juvenile justice, mental health services, education, and social services. Coordinating efforts across these systems can be challenging, particularly when there are differing priorities, policies, and procedures.

D. Long-Term Monitoring and Support

- Rehabilitation does not end with the completion of a program; ongoing monitoring and support are essential for maintaining progress and preventing relapse. Ensuring that juveniles have access to continued services and support after they leave the justice system is crucial for their long-term success.

Rehabilitation approaches for juvenile offenders must be tailored to the unique needs and circumstances of each individual. By combining cognitive-behavior

al therapy, family-based interventions, educational and vocational programs, and restorative justice practices, professionals in juvenile justice can create comprehensive rehabilitation plans that address the root causes of delinquency and promote positive, long-lasting change. Through these efforts, juvenile offenders can be guided toward a brighter future, free from the cycle of crime and reoffending.

4.3 Case Study: Developmental Assessment of Juvenile Offenders

This case study illustrates the process of conducting a developmental assessment for a juvenile offender, highlighting the importance of understanding the various factors that contribute to delinquent behavior. By examining the developmental, psychological, and social aspects of the youth's life, professionals can design targeted interventions that address the underlying causes of their behavior and support their rehabilitation.

1. Background

A. Subject Overview

- Name: Emily

- Age: 15 years old

- Offenses: Multiple counts of theft, truancy, and vandalism

- Family Situation: Emily's parents recently divorced, and she now lives with her mother, who works long hours and is minimally involved in her daily life. Emily has a strained relationship with her father, who is largely absent. She has no siblings and few close friends, leading to feelings of isolation.

B. Developmental Concerns

- Adolescence: Emily's behavior began to deteriorate following her parents' separation, coinciding with the onset of adolescence—a period marked by significant cognitive, emotional, and social changes. Adolescents often experience heightened emotions and a stronger desire for independence, which can lead to risky behaviors if not properly guided.

- Academic Struggles: Emily has a history of academic difficulties, including poor grades, frequent absences, and behavioral issues at school. These challenges have led to frustration and disengagement from her studies, further isolating her from positive peer influences.

C. Social Environment

- Peer Influence: In the absence of strong family support, Emily has gravitated towards peers who engage in delinquent behaviors. Her desire for acceptance and belonging has led her to participate in theft and vandalism, actions that she views as a way to gain approval from her peers.

- Community: Emily lives in a community with limited access to recreational activities, youth programs, and other positive outlets for her energy and creativity. The lack of supportive community resources has left her with few alternatives to delinquent behavior.

2. Assessment Process

A. Developmental Evaluation

- Cognitive Development: A cognitive assessment was conducted to evaluate Emily's intellectual functioning and identify any learning disabilities that might be contributing to her academic struggles. The assessment revealed that Emily has mild dyslexia, which has impacted her reading comprehension and overall academic performance. This learning disability had not been previously diagnosed, contributing to her frustration and disengagement from school.

- Emotional and Social Development: Emily's emotional development was assessed through interviews and standardized tests that measured her emotional regulation, self-esteem, and social skills. The assessment indicated that Emily struggles with low self-esteem, difficulty managing her emotions, and a lack of effective social skills. These issues have contributed to her defiant behavior and her reliance on negative peer influences.

- Moral Development: Emily's understanding of right and wrong was also assessed, focusing on her moral reasoning and decision-making processes. The evaluation showed that Emily's moral development is at a stage where she is heavily influenced by peer approval, often prioritizing her friends' opinions over established social norms and rules.

B. Psychological Evaluation

- Mental Health Assessment: A comprehensive psychological evaluation was conducted to assess Emily's mental health status. The evaluation included interviews with Emily, her mother, and her teachers, as well as standardized questionnaires. Emily was found to be experiencing symptoms of depression, including sadness, irritability, and withdrawal from activities she previously enjoyed. These symptoms were linked to her parents' divorce and her subsequent feelings of abandonment and insecurity.

- Behavioral Assessment: Emily's behavioral patterns were evaluated to understand the frequency, intensity, and triggers of her delinquent actions. The assessment revealed that Emily's delinquent behavior often occurred in response to feelings of rejection, loneliness, and anger. These emotions were particularly strong in situations where she felt criticized or neglected by her family or teachers.

3. Intervention and Recommendations

A. Therapeutic Interventions

- Individual Therapy: It was recommended that Emily participate in individual therapy to address her depression, low self-esteem, and difficulties with emotional regulation. Cognitive-behavioral therapy (CBT) was suggested as the primary approach, focusing on helping Emily develop healthier thought patterns and coping strategies.

- Family Therapy: Family therapy was also recommended to improve communication and strengthen the relationship between Emily and her mother. The therapy sessions would focus on addressing the unresolved issues from the parents' divorce and helping the family establish a more supportive and nurturing home environment.

B. Educational Support

- Special Education Services: Given her diagnosis of mild dyslexia, Emily was referred to special education services to receive the support she needs in her academic work. This included tutoring, accommodations in the classroom (such as extra time on tests), and individualized learning plans to help her succeed in school.

- Vocational Counseling: Vocational counseling was recommended to help Emily explore potential career interests and develop a sense of purpose. This counseling would provide guidance on choosing educational pathways that align with her strengths and interests, helping her see a positive future beyond her current struggles.

C. Social Interventions

- Peer Group Therapy: To address her social isolation and reliance on negative peer influences, Emily was encouraged to participate in peer group therapy. This group setting would allow her to develop better social skills, build positive relationships, and receive support from peers facing similar challenges.

- Extracurricular Activities: Emily was also encouraged to join extracurricular activities, such as a school club or a community youth group, to provide her with positive outlets for her energy and opportunities to form healthy relationships with her peers.

4. Outcomes

A. Progress and Challenges

- Initial Improvements: Over several months of therapy and educational support, Emily began to show improvements in her behavior, academic performance, and emotional well-being. She became more engaged in school, her grades improved, and she started to form positive relationships with new peers.

- Setbacks: Despite these improvements, Emily experienced setbacks, particularly during times of stress, such as when her mother's work schedule became more demanding, limiting her ability to participate in family therapy. These setbacks highlighted the importance of continued support and monitoring.

B. Long-Term Recommendations

- Continued Therapy: Ongoing individual and family therapy were recommended to ensure that Emily continues to build on the progress she has made. The focus of therapy would shift towards long-term goals, such as planning for her future and strengthening her coping strategies.

- Educational Monitoring: Regular check-ins with her teachers and special education staff were recommended to monitor Emily's academic progress and adjust her learning plan as needed. Ensuring that she continues to receive the support she needs in school is crucial for maintaining her academic success.

- Social Support: Emily's involvement in positive peer groups and extracurricular activities should be encouraged and supported over the long term. These activities will help her build a strong social network and provide a buffer against potential future challenges.

This case study demonstrates the importance of conducting a thorough developmental and psychological assessment for juvenile offenders. By understanding the individual's cognitive, emotional, and social development, professionals can design targeted interventions that address the root causes of delinquent behavior and support the youth's successful rehabilitation and reintegration into society.

4.4 Practical Exercise: Designing a Juvenile Rehabilitation Program

This practical exercise is designed to help you apply the knowledge gained in this chapter by creating a comprehensive rehabilitation program for a hypothetical juvenile offender. By considering the unique needs and circumstances of the youth, you will develop a tailored intervention plan that addresses the underlying causes of delinquent behavior and supports the youth's successful reintegration into society.

1. Scenario Description

A. Case Overview

- Subject: Jordan, a 16-year-old male, has been adjudicated for multiple offenses, including vandalism, shoplifting, and assault. Jordan has a history of gang involvement, truancy, and substance abuse. He lives with his single mother, who works multiple jobs and is often absent. Jordan has been in and out of foster care and has frequent conflicts with authority figures, including teachers and law enforcement.

B. Background Information

- Family Environment: Jordan's father left when he was young, and his mother has struggled to provide stability due to financial hardships and work demands. The absence of parental guidance has led Jordan to seek belonging and support from his peers, many of whom are involved in criminal activities.

- Educational History: Jordan has a poor academic record, with frequent absences and failing grades. He has been suspended multiple times for disruptive behavior and has expressed little interest in school. Jordan's teachers describe him as intelligent but disengaged, with a tendency to act out when he feels threatened or disrespected.

- Social Environment: Jordan's social circle primarily consists of peers involved in gang activities. He has been arrested several times for minor offenses, but his involvement in more serious crimes has escalated over time. Jordan has expressed feelings of anger and frustration, often citing his lack of opportunities and support as reasons for his behavior.

2. *Program Design Process*

A. Assess Jordan's Needs

1. *Psychological and Behavioral Needs*

- Mental Health Assessment: Jordan may benefit from a thorough psychological evaluation to identify any underlying mental health issues, such as depression, anxiety, or conduct disorder. Understanding his emotional state and behavioral tendencies is crucial for developing effective interventions.

- Substance Abuse: Given his history of substance abuse, Jordan's rehabilitation program should include a substance abuse assessment and treatment plan. Addressing his drug and alcohol use is essential for his overall rehabilitation.

2. Educational and Vocational Needs

- Educational Support: Jordan's disengagement from school suggests a need for specialized educational support. This might include tutoring, special education services, or an alternative education program that offers a more flexible and supportive learning environment.

- Vocational Training: Since Jordan has expressed little interest in traditional schooling, vocational training could provide a meaningful alternative. Identifying his interests and strengths can help guide him towards a career path that is both practical and fulfilling.

3. Social and Family Needs

- Family Counseling: Improving Jordan's relationship with his mother and addressing the family dynamics is critical. Family counseling could help them develop better communication and support each other's needs. If his mother's work schedule is a barrier, involving extended family or community resources may be necessary.

- Peer Relationships: Jordan's involvement with delinquent peers is a significant risk factor. His rehabilitation plan should include strategies for distancing him from these influences and helping him build positive relationships. Mentorship programs or involvement in structured group activities could provide alternative social networks.

4. Community and Environmental Needs

- Restorative Justice: Incorporating restorative justice practices, such as victim-offender mediation or community service, could help Jordan understand the impact of his actions and foster a sense of responsibility. These programs also encourage him to make amends and reintegrate into his community.

- Recreational Activities: Providing Jordan with access to positive recreational activities, such as sports, arts, or youth clubs, can help him channel his energy into constructive outlets and reduce his involvement in criminal activities.

B. Select Rehabilitation Approaches

1. Cognitive-Behavioral Therapy (CBT)

- Focus: Implement CBT to address Jordan's negative thought patterns and behaviors. The therapy sessions should focus on helping him develop healthier coping mechanisms, improve his emotional regulation, and make better decisions in stressful situations.

2. Family-Based Interventions

- Focus: Engage Jordan and his mother in family therapy to improve communication and address underlying issues contributing to his delinquent behavior. The therapy should also explore ways to strengthen their relationship and establish a more supportive home environment.

3. Educational and Vocational Programs

- Focus: Enroll Jordan in a vocational training program aligned with his interests. This program should offer practical skills training and mentorship to help him build a career path. Simultaneously, provide him with tutoring or alternative education options to ensure he completes his basic education.

4. Restorative Justice and Community Involvement

- Focus: Involve Jordan in a restorative justice program where he can engage in community service and participate in victim-offender mediation. These activities will help him understand the consequences of his actions and encourage him to take responsibility for his behavior.

C. Develop a Comprehensive Plan

1. Short-Term Goals

- Psychological Stability: Achieve a reduction in Jordan's substance use and improve his emotional regulation through consistent participation in CBT.

- Family Reconciliation: Improve communication and reduce conflict between Jordan and his mother through regular family therapy sessions.

2. Long-Term Goals

- Educational Attainment: Help Jordan obtain his GED or complete an alternative education program while exploring vocational training opportunities that align with his interests.

- Positive Social Integration: Establish a new social network for Jordan through mentorship programs and positive peer group activities, reducing his reliance on delinquent peers.

3. Monitoring and Evaluation

- Ongoing Assessment: Implement regular check-ins with Jordan's therapists, educators, and family to monitor his progress and adjust the rehabilitation plan as needed.

- Outcome Measurement: Track Jordan's participation in therapy, educational progress, and engagement in community service. Success indicators include a reduction in criminal behavior, improved family relationships, and the achievement of educational and vocational milestones.

D. Evaluate and Adjust

1. Regular Progress Reviews

   - Frequency: Schedule bi-weekly reviews with all stakeholders, including Jordan, his family, therapists, and educators, to assess progress and make necessary adjustments to the program.

   - Feedback Loop: Encourage open communication during reviews to ensure that Jordan's needs are being met and that he feels supported throughout the process.

2. Flexibility in Approach

   - Adapting to Change: Be prepared to adjust the rehabilitation plan if Jordan encounters setbacks or if his circumstances change. Flexibility is key to ensuring that the program remains effective and responsive to his evolving needs.

3. Reflection and Feedback

A. Reflect on the Design Process

- Consider the following questions:

   - How did you prioritize the different needs and challenges Jordan faces?

   - What strategies did you use to ensure that the program is holistic and addresses both immediate and long-term goals?

   - How might the program be adjusted if Jordan encounters setbacks or if his needs change over time?

B. Feedback for Improvement

- Seek feedback: After presenting the rehabilitation plan, seek feedback from peers, mentors, or professionals in the field. This feedback can provide valuable insights into areas of the plan that may need refinement or further development.

C. Application to Future Cases

- Consider how the skills and insights gained from this exercise can be applied to future cases in forensic psychology. Reflect on the importance of a comprehensive, individualized approach to juvenile rehabilitation and how this approach can lead to more effective outcomes.

This practical exercise in designing a juvenile rehabilitation program is intended to deepen your understanding of the complexities involved in addressing delinquent behavior. By applying theoretical knowledge to a real-world scenario, you can develop the skills necessary to create tailored interventions that support the rehabilitation and reintegration of juvenile offenders, ultimately contributing to a safer and more just society.

Chapter 4 Review

Chapter 4 delves into the complexities of juvenile and developmental forensic psychology, offering insights into the causes of juvenile delinquency, effective rehabilitation approaches, and the importance of developmental assessments in shaping interventions. This review summarizes the key points and takeaways from each section of the chapter.

4.1 Causes of Juvenile Delinquency

- Family Dynamics: Dysfunctional family environments, including neglect, abuse, and poor parental role models, are significant contributors to juvenile delinquency. The lack of a supportive home environment often drives juveniles to seek acceptance through delinquent behavior.

- Peer Influence: Adolescents are highly influenced by their peers, and involvement in gangs or delinquent peer groups can lead to criminal behavior. Peer pressure plays a crucial role in shaping the actions and decisions of young offenders.

- Socioeconomic Factors: Poverty, educational disengagement, and limited opportunities increase the risk of delinquency. Juveniles from disadvantaged backgrounds often turn to crime as a means of survival or achieving status.

- Psychological Factors: Mental health issues, such as conduct disorder and ADHD, can predispose youths to delinquent behavior. Emotional regulation difficulties and untreated psychological disorders are key risk factors.

- Environmental Factors: High-crime neighborhoods and exposure to violence normalize delinquent behavior for juveniles, making crime seem like a necessary or acceptable means of achieving goals.

4.2 Assessment Methods

- Risk and Needs Assessments: Tools like the YLS/CMI and SAVRY help professionals evaluate the risk factors and needs of juvenile offenders, guiding the development of individualized treatment plans.

- Developmental Assessments: These assessments focus on cognitive, emotional, and social development, identifying any delays or disorders that may contribute to delinquent behavior. They are crucial for tailoring interventions to the juvenile's developmental stage.

- Psychological Evaluations: Comprehensive psychological evaluations assess mental health status and identify disorders that may influence behavior. These evaluations are critical for informing treatment plans that address the specific mental health needs of the juvenile.

4.3 Rehabilitation Approaches for Juvenile Offenders

- Cognitive-Behavioral Therapy (CBT): CBT is effective in reducing recidivism by helping juveniles change negative thought patterns and behaviors. It focuses on emotional regulation, decision-making, and developing healthier ways of thinking.

- Family-Based Interventions: Programs like FFT, MST, and PMT address family dynamics that contribute to delinquency. These interventions improve communication, resolve conflicts, and strengthen family bonds, creating a supportive environment for the juvenile.

- Educational and Vocational Programs: Providing education and job training is critical for rehabilitation. These programs help juveniles build self-esteem, develop skills, and find alternative paths to success, reducing the likelihood of reoffending.

- Restorative Justice Programs: Restorative justice focuses on repairing harm and restoring relationships between the offender, the victim, and the community. These programs encourage accountability, empathy, and making amends, leading to lower recidivism rates.

4.4 Case Study: Developmental Assessment of Juvenile Offenders

- The case study of Emily illustrates the importance of conducting a thorough developmental and psychological assessment. By understanding the individual's cognitive, emotional, and social development, professionals can design targeted interventions that address the root causes of delinquent behavior.

- The assessment process revealed Emily's struggles with depression, low self-esteem, and undiagnosed learning disabilities, leading to recommendations for individual therapy, special education services, and social support. The case study highlights the need for comprehensive and tailored interventions to support successful rehabilitation.

4.5 Practical Exercise: Designing a Juvenile Rehabilitation Program

- The practical exercise involved creating a comprehensive rehabilitation program for a hypothetical juvenile offender, Jordan. The exercise emphasized the importance of assessing psychological, educational, social, and environmental needs to develop a holistic intervention plan.

- Key strategies included CBT, family-based interventions, vocational training, and restorative justice practices. The exercise highlighted the need for ongoing monitoring, flexibility, and collaboration among stakeholders to ensure the program's success.

Key Takeaways

- Holistic Approach: Effective rehabilitation requires a holistic approach that addresses the multiple factors contributing to juvenile delinquency, including family dynamics, peer influence, socioeconomic status, psychological issues, and environmental factors.

- Tailored Interventions: Each juvenile offender's needs and circumstances are unique, necessitating individualized treatment plans that consider their developmental stage, mental health, and social environment.

- Importance of Family and Community: Engaging the family and community in the rehabilitation process is crucial for creating a supportive network that encourages positive behavior change and reduces the risk of reoffending.

- Restorative Practices: Restorative justice programs offer a valuable alternative to punitive measures, focusing on healing, accountability, and the reintegration of juveniles into society.

Chapter 4 provides a comprehensive overview of juvenile and developmental forensic psychology, emphasizing the importance of understanding the root causes of delinquent behavior and implementing tailored, multi-faceted rehabilitation approaches. By applying the concepts and strategies discussed in this chapter, professionals can support the successful rehabilitation of juvenile offenders and contribute to a safer, more just society.

Chapter 5: Legal Processes and Forensic Psychology

The intersection of law and psychology forms the foundation of forensic psychology, a field that demands a deep understanding of both legal processes and human behavior. Chapter 5 delves into the intricate relationship between the criminal justice system and forensic psychology, exploring how forensic psychologists contribute to legal proceedings, influence courtroom dynamics, and ensure that psychological insights are integrated into the pursuit of justice. This chapter provides a comprehensive analysis of the roles forensic psychologists play within legal settings, the challenges they face, and the ethical considerations that guide their work. Through detailed exploration and real-world examples, this chapter equips readers with the knowledge needed to navigate the complex legal landscape and apply psychological expertise effectively in forensic contexts.

5.1 The Criminal Justice System: An Overview

Understanding the criminal justice system is essential for anyone working in forensic psychology, as it provides the framework within which legal decisions are made and justice is administered. This section offers a comprehensive overview of the criminal justice system, highlighting its key components, the roles of various professionals, and the processes that govern the administration of justice.

1. Key Components of the Criminal Justice System

A. Law Enforcement

- Law enforcement agencies, including the police and federal agencies, are responsible for investigating crimes, gathering evidence, and apprehending suspects.

B. The Judiciary

- The judiciary interprets and applies the law, overseeing legal proceedings, ensuring due process, and ultimately delivering justice through the court system.

C. Corrections

- The corrections system manages the punishment, rehabilitation, and reintegration of convicted individuals, encompassing prisons, probation, and parole.

2. Legal Processes

A. Investigation and Arrest

- The criminal justice process typically begins with the investigation of a crime, followed by the arrest of a suspect based on probable cause.

B. Charging and Prosecution

- After an arrest, the prosecution decides whether to file charges and proceed with a case, based on the evidence collected and the likelihood of securing a conviction.

C. Trial and Sentencing

- If the case goes to trial, the court evaluates the evidence presented by both the prosecution and defense before delivering a verdict. If the defendant is found guilty, sentencing follows, determining the appropriate punishment.

3. Roles and Responsibilities in the Criminal Justice System

A. Judges and Magistrates

- Judges and magistrates play a crucial role in ensuring that legal proceedings are fair and just, interpreting the law, and delivering sentences that reflect the severity of the crime.

B. Prosecutors and Defense Attorneys

- Prosecutors represent the state or government, seeking to prove the defendant's guilt, while defense attorneys advocate on behalf of the accused, challenging the prosecution's evidence and protecting the defendant's rights.

C. Forensic Psychologists

- Forensic psychologists contribute by providing expert assessments, offering insights into the psychological aspects of cases, and sometimes testifying in court to inform legal decisions.

By understanding the key components and processes of the criminal justice system, forensic psychologists can more effectively navigate the legal landscape, ensuring that their contributions are relevant, accurate, and aligned with the pursuit of justice. This foundational knowledge is critical for applying psychological principles within a legal context and for collaborating with other professionals within the system.

5.2 Role of Forensic Psychologists in Legal Settings

Forensic psychologists play a pivotal role in legal settings, bridging the gap between psychology and the law. Their expertise is called upon in various stages of the legal process, where they provide critical insights that can influence the outcomes of cases. This section delves into the diverse functions of forensic psychologists within the legal system, highlighting their contributions to both criminal and civil cases.

1. Assessment and Evaluation

A. Competency Evaluations

- Forensic psychologists conduct competency evaluations to determine whether a defendant is mentally fit to stand trial. This involves assessing the individual's ability to understand the charges against them and participate in their defense.

B. Risk Assessment

- They assess the risk of reoffending, particularly in cases involving violent or sexual crimes. This evaluation helps inform sentencing decisions, parole eligibility, and the development of treatment plans.

C. Psychological Profiling

- In some cases, forensic psychologists may assist law enforcement by developing psychological profiles of suspects, helping to narrow down the search and understand the motivations behind a crime.

2. Expert Testimony

A. Providing Expert Opinions

- Forensic psychologists often serve as expert witnesses in court, offering testimony on matters such as a defendant's mental state at the time of the crime, the likelihood of future dangerousness, or the psychological impact of an event on a victim.

B. Educating the Court

- They educate judges, juries, and attorneys on psychological concepts that are pertinent to the case, such as the effects of trauma, memory reliability, or the characteristics of mental illness.

C. Cross-Examination and Challenges

- Forensic psychologists must be prepared to defend their findings and opinions under cross-examination, demonstrating the validity and reliability of their assessments in the face of scrutiny from opposing counsel.

3. Consultation and Collaboration

A. Assisting Legal Teams

- Forensic psychologists work closely with legal teams to develop case strategies, providing insights into the psychological aspects that may influence the jury's perception or the client's behavior.

B. Jury Selection and Consultation

- They may assist in the jury selection process, using their understanding of human behavior to identify potential biases or predict how jurors might respond to certain arguments.

C. Collaboration with Law Enforcement

- Forensic psychologists collaborate with law enforcement agencies, offering guidance during criminal investigations, particularly in cases involving serial offenders or complex psychological factors.

4. Treatment and Rehabilitation

A. Designing Treatment Plans

- Forensic psychologists are involved in the treatment and rehabilitation of offenders, creating tailored programs that address the underlying psychological issues contributing to criminal behavior.

B. Monitoring Progress

- They monitor the progress of individuals undergoing court-mandated treatment, providing reports to the court on their compliance and improvements, which can influence parole or probation decisions.

C. Rehabilitation and Reintegration

- Their work extends to helping offenders reintegrate into society post-incarceration, focusing on reducing recidivism through ongoing psychological support and intervention.

By understanding the multifaceted role of forensic psychologists in legal settings, professionals in this field can better navigate the complex interplay between psychological expertise and legal requirements. Their contributions are integral to ensuring that justice is served in a manner that considers both the legal and psychological dimensions of each case.

5.3 Expert Witness Testimony and Courtroom Dynamics

Expert witness testimony is one of the most visible and impactful roles that forensic psychologists undertake within the legal system. Their involvement in courtroom proceedings requires not only a deep understanding of psychological principles but also the ability to communicate complex information effectively to judges, juries, and attorneys. This section explores the intricacies of providing expert testimony, the challenges that forensic psychologists face in the courtroom, and the strategies they employ to ensure their testimony is both credible and persuasive.

1. Preparation for Testimony

A. Thorough Case Review

- Before appearing in court, forensic psychologists conduct an exhaustive review of all relevant case materials, including psychological evaluations, medical records, and any prior testimonies. This preparation ensures that their testimony is well-informed and based on a comprehensive understanding of the case.

B. Developing Clear and Concise Explanations

- One of the key challenges in expert testimony is explaining psychological concepts in a way that is accessible to non-experts. Forensic psychologists must distill complex ideas into clear, concise explanations that can be easily understood by the jury and the court.

C. Anticipating Cross-Examination

- Forensic psychologists must anticipate the questions and challenges that may arise during cross-examination. They prepare to defend their assessments and opinions against opposing counsel's attempts to undermine their credibility or findings.

2. The Testimony Process

A. Establishing Credibility

- From the moment they take the stand, forensic psychologists work to establish their credibility. This involves outlining their qualifications, experience, and the methodology used in their evaluations. A clear, confident demeanor is crucial in building trust with the court.

B. Delivering Testimony

- During testimony, forensic psychologists present their findings in response to questions from both the prosecuting and defense attorneys. They must remain composed and professional, avoiding technical jargon and focusing on conveying their expert opinions in a straightforward manner.

C. Responding to Cross-Examination

- Cross-examination is designed to test the reliability and accuracy of the expert's testimony. Forensic psychologists must remain calm under pressure, responding thoughtfully to challenging questions and avoiding traps set by opposing counsel. They must maintain consistency in their testimony while being adaptable to the flow of questioning.

3. Courtroom Dynamics

A. Understanding the Audience

- Forensic psychologists must be attuned to the dynamics of the courtroom, including the attitudes and reactions of the jury, judge, and attorneys. Understanding these dynamics helps them tailor their testimony to be more effective and impactful.

B. Building Rapport with the Jury

- Establishing a connection with the jury is essential. Forensic psychologists can build rapport by maintaining eye contact, using body language that conveys confidence and openness, and addressing the jury directly when appropriate.

C. Navigating Objections and Interruptions

- Courtroom testimony can be interrupted by objections from attorneys. Forensic psychologists must be prepared to pause, wait for the judge's ruling, and then continue their testimony smoothly. They must also know how to reframe their answers if the court sustains an objection.

4. Ethical Considerations

A. Maintaining Objectivity

- It is crucial for forensic psychologists to maintain objectivity throughout their testimony. They must present their findings based on evidence and professional judgment, avoiding any bias or alignment with either party.

B. Confidentiality and Privacy

- Forensic psychologists must navigate the ethical complexities of confidentiality, ensuring that sensitive information is disclosed only as necessary and in compliance with legal standards.

C. Handling Pressure from Legal Teams

- Legal teams may attempt to influence the expert's testimony to favor their case. Forensic psychologists must adhere strictly to their ethical obligations, providing testimony that is truthful and based on their independent professional assessment.

By mastering the art of expert witness testimony and understanding the nuances of courtroom dynamics, forensic psychologists can significantly influence legal outcomes. Their ability to communicate psychological expertise effectively within the constraints of the legal system is essential to ensuring that their testimony contributes meaningfully to the pursuit of justice.

5.4 Interactive Exercise: Preparing for Testimony

This interactive exercise is designed to simulate the experience of preparing for expert witness testimony in a courtroom setting. By engaging in this exercise, forensic psychology professionals and students can develop the skills needed to deliver effective and credible testimony. The exercise will guide you through the key steps of preparation, from reviewing case materials to anticipating cross-examination, providing practical insights into the dynamics of expert testimony.

1. Case Review and Analysis

A. Reviewing Case Materials

- Begin by thoroughly reviewing all relevant case materials. This includes psychological evaluations, medical records, witness statements, and any prior testimonies related to the case. Focus on understanding the context of the case, the individuals involved, and the specific psychological issues at play.

  - Task: Summarize the key psychological findings and how they relate to the legal questions at hand. Identify any potential weaknesses or areas that may be challenged during cross-examination.

B. Identifying Core Issues

- Next, identify the core psychological issues that will be central to your testimony. Determine how these issues align with the legal questions and what your expert opinion will contribute to the case.

- Task: Outline the primary psychological concepts and evidence that support your expert opinion. Consider how these concepts can be explained clearly to a lay audience.

C. Formulating Clear Explanations

- Develop clear and concise explanations for the psychological concepts you will discuss in court. These explanations should be accessible to individuals without a background in psychology, such as jurors and judges.

- Task: Practice explaining complex psychological terms and diagnoses in plain language. Test your explanations with a peer or mentor to ensure clarity.

2. Crafting Your Testimony

A. Structuring Your Testimony

- Organize your testimony in a logical structure that guides the court through your findings. Begin with your qualifications and methodology, followed by your analysis and conclusions.

- Task: Create an outline of your testimony, including an introduction that establishes your credibility and a conclusion that reinforces your key points.

B. Anticipating Questions

- Anticipate the types of questions you might face from both the prosecution and defense. Consider how you will respond to questions that challenge your findings or attempt to undermine your credibility.

- Task: Write down potential cross-examination questions and formulate thoughtful, evidence-based responses. Practice delivering these responses confidently and without hesitation.

C. Preparing for Objections

- Be prepared for objections from opposing counsel during your testimony. Understand common objections related to expert testimony, such as hearsay or leading questions, and how to navigate them.

   - Task: Review legal guidelines on expert witness testimony and familiarize yourself with the rules of evidence. Role-play scenarios where objections are raised, and practice maintaining composure while waiting for the judge's ruling.

3. Role-Playing the Testimony

A. Simulated Courtroom Setting

- Engage in a role-playing exercise that simulates a courtroom setting. Have a peer or mentor act as the attorney, asking you questions based on your prepared testimony. This exercise should include both direct examination and cross-examination.

   - Task: Record the role-play session and review your performance. Pay attention to your body language, tone of voice, and clarity of responses. Identify areas for improvement.

B. Building Confidence

- Focus on building confidence in your ability to testify effectively. Confidence is key to establishing credibility in the courtroom, so practice maintaining a calm and authoritative presence.

   - Task: Repeat the role-playing exercise multiple times, incorporating feedback from previous sessions. Aim to refine your delivery and reduce any signs of nervousness.

C. Receiving Feedback

- After the role-playing exercise, seek feedback from your peers, mentors, or supervisors. Constructive feedback is invaluable for improving your testimony skills and addressing any weaknesses.

  - Task: Implement the feedback into your next practice session, focusing on the specific areas highlighted for improvement.

4. Reflecting on the Experience

A. Self-Assessment

- After completing the interactive exercise, take time to reflect on your experience. Consider what you learned about the preparation process and how you can apply these skills in real courtroom settings.

  - Task: Write a brief reflection on what you found challenging and what aspects of your testimony preparation were most effective. Set goals for further development of your courtroom skills.

B. Continuous Improvement

- Testifying as an expert witness is a skill that improves with experience and practice. Commit to ongoing learning and development in this area, whether through additional exercises, continuing education, or real-world experience.

  - Task: Identify resources, such as workshops, seminars, or mentorship opportunities, that can help you continue to build your expertise in forensic testimony.

This interactive exercise provides a practical framework for preparing expert witness testimony, helping forensic psychologists develop the skills needed to navigate the complexities of the courtroom with confidence and professionalism. By engaging in this exercise, you can refine your testimony techniques and enhance your effectiveness as an expert witness in legal settings.

5.5 Case Study: Mock Trial Preparation

In this section, we delve into a comprehensive case study that illustrates the process of preparing for a mock trial as a forensic psychologist. This case study is designed to provide you with practical insights and a deep understanding of the steps involved in trial preparation, emphasizing the application of forensic psychology within a legal context.

1. Case Overview

A. Background Information

- The mock trial centers around a criminal case involving allegations of assault where the defendant's mental state at the time of the offense is a crucial factor.

    - Details: The defendant, a 35-year-old male with a history of mental illness, is accused of assaulting a neighbor during a dispute. The defense is arguing that the defendant was not in control of his actions due to a psychotic episode.

B. Psychological Evaluations

- As the forensic psychologist, your role is to conduct a comprehensive psychological evaluation of the defendant to assess his mental state during the incident.

    - Process: This involves clinical interviews, psychological testing, and reviewing the defendant's medical and psychiatric history. Key assessments include evaluating cognitive functioning, diagnosing any relevant mental disorders, and determining the impact of these disorders on the defendant's behavior at the time of the alleged offense.

C. Legal Implications

- The findings from your evaluation will play a significant role in the trial, particularly in determining whether the defendant meets the legal criteria for insanity or diminished capacity.

- Objective: To present an objective, evidence-based opinion that helps the court understand the psychological factors that may have influenced the defendant's actions, and how these factors relate to legal standards of criminal responsibility.

2. Preparation for Testimony

A. Developing the Testimony

- Based on your evaluations, the next step is to prepare your testimony, focusing on clear communication of your findings and their implications for the case.

  - Content: Your testimony should include a detailed explanation of the defendant's mental health condition, the methodology used in your evaluation, and how these findings relate to the defendant's ability to form intent or control his actions during the incident.

B. Anticipating Cross-Examination

- Anticipate the areas of your testimony that may be challenged during cross-examination by the prosecution.

  - Preparation: Identify potential weaknesses in your assessment, such as the reliability of psychological tests or alternative explanations for the defendant's behavior. Prepare reasoned responses to questions that may attempt to undermine your credibility or the validity of your findings.

C. Mock Testimony Practice

- Engage in practice sessions where you deliver your testimony in a simulated courtroom setting. This helps in refining your delivery and preparing for the dynamics of cross-examination.

  - Simulation: Have colleagues or mentors act as attorneys, posing challenging questions and objections to simulate the pressure of a real trial. Focus on maintaining composure, clarity, and adherence to the facts during these mock sessions.

3. Collaboration with Legal Team

A. Strategy Development

- Work closely with the defense attorneys to develop a cohesive strategy that integrates your psychological findings into the broader defense narrative.

　- Coordination: Discuss how your testimony will support key defense arguments, such as the impact of the defendant's mental state on his criminal intent. Ensure that your findings are aligned with the legal theories the defense plans to present.

B. Pre-Trial Meetings

- Participate in pre-trial meetings with the legal team to go over the specifics of your testimony, including the sequence of questioning and key points to emphasize.

　- Discussion: Review any legal precedents or statutes relevant to your testimony. Clarify the defense's expectations regarding how your testimony will be used in closing arguments or motions.

C. Refining the Testimony

- Based on feedback from the legal team, make any necessary adjustments to your testimony to ensure it is as effective and persuasive as possible.

　- Adjustment: This might involve simplifying complex psychological concepts or focusing more on certain aspects of the evaluation that are particularly relevant to the defense's case.

4. Trial Simulation

A. Mock Trial Execution

- Participate in a full mock trial where your testimony is presented in a realistic courtroom environment. This provides an opportunity to experience the flow of a trial and the interactions between different courtroom participants.

   - Role Play: Engage in direct examination, cross-examination, and re-direct examination as part of the simulation. Practice responding to objections and interacting with the judge and jury.

B. Feedback and Analysis

- After the mock trial, engage in a debriefing session where you receive feedback from peers, mentors, and legal professionals.

   - Evaluation: Analyze your performance, focusing on areas such as clarity, persuasiveness, and how well you handled cross-examination. Identify strengths and areas for improvement.

C. Applying Lessons Learned

- Use the insights gained from the mock trial to refine your approach to future testimonies.

   - Implementation: Incorporate feedback into your ongoing preparation process. Consider how to apply these lessons in real-world courtroom settings to enhance your effectiveness as an expert witness.

5. Reflection and Continuous Improvement

A. Reflective Practice

- Reflect on your experience throughout the mock trial preparation and simulation process.

- Self-Assessment: Consider what aspects of the preparation were most challenging and how you addressed these challenges. Reflect on your growth in handling courtroom dynamics and expert testimony.

B. Ongoing Learning

- Commit to continuous improvement in your role as a forensic psychologist by seeking out additional training, mentorship, and opportunities for mock trial participation.

  - Professional Development: Engage in continuing education focused on forensic testimony and legal processes. Stay updated on the latest research and best practices in forensic psychology to enhance your credibility and effectiveness in the courtroom.

This case study on mock trial preparation provides a practical, in-depth exploration of the processes involved in delivering expert testimony in a legal setting. By applying these strategies and techniques, forensic psychologists can strengthen their courtroom presence and contribute valuable insights to the legal process.

Chapter 5 Review: Legal Processes and Forensic Psychology

Chapter 5 of *HowExpert Guide to Forensic Psychology* delves into the intricate relationship between the criminal justice system and forensic psychology, exploring the pivotal role that forensic psychologists play in legal settings. This chapter provides a comprehensive overview of the criminal justice system, the responsibilities of forensic psychologists, the dynamics of expert witness testimony, and practical exercises like preparing for mock trials.

5.1 The Criminal Justice System: An Overview

- Understanding the System: This section offers a foundational overview of the criminal justice system, highlighting the different stages from investigation to trial and the various players involved, such as law enforcement, attorneys, judges, and juries.

- Psychological Aspects: It emphasizes how forensic psychology intersects with these stages, particularly in assessing defendants' mental states, providing insights into criminal behavior, and assisting in the formulation of legal strategies.

5.2 Role of Forensic Psychologists in Legal Settings

- Key Responsibilities: Forensic psychologists are tasked with various responsibilities, including conducting psychological evaluations, providing expert testimony, and consulting on cases.

- Ethical Considerations: The section delves into the ethical obligations of forensic psychologists, such as maintaining objectivity, ensuring confidentiality, and adhering to legal standards.

- Impact on Legal Outcomes: It also explores how their work can significantly influence legal outcomes, from competency evaluations to risk assessments and sentencing recommendations.

5.3 Expert Witness Testimony and Courtroom Dynamics

- Preparation for Testimony: This section outlines the process of preparing for courtroom testimony, emphasizing the importance of thorough evaluation, clear communication, and understanding legal terminology.

- Courtroom Challenges: It discusses the challenges forensic psychologists may face during cross-examination, such as maintaining composure under pressure and defending their findings against scrutiny.

- Enhancing Credibility: Strategies for enhancing credibility as an expert witness are also covered, including the importance of professional demeanor, the clarity of explanations, and the use of supporting evidence.

5.4 Interactive Exercise: Preparing for Testimony

- Practical Application: This interactive exercise provides a hands-on approach to preparing for testimony, guiding readers through the steps of creating and delivering effective expert testimony.

- Simulation Techniques: The section encourages the use of mock trials and role-playing exercises to simulate courtroom conditions, helping forensic psychologists refine their testimony skills and anticipate potential challenges.

5.5 Case Study: Mock Trial Preparation

- Real-World Application: The case study offers a detailed exploration of the preparation process for a mock trial, providing practical insights into how forensic psychologists can prepare for actual court cases.

- Collaborative Effort: It highlights the importance of collaboration with legal teams, understanding the nuances of the case, and tailoring testimony to support the defense or prosecution's arguments.

- Reflective Practice: The section concludes with a focus on reflective practice, encouraging forensic psychologists to continually assess and improve their courtroom performance based on feedback and self-evaluation.

Chapter 5 emphasizes the critical role that forensic psychologists play in the legal system. From understanding the criminal justice process to preparing for and delivering expert testimony, forensic psychologists must navigate a complex landscape where psychological expertise intersects with legal standards. The chapter's in-depth analysis of the responsibilities, challenges, and practical applications of forensic psychology in legal settings provides valuable guidance for professionals looking to excel in this field. Through detailed explanations, practical exercises, and case studies, readers gain a nuanced understanding of how to effectively contribute to legal processes, enhancing both their professional practice and the outcomes of the cases they work on.

Chapter 6: Psychological Assessments and Legal Implications

Chapter 6 delves into the critical role of psychological assessments within the legal system. It explores various types of assessments, their implications for legal outcomes, and provides practical tools and exercises for conducting these assessments effectively.

6.1 Types of Psychological Assessments

Psychological assessments are foundational tools in forensic psychology, playing a pivotal role in shaping legal decisions. These assessments provide a systematic approach to evaluating mental state, cognitive abilities, and personality traits, all of which are critical in legal contexts. The accuracy and reliability of these assessments can significantly influence outcomes in cases involving criminal responsibility, competency to stand trial, and risk of reoffending. A deep understanding of the various types of psychological assessments is essential for forensic psychologists, legal professionals, and researchers seeking to make informed, evidence-based judgments within the justice system.

1. Personality Assessments

A. Overview

- Personality assessments aim to evaluate enduring patterns of thinking, feeling, and behaving that characterize an individual. In forensic settings, these assessments are particularly valuable in understanding how personality traits might influence behavior, especially in relation to criminal activity. The insights gained from personality assessments can help forensic psychologists identify psychological disorders, predict future behavior, and provide critical information that may affect legal decisions such as sentencing, parole, or treatment.

B. Common Tools

- Minnesota Multiphasic Personality Inventory-2 (MMPI-2): This is one of the most widely used and researched personality assessment tools in forensic psychology. The MMPI-2 is designed to assess a broad range of psychological conditions, including mood disorders, anxiety disorders, psychopathy, and paranoia. It includes validity scales that help detect malingering, exaggeration, or defensiveness, which are common concerns in forensic assessments.

- Personality Assessment Inventory (PAI): The PAI is another extensively used tool that assesses various aspects of personality and psychopathology, including anxiety, depression, aggression, and substance abuse. It is particularly effective in diagnosing mental disorders and evaluating traits relevant to legal cases, such as the potential for violent behavior or susceptibility to stress.

C. Legal Relevance

- Personality assessments are critical in cases involving questions of criminal responsibility, risk of reoffending, and the mental state of defendants at the time of the offense. For instance, in cases where a defendant pleads not guilty by reason of insanity (NGRI), personality assessments can provide evidence about the defendant's mental state at the time of the crime. Additionally, these assessments can inform risk assessments, helping courts decide on appropriate interventions, such as rehabilitation or confinement, based on the likelihood of future criminal behavior.

D. Critical Analysis

- While personality assessments are valuable, they are not without limitations. For example, self-report inventories like the MMPI-2 and PAI rely on the honesty and self-awareness of the individual being assessed. In forensic contexts, where individuals may have a strong incentive to present themselves in a certain light, the validity of these assessments can be compromised. Additionally, cultural and contextual factors may influence responses, leading to potential biases in interpretation. Forensic psychologists must be adept at recognizing these limitations and using multiple sources of information to form a comprehensive assessment.

2. Cognitive Assessments

A. Purpose

- Cognitive assessments are designed to measure various aspects of intellectual functioning, including memory, attention, problem-solving, and language abilities. In forensic psychology, these assessments are crucial for evaluating a person's cognitive capacities, which can significantly impact their competency to stand trial, ability to understand legal proceedings, and overall mental functioning.

B. Examples

- Wechsler Adult Intelligence Scale (WAIS-IV): The WAIS-IV is one of the most commonly used cognitive assessment tools. It provides a comprehensive evaluation of intellectual abilities through subtests that measure verbal comprehension, perceptual reasoning, working memory, and processing speed. This tool is particularly useful in cases where intellectual impairment might affect a defendant's ability to participate in their defense.

- Cognitive Assessment System (CAS): The CAS focuses on cognitive processing capabilities, particularly executive functions like planning, attention, and problem-solving. It is often used in forensic evaluations where cognitive deficits are suspected to play a role in the individual's behavior or legal competence.

C. Applications

- Cognitive assessments are particularly crucial in determining competency to stand trial, assessing cognitive impairments due to neurological conditions, and evaluating the intellectual functioning of defendants who may have mental disabilities. For example, a defendant with an intellectual disability may lack the cognitive capacity to understand the charges against them, communicate effectively with their attorney, or grasp the consequences of a guilty plea. In such cases, the results of cognitive assessments can lead to modifications in how the legal process is handled, including the possibility of a competency restoration program.

D. Critical Analysis

- Cognitive assessments are not immune to challenges. For example, factors such as anxiety, fatigue, or lack of cooperation during testing can skew results, leading to either an overestimation or underestimation of cognitive abilities. Moreover, standard cognitive assessments may not adequately capture the complexities of cognitive functioning in individuals with severe mental illness, brain injuries, or developmental disorders. Forensic psychologists must be skilled in interpreting these assessments in the context of the individual's overall psychological and neurological profile, often integrating findings from multiple assessments to draw accurate conclusions.

3. Neuropsychological Assessments

A. Focus

- Neuropsychological assessments evaluate the relationship between brain function and behavior. These assessments are used to identify cognitive deficits that may be linked to neurological conditions, such as traumatic brain injury, dementia, or developmental disorders. In forensic settings, neuropsychological assessments can be critical in cases where brain dysfunction is suspected to have played a role in criminal behavior or where cognitive deficits may impact legal competence.

B. Methods

- Halstead-Reitan Neuropsychological Battery: This battery is a comprehensive set of tests that assess a wide range of cognitive functions, including memory, attention, language, and executive functioning. It is often used to assess the impact of brain injuries and neurological diseases on cognitive performance.

- Luria-Nebraska Neuropsychological Battery: This tool evaluates neuropsychological functioning through tests that assess motor skills, spatial abilities, and problem-solving. It is particularly useful in identifying localized brain damage and understanding its impact on behavior and cognitive abilities.

C. Legal Context

- Neuropsychological assessments are critical in cases where cognitive deficits may influence criminal behavior, decision-making capabilities, or the ability to understand legal proceedings. For example, a defendant with a traumatic brain injury may exhibit impulsivity, poor judgment, or difficulties with memory, all of which could impact their culpability or competency to stand trial. These assessments provide the court with essential information on how neurological conditions may affect a defendant's actions and responsibilities.

D. Critical Analysis

- The use of neuropsychological assessments in forensic settings requires careful consideration of the interplay between neurological impairments and behavior. One challenge is the interpretation of results, particularly in cases where brain imaging and neuropsychological findings may not align. Additionally, there is a need for greater standardization in the administration and interpretation of these assessments across different forensic contexts. Forensic psychologists must stay current with the latest research and best practices in neuropsychology to ensure that their assessments are both accurate and legally defensible.

4. Integrating Assessment Findings

A. Comprehensive Evaluation

- In forensic psychology, no single assessment tool should be relied upon exclusively. Instead, forensic psychologists must integrate findings from multiple assessments to provide a comprehensive evaluation of an individual's psychological and cognitive functioning. This integration involves synthesizing data from personality, cognitive, and neuropsychological assessments, along with collateral information from interviews, medical records, and other relevant sources.

B. Challenges and Considerations

- Integrating assessment findings can be challenging, particularly when different assessments yield conflicting results. Forensic psychologists must be adept at identifying potential sources of bias, inconsistencies, or limitations in the data and use their professional judgment to reconcile these discrepancies. Additionally, the forensic context often requires psychologists to present their findings in a manner that is accessible to non-expert audiences, such as judges and juries, while maintaining the scientific rigor and accuracy of their conclusions.

C. Impact on Legal Decisions

- The integration of assessment findings plays a crucial role in informing legal decisions. Whether determining a defendant's competency to stand trial, assessing the risk of reoffending, or evaluating the validity of an insanity defense, the ability to provide a nuanced, evidence-based assessment is essential. Forensic psychologists must communicate their findings clearly and effectively, ensuring that their assessments contribute to fair and just legal outcomes.

By utilizing these various types of psychological assessments and critically analyzing their findings, forensic psychologists can offer courts comprehensive insights into an individual's mental state, cognitive abilities, and personality traits. These assessments are indispensable in making informed legal decisions, impacting outcomes related to competency, criminal responsibility, and sentencing.

6.2 Risk Assessments and Competency Evaluations

Risk assessments and competency evaluations are crucial elements in forensic psychology, used to inform legal decisions that have significant implications for both public safety and individual rights. These assessments help in determining the potential risk posed by an individual and their ability to participate meaningfully in legal proceedings. Understanding these assessments is essential for professionals involved in the criminal justice system.

1. Risk Assessments

A. Overview

- Risk assessments evaluate the likelihood that an individual will engage in future harmful behaviors, such as reoffending or violent actions. These assessments are used to inform decisions related to sentencing, parole, and treatment, ensuring that appropriate measures are taken to protect society while addressing the needs of the individual.

B. Types of Risk Factors

- Static Risk Factors: These are unchangeable factors, such as past criminal history or demographic characteristics, that provide a baseline risk level.

- Dynamic Risk Factors: These include changeable elements, such as current mental health status or substance abuse, which can fluctuate over time and influence the likelihood of reoffending.

- Protective Factors: These are characteristics or conditions that decrease the likelihood of reoffending, such as stable employment, strong social support, or engagement in rehabilitation programs.

C. Assessment Tools

- Actuarial Tools: These tools use statistical data to predict risk, such as the Static-99 for sex offenders or the Violence Risk Appraisal Guide (VRAG) for predicting violent behavior.

- Structured Professional Judgment (SPJ): This method combines actuarial data with clinical expertise, using tools like the HCR-20 to assess the risk of future violence by considering a combination of historical, clinical, and risk management factors.

- Unstructured Clinical Judgment: This method relies on the clinician's experience and intuition, allowing for a more individualized approach, though it is generally less reliable than structured methods.

D. Legal Applications

- Risk assessments are instrumental in legal decisions related to sentencing, parole, and the implementation of treatment plans. They ensure that the measures taken are proportionate to the risk posed by the individual, balancing public safety with rehabilitation and fair treatment.

2. Competency Evaluations

A. Overview

- Competency evaluations assess an individual's ability to understand and participate in legal proceedings. These evaluations are crucial in ensuring that defendants can engage meaningfully in their defense and that legal processes are fair and just.

B. Types of Competency

- Competency to Stand Trial: This evaluation determines whether a defendant has the mental capacity to comprehend the charges against them, understand the legal process, and assist in their defense.

- Competency to Plead Guilty: This assessment ensures that a defendant fully understands the consequences of pleading guilty and can make an informed decision.

- Competency to be Executed: In capital cases, this evaluation determines whether an individual understands the nature and reason for their execution, ensuring that the execution is legally and ethically permissible.

C. Assessment Methods

- Clinical Interviews: These are in-depth interviews conducted by mental health professionals to gather information about the individual's mental state and understanding of the legal process.

- Psychological Testing: Tools like the Competence Assessment for Standing Trial for Defendants with Mental Retardation (CAST-MR) or the MacArthur Competence Assessment Tool-Criminal Adjudication (MacCAT-CA) are used to evaluate specific competencies.

- Collateral Information: Information from family members, medical records, and previous legal interactions is often gathered to provide a comprehensive picture of the individual's mental state and abilities.

D. Legal Relevance

- Competency evaluations are vital in protecting the rights of defendants and ensuring that legal proceedings are conducted fairly. If a defendant is found incompetent, they may receive treatment to restore competency before proceedings can continue, or alternative legal measures may be taken.

By integrating risk assessments and competency evaluations, forensic psychologists provide critical insights that help balance public safety with the rights and needs of individuals within the justice system. These assessments ensure that legal decisions are informed, ethical, and just.

6.3 Insanity Defense Evaluations and Legal Outcomes

Insanity defense evaluations are a critical aspect of forensic psychology, where the mental state of a defendant at the time of the offense is assessed to determine whether they can be held legally responsible for their actions. These evaluations play a pivotal role in the criminal justice system, influencing both the outcomes of trials and the sentencing of individuals. Understanding the complexities of insanity defense evaluations and their legal implications is essential for forensic psychologists and legal professionals alike.

1. Overview of Insanity Defense

A. Legal Definition

- The insanity defense is a legal argument used by defendants who claim that, due to a severe mental illness or defect, they were unable to understand the nature of their actions or distinguish right from wrong at the time of the crime. This defense is grounded in the principle that individuals should not be held criminally responsible if they lack the capacity for rational judgment.

B. Standards and Tests

- Different jurisdictions use various standards to determine legal insanity. The most common include:

  - M'Naghten Rule: Focuses on whether the defendant knew what they were doing or understood that it was wrong.

  - Irresistible Impulse Test: Considers whether the defendant was unable to control their actions despite knowing they were wrong.

  - Durham Rule: Evaluates whether the crime was a product of mental illness.

  - Model Penal Code (MPC) Test: Assesses whether the defendant lacked substantial capacity to appreciate the criminality of their conduct or conform their conduct to the requirements of the law.

C. Legal Relevance

- The insanity defense is not commonly used and is successful in only a small percentage of cases. However, when it is applied, it can lead to significant legal outcomes, such as a verdict of not guilty by reason of insanity (NGRI), which often results in commitment to a mental health facility rather than a prison sentence.

2. Conducting Insanity Defense Evaluations

A. Assessment Process

- Forensic psychologists conducting insanity defense evaluations must gather comprehensive information about the defendant's mental state, including:

  - Clinical Interviews: In-depth discussions with the defendant to understand their mental health history and current psychological state.

  - Collateral Information: Gathering data from medical records, family members, and others who have observed the defendant's behavior.

  - Psychological Testing: Utilizing standardized tools to assess cognitive and emotional functioning, such as the Rorschach Inkblot Test, MMPI-2, or the Wechsler Adult Intelligence Scale (WAIS).

B. Challenges in Evaluation

- Evaluating insanity defenses presents unique challenges, including:

  - Retrospective Analysis: Assessing the defendant's mental state at the time of the crime, which may have occurred months or even years before the evaluation.

  - Malingering: The possibility that the defendant is exaggerating or feigning mental illness to avoid legal consequences.

  - Complex Diagnoses: Distinguishing between genuine mental illness and other factors that may influence behavior, such as substance abuse or personality disorders.

C. Report Writing and Testimony

- Forensic psychologists must present their findings clearly and concisely, often in written reports that will be scrutinized in court. They may also provide expert testimony, explaining their evaluation and conclusions to the judge and jury in a way that is accessible and understandable.

3. *Legal Outcomes of Insanity Defense*

A. Verdict Options

- Based on the findings of the insanity defense evaluation, several legal outcomes are possible:

  - Not Guilty by Reason of Insanity (NGRI): The defendant is acquitted of the charges but typically committed to a mental health facility for treatment.

  - Guilty but Mentally Ill (GBMI): The defendant is found guilty but is recognized as suffering from a mental illness, leading to a sentence that includes both imprisonment and psychiatric treatment.

  - Competency Restoration: In cases where the defendant is found incompetent to stand trial, they may undergo treatment to restore competency before the trial proceeds.

B. Implications for Sentencing

- The outcome of an insanity defense can significantly affect sentencing, as those found NGRI may spend longer in a mental health facility than they would have in prison. Conversely, those found GBMI may receive a combination of treatment and incarceration, reflecting both the need for public safety and the need for mental health care.

C. Public Perception and Ethical Considerations

- The insanity defense often sparks public debate, with concerns about the potential for misuse or the perception that it allows dangerous individuals to avoid justice. Forensic psychologists must navigate these ethical challenges, ensuring that their evaluations are objective, thorough, and grounded in scientific evidence.

By mastering the complexities of insanity defense evaluations, forensic psychologists can provide critical insights that influence legal outcomes, ensuring that justice is served while addressing the mental health needs of defendants. These evaluations require a deep understanding of both psychological principles and legal standards, making them a vital component of forensic psychology practice.

6.4 Toolkit: Sample Assessment Tools

In forensic psychology, the application of reliable and valid assessment tools is crucial for conducting accurate evaluations that inform legal decisions. This section provides a comprehensive toolkit of sample assessment tools commonly used in forensic settings. These tools are designed to assess various aspects of mental health, cognitive functioning, and personality, and are essential for professionals conducting evaluations related to criminal cases, competency, and risk assessments.

1. Overview of Assessment Tools

A. Purpose and Application

- Objective Measurement: Assessment tools in forensic psychology serve to objectively measure different psychological constructs that are relevant in legal contexts.

- Data Support: These tools help forensic psychologists gather data that supports their evaluations, whether for determining competency, assessing risk, or evaluating mental state at the time of the offense.

B. Selection Criteria

- Relevance: The tool must be appropriate for the specific legal question being addressed.

- Reliability and Validity: The tool must have established reliability (consistency of results) and validity (accuracy in measuring what it is intended to measure).

- Standardization: The tool should be standardized, meaning it has been tested on a large sample and has established norms for interpretation.

2. Cognitive Assessment Tools

A. Wechsler Adult Intelligence Scale (WAIS-IV)

- Purpose: Measures overall cognitive ability and provides a full-scale IQ score along with subscale scores for verbal comprehension, perceptual reasoning, working memory, and processing speed.

- Application: Commonly used in evaluations of intellectual functioning, especially in cases where cognitive impairment may be a factor in competency evaluations or criminal responsibility.

B. Mini-Mental State Examination (MMSE)

- Purpose: A brief screening tool used to assess cognitive function, including orientation, memory, attention, calculation, language, and visuospatial skills.

- Application: Often used in preliminary assessments of cognitive impairment, particularly in older adults, and can be a component of competency evaluations.

3. Personality and Psychopathology Assessment Tools

A. Minnesota Multiphasic Personality Inventory-2 (MMPI-2)

- Purpose: A widely used personality assessment tool that measures a range of psychological conditions, including depression, anxiety, psychopathy, and paranoia.

- Application: Frequently used in forensic settings to assess personality traits and psychopathology, particularly in cases involving the insanity defense or risk assessments.

B. Personality Assessment Inventory (PAI)

- Purpose: Assesses various aspects of personality and psychopathology, including anxiety, depression, aggression, and substance abuse.

- Application: Useful in evaluating mental health issues that may impact legal decisions, such as competency to stand trial or the likelihood of reoffending.

C. Rorschach Inkblot Test

- Purpose: A projective test that presents a series of inkblots to the individual, who is asked to describe what they see. The responses are analyzed to uncover underlying thoughts, feelings, and personality traits.

- Application: Although controversial, the Rorschach is sometimes used in forensic assessments to explore deeper, unconscious aspects of the individual's personality.

4. Risk Assessment Tools

A. Static-99

- Purpose: An actuarial risk assessment tool used to estimate the likelihood of sexual reoffending among adult male offenders.

- Application: Widely used in legal settings to inform decisions about sentencing, parole, and treatment for sex offenders.

B. HCR-20 (Historical, Clinical, Risk Management-20)

- Purpose: A structured professional judgment tool used to assess the risk of violence.

- Application: Evaluates the potential for future violent behavior, considering historical factors (e.g., previous violence), clinical factors (e.g., mental illness), and risk management factors (e.g., plans for future behavior).

C. Violence Risk Appraisal Guide (VRAG)

- Purpose: An actuarial tool designed to predict the risk of violent recidivism among offenders with mental disorders.

- Application: Commonly used in forensic evaluations to assist in determining the likelihood of future violent behavior, aiding in decisions related to sentencing, parole, and treatment.

5. Competency Assessment Tools

A. MacArthur Competence Assessment Tool-Criminal Adjudication (MacCAT-CA)

- Purpose: Assesses a defendant's competence to stand trial by evaluating their understanding of legal proceedings, ability to assist in their defense, and reasoning abilities.

- Application: A key tool in forensic psychology for determining whether a defendant has the mental capacity to participate in legal proceedings.

B. Competence Assessment for Standing Trial for Defendants with Mental Retardation (CAST-MR)

- Purpose: Specifically designed to assess competency to stand trial in defendants with intellectual disabilities.

- Application: Used in cases where intellectual disabilities are present, helping to ensure that the defendant's rights are protected during legal proceedings.

6. Best Practices for Using Assessment Tools

A. Ethical Considerations

- Adherence to Guidelines: Forensic psychologists must use assessment tools in accordance with ethical guidelines, ensuring appropriate use, accurate interpretation, and confidentiality.

- Confidentiality: Ensure that sensitive information is protected throughout the assessment and reporting process.

B. Integration of Findings

- Holistic Evaluation: The results from various assessment tools should be integrated to provide a comprehensive evaluation.

- Multiple Tools: A combination of tools should be used to create a holistic understanding of the individual's mental state and behavior.

C. Documentation and Reporting

- Accurate Documentation: Accurate documentation and clear reporting of assessment findings are critical.

- Detailed Reports: Reports should explain the tools used, the results obtained, and their relevance to the legal questions at hand.

By utilizing these sample assessment tools effectively, forensic psychologists can conduct thorough and reliable evaluations that contribute to informed legal decisions. These tools are an essential part of the forensic psychologist's toolkit, enabling them to provide critical insights that impact the outcomes of criminal cases.

6.5 Practical Exercise: Conducting a Mock Assessment

Practical exercises are invaluable for honing the skills necessary to perform forensic psychological assessments effectively. This section provides a step-by-step guide to conducting a mock assessment, allowing readers to apply the concepts and tools discussed in the previous sections. Engaging in this exercise will help develop the practical skills required for real-world forensic evaluations, including gathering information, administering assessment tools, and integrating findings into a coherent report.

1. Preparation for the Mock Assessment

A. Choosing a Case Scenario

- Select a Case: Begin by selecting a fictional case scenario that requires a comprehensive forensic psychological assessment. This could involve evaluating a defendant's competency to stand trial, assessing the risk of reoffending, or conducting an insanity defense evaluation.

- Define the Legal Question: Clearly define the legal question that your assessment will address. For example, "Is the defendant competent to stand trial?" or "Does the defendant meet the criteria for an insanity defense?"

B. Gathering Background Information

- Case History: Review the background information provided in the case scenario, including the defendant's personal history, criminal record, and any relevant medical or psychological history.

- Collateral Information: Collect additional information from sources such as family members, medical records, and past legal interactions to create a comprehensive understanding of the defendant's background.

C. Selecting Assessment Tools

- Tool Selection: Based on the legal question and the case details, select appropriate assessment tools from the toolkit provided in Section 6.4. Ensure that the tools chosen are relevant to the case scenario and the specific aspects of the defendant's mental state or behavior that need to be evaluated.

2. Conducting the Mock Assessment

A. Administering the Assessments

- Clinical Interview: Conduct a simulated clinical interview with the defendant, focusing on gathering information relevant to the legal question. Use open-ended questions to explore the defendant's mental state, understanding of the legal process, and any symptoms of mental illness.

- Psychological Testing: Administer the selected assessment tools, such as the MMPI-2 for personality assessment, the WAIS-IV for cognitive evaluation, or the MacCAT-CA for competency assessment. Simulate the testing environment and interpret the results as if they were from an actual case.

B. Analyzing the Results

- Interpreting Data: Analyze the data collected from the clinical interview and psychological testing. Identify patterns in the results that align with or contradict the initial case history and collateral information.

- Integrating Findings: Integrate the findings from different assessment tools to form a comprehensive picture of the defendant's mental state, risk level, or competency. Consider how these findings relate to the legal question at hand.

C. Addressing Challenges

- Malingering: Consider the possibility of malingering (exaggerating or faking symptoms) in the scenario and how it might affect the assessment. Discuss strategies for detecting malingering and ensuring the accuracy of the evaluation.

- Ethical Considerations: Reflect on the ethical issues that may arise during the assessment process, such as maintaining objectivity, ensuring confidentiality, and the potential impact of the evaluation on the defendant's legal outcomes.

3. *Writing the Assessment Report*

A. Report Structure

- Introduction: Begin the report with an introduction that outlines the legal question, the purpose of the assessment, and the tools used.

- Findings: Present the findings from the clinical interview, psychological testing, and collateral information. Provide a detailed analysis of how these findings address the legal question.

- Conclusion and Recommendations: Conclude with a summary of the assessment results, providing clear answers to the legal question. Offer recommendations for further action, such as treatment options or considerations for the court.

B. Review and Feedback

- Self-Review: After completing the report, review it for clarity, accuracy, and completeness. Ensure that the conclusions are well-supported by the data and that the report is free of biases or assumptions.

- Peer Review: If possible, share the report with a peer or mentor for feedback. Discuss any areas for improvement and consider how the assessment could be refined or expanded in future cases.

4. Reflecting on the Mock Assessment Experience

A. Self-Reflection

- Skills Assessment: Reflect on the skills you developed during the mock assessment, including conducting interviews, administering tests, and writing reports. Identify areas where you excelled and areas that may need further practice.

- Understanding the Role: Consider how the exercise has enhanced your understanding of the role of a forensic psychologist and the complexities involved in conducting forensic assessments.

B. Applying Lessons Learned

- Real-World Application: Think about how the lessons learned from the mock assessment can be applied in real-world forensic settings. Consider how the experience has prepared you for future assessments and the challenges you might face.

By engaging in this practical exercise, you will gain hands-on experience in conducting forensic psychological assessments, from selecting appropriate tools to integrating findings into a coherent and legally relevant report. This mock assessment serves as a valuable practice tool, helping you to build confidence and competence in your forensic psychology skills.

Chapter 6 Review: Psychological Assessments and Legal Implications

Chapter 6 of *HowExpert Guide to Forensic Psychology* offers an in-depth analysis of the psychological assessments utilized in forensic settings, focusing on their application in evaluating mental state, cognitive abilities, and personality traits within the legal context. The chapter is systematically organized into key sections, each detailing the types of assessments, their legal relevance, and practical applications in forensic psychology.

6.1 Types of Psychological Assessments

- Personality Assessments:

  - Tools such as the Minnesota Multiphasic Personality Inventory-2 (MMPI-2) and the Personality Assessment Inventory (PAI) are highlighted for their role in diagnosing mental disorders and assessing personality traits that may influence criminal behavior.

  - The section emphasizes the legal significance of these assessments, particularly in cases involving questions of criminal responsibility and the risk of reoffending.

- Cognitive Assessments:

  - This section covers assessments like the Wechsler Adult Intelligence Scale (WAIS-IV) and the Cognitive Assessment System (CAS), which are essential for evaluating intellectual functioning, memory, and problem-solving abilities.

  - The role of cognitive assessments in determining a defendant's competency to stand trial is discussed, alongside the challenges in interpreting these results within the legal framework.

- Neuropsychological Assessments:

  - The focus here is on the relationship between brain function and behavior, with tools such as the Halstead-Reitan Neuropsychological Battery and the Luria-Nebraska Neuropsychological Battery being key in assessing the impact of neurological impairments on legal competence and criminal behavior.

- The section explores how these assessments are particularly relevant in cases involving brain injuries, dementia, or other neurological conditions.

6.2 Risk Assessments and Competency Evaluations

- Risk Assessments:

- The chapter explores methods for evaluating the likelihood of future harmful behaviors using structured professional judgment and actuarial tools. These assessments are crucial in informing decisions about sentencing, parole, and treatment.

- Emphasis is placed on the importance of accurately assessing both static (unchangeable) and dynamic (changeable) risk factors to provide a reliable prediction of future behavior.

- Competency Evaluations:

- This section delves into the tools and processes used to assess a defendant's competency to stand trial, including the MacArthur Competence Assessment Tool-Criminal Adjudication (MacCAT-CA).

- It discusses the implications of competency evaluations on legal proceedings, ensuring that defendants are capable of participating meaningfully in their defense and understanding the charges against them.

6.3 Insanity Defense Evaluations and Legal Outcomes

- Insanity Defense Evaluations:

- The chapter examines the methods used to determine whether a defendant was legally insane at the time of the offense, focusing on the application of standards like the M'Naghten Rule and the Model Penal Code Test.

- Challenges of these evaluations, such as the retrospective assessment of the defendant's mental state during the crime, are also discussed.

- Legal Outcomes:

- This section analyzes the potential legal outcomes of insanity defense evaluations, including verdicts like Not Guilty by Reason of Insanity (NGRI) and Guilty but Mentally Ill (GBMI).

- It explores how these outcomes affect sentencing, treatment options, and public perception, providing a critical perspective on the impact of forensic psychology on legal decisions.

6.4 Toolkit: Sample Assessment Tools

- *Sample Tools:*

- The chapter includes a practical toolkit of commonly used psychological assessments, offering detailed descriptions of each tool's purpose, applications, and limitations.

- This section serves as a practical resource for forensic psychologists, helping them select and implement the most appropriate assessment tools in various legal contexts.

6.5 Practical Exercise: Conducting a Mock Assessment

- *Mock Assessment:*

- The chapter concludes with a hands-on exercise designed to help readers apply the concepts learned by conducting a mock psychological assessment.

- The exercise guides readers through selecting assessment tools, conducting evaluations, and integrating findings into a comprehensive and coherent report, reinforcing the key lessons of the chapter.

Chapter 6 underscores the vital role that psychological assessments play in forensic psychology, particularly in influencing legal decisions regarding competency, criminal responsibility, and risk of reoffending. By integrating multiple assessment tools and addressing the challenges inherent in forensic evaluations, forensic psychologists can ensure that their assessments are both scientifically rigorous and legally defensible. The chapter provides practical guidance on selecting appropriate tools, conducting thorough evaluations, and clearly communicating findings to contribute effectively to the justice system. Through detailed explanations and practical exercises, readers gain a comprehensive understanding of the application of psychological assessments in legal contexts, enhancing their ability to make informed and impactful contributions to forensic psychology.

Chapter 7: Victimology and Trauma Response

Chapter 7 delves into the complex and crucial area of victimology, exploring how crime impacts victims and the psychological assessments used to understand and address their needs. This chapter is structured to provide a comprehensive understanding of the trauma experienced by victims and the role forensic psychologists play in supporting them through the legal process. Each section builds upon the previous one, offering insights into the psychological effects of crime, the methodologies for assessing victims, and the strategies for providing effective support.

7.1 Understanding the Impact of Crime on Victims

Understanding the impact of crime on victims is a fundamental aspect of victimology, providing insights into the psychological, emotional, and social effects that individuals experience following a crime. This section explores the various ways crime affects victims, emphasizing the diversity of responses based on the nature of the crime, the victim's characteristics, and broader social and cultural contexts. Forensic psychologists play a crucial role in assessing and addressing these impacts, ensuring that victims receive appropriate support and that their experiences are adequately represented in the legal process.

1. Psychological Effects of Crime on Victims

A. Acute Stress Reaction

- Immediate Response: Victims often experience an acute stress reaction immediately following a crime, which includes feelings of shock, disbelief, fear, and confusion. These reactions are typically intense and can subside over time with proper support and intervention.

- Potential Evolution: If not properly addressed, these initial reactions can evolve into more serious psychological conditions, leading to long-term emotional difficulties.

B. Post-Traumatic Stress Disorder (PTSD)

- Symptoms of PTSD: PTSD is a severe psychological impact of crime, characterized by intrusive thoughts, flashbacks, nightmares, hypervigilance, and avoidance behaviors. These symptoms can significantly impair daily functioning and require targeted intervention.

- Long-Term Impact: Without treatment, PTSD symptoms can persist, affecting the victim's ability to return to normal life activities, maintain relationships, and work effectively.

C. Anxiety and Depression

- Anxiety Symptoms: Crime victims often experience elevated levels of anxiety, which can manifest as generalized anxiety, panic attacks, or specific phobias related to the crime. This anxiety can interfere with daily activities and overall well-being.

- Depression Symptoms: Depression in victims can present as feelings of hopelessness, worthlessness, and a loss of interest in previously enjoyed activities. In severe cases, this can lead to suicidal ideation or attempts, making early intervention critical.

2. Emotional and Behavioral Responses

A. Guilt and Shame

- Self-Blame: Victims may experience intense feelings of guilt or shame, particularly in cases of sexual assault or domestic violence. This self-blame can be a barrier to seeking help and recovering from the trauma.

- Psychological Impact: These emotions can lead to further psychological distress, including depression and anxiety, and may hinder the healing process.

B. Anger and Resentment

- Directed Anger: Victims often direct their anger at the perpetrator, the justice system, or themselves. This anger can manifest as resentment and lead to difficulties in interpersonal relationships.

- Coping Challenges: Unresolved anger can complicate the victim's ability to cope with the aftermath of the crime, potentially leading to additional mental health issues.

C. Social Withdrawal and Behavioral Changes

- Withdrawal from Social Interaction: Victims may withdraw from social interactions due to fear, depression, or a sense of isolation. This can result in a loss of support systems, exacerbating feelings of loneliness.

- Behavioral Changes: Victims may also exhibit significant behavioral changes, such as increased substance use, changes in sleep patterns, or the development of obsessive-compulsive behaviors aimed at regaining a sense of control.

3. Social and Cultural Influences

A. Stigma and Victim Blaming

- Social Judgment: Victims, particularly of crimes like sexual assault, may face societal judgment or disbelief, leading to additional emotional distress and reluctance to seek help.

- Impact on Recovery: This stigma can discourage victims from reporting the crime or accessing necessary support services, thereby prolonging their suffering and hindering recovery.

B. Cultural Perceptions of Victimhood

- Cultural Influence: Cultural norms and values can shape how victims perceive their experiences and how they are treated by others. In some cultures, there may be pressure to remain silent about certain types of victimization, while in others, community support may be more readily available.

- Tailored Interventions: Forensic psychologists must understand these cultural dynamics to provide culturally sensitive assessments and interventions that are appropriate for the victim's context.

C. Access to Resources

- Resource Availability: The availability of resources, such as counseling services, legal aid, and social support, can significantly influence a victim's recovery process. In resource-scarce areas, victims may struggle to find the help they need.

- Impact on Recovery: A lack of culturally appropriate services can lead to prolonged suffering and unaddressed trauma, making access to resources a crucial factor in the victim's overall recovery.

This section provides a comprehensive overview of how crime impacts victims, with each point including essential details that are necessary for understanding the topic. The structure and content are aligned with your request for bullet points that convey clear, actionable information relevant to forensic psychology.

7.2 Psychological Assessment of Victims

Psychological assessment of victims is a critical component in victimology, providing forensic psychologists with the necessary tools to evaluate the mental and emotional state of individuals who have experienced trauma. These assessments are essential for understanding the extent of psychological harm, guiding therapeutic interventions, and informing legal decisions. This section explores the various tools and methods used to assess victims, emphasizing their applications in forensic settings and the importance of sensitivity and accuracy in the assessment process.

1. Purpose of Psychological Assessments

A. Evaluating Psychological Impact

- Determining Severity: The primary purpose of psychological assessments is to evaluate the impact of crime on a victim's mental health. These assessments help determine the presence and severity of conditions such as PTSD, anxiety, depression, and other trauma-related disorders.

B. Guiding Treatment Plans

- Tailoring Interventions: Assessments are instrumental in developing effective treatment plans tailored to the specific needs of each victim. By understanding the psychological effects of the crime, forensic psychologists can recommend appropriate therapeutic interventions to support the victim's recovery.

C. Informing Legal Proceedings

- Providing Evidence: In legal contexts, psychological assessments provide critical evidence regarding the extent of psychological harm suffered by the victim. This information can influence decisions related to compensation claims, sentencing of the offender, and the victim's participation in legal proceedings.

2. Common Assessment Tools

A. Impact of Event Scale-Revised (IES-R)

- Purpose: The IES-R is a widely used tool for assessing symptoms of PTSD and other trauma-related conditions. It measures the severity of symptoms such as intrusion, avoidance, and hyperarousal, providing a quantitative assessment of the victim's psychological distress.

- Application: The IES-R is often administered in the aftermath of a traumatic event to gauge the immediate impact on the victim and to monitor changes in symptoms over time. It is particularly useful in cases where PTSD is suspected.

B. Beck Depression Inventory (BDI)

- Purpose: The BDI is a standardized tool used to assess the presence and severity of depressive symptoms. It covers a range of symptoms, including mood, cognitive patterns, and physical complaints related to depression.

- Application: The BDI is commonly used in forensic settings to evaluate the psychological state of victims who exhibit signs of depression, particularly when depression may impact their ability to participate in legal proceedings or influence their overall well-being.

C. Trauma Symptom Inventory (TSI)

- Purpose: The TSI is designed to assess a broad range of trauma-related symptoms, including anxiety, depression, anger, and dissociation. It provides a comprehensive evaluation of the psychological effects of trauma on the victim.

- Application: The TSI is often used in cases involving severe trauma, such as sexual assault or domestic violence, where a detailed assessment of multiple symptom domains is necessary. It helps in understanding the full scope of the victim's psychological distress and in planning appropriate interventions.

3. Challenges in Assessing Victims

A. Sensitivity and Re-Traumatization

- Sensitivity: Conducting psychological assessments with victims requires a high degree of sensitivity. Victims are often in a vulnerable state, and the assessment process must be handled with care to avoid causing additional distress.

- Re-Traumatization: One of the significant challenges in assessing victims is the risk of re-traumatization. Asking victims to recount their experiences or relive the trauma during assessments can exacerbate their symptoms. Forensic psychologists must be trained to recognize signs of distress and to adjust their approach accordingly.

B. Cultural and Contextual Factors

- Cultural Sensitivity: Victims from different cultural backgrounds may have varying responses to trauma and may interpret or express symptoms differently. Assessments must be culturally sensitive and adapted to the victim's cultural context to ensure accurate and meaningful results.

- Contextual Factors: The context in which the crime occurred, such as the victim's environment or social support system, can also influence the assessment. Forensic psychologists must consider these factors when interpreting the results of psychological assessments.

C. Limitations of Assessment Tools

- Tool Limitations: No single assessment tool can capture the full complexity of a victim's psychological state. Each tool has its limitations, and forensic psychologists must use a combination of assessments and clinical judgment to form a comprehensive understanding of the victim's mental health.

- Reliability and Validity: Ensuring the reliability and validity of assessment tools is crucial in forensic settings. The tools used must have strong empirical support and be appropriate for the specific population being assessed to provide accurate and legally defensible results.

7.3 Supporting Victims Through the Legal Process

Supporting victims through the legal process is a crucial aspect of forensic psychology, as it involves providing both emotional support and practical guidance to individuals who are navigating the complexities of the justice system. Forensic psychologists play a key role in ensuring that victims are not only prepared for the legal proceedings but are also supported in a way that minimizes the psychological impact of their involvement. This section explores the strategies and responsibilities of forensic psychologists in assisting victims throughout the legal process.

1. Role of Forensic Psychologists

A. Emotional Support

- Providing Counseling: Forensic psychologists offer counseling to help victims cope with the emotional stress associated with legal proceedings. This support is essential in helping victims manage anxiety, fear, and other emotions that may arise during the process.

- Building Trust and Rapport: Establishing a trusting relationship with the victim is crucial. Forensic psychologists must create a safe and supportive environment where victims feel comfortable discussing their experiences and concerns.

B. Education and Preparation

- Explaining the Legal Process: Many victims are unfamiliar with the legal system, which can be intimidating and overwhelming. Forensic psychologists help by explaining the legal process, including what to expect during court proceedings, the roles of various legal professionals, and the potential outcomes.

- Preparing for Testimony: If the victim is required to testify, forensic psychologists can help prepare them for the experience. This preparation includes role-playing courtroom scenarios, discussing potential questions, and teaching techniques to manage stress while on the stand.

C. Advocacy

- Legal Advocacy: Forensic psychologists often act as advocates for victims, ensuring that their rights are protected throughout the legal process. This can include working with legal professionals to ensure that the victim's needs are considered in legal decisions, such as the timing of court appearances or the provision of accommodations for vulnerable individuals.

- Support During Court Proceedings: During court proceedings, forensic psychologists may provide real-time support, helping victims manage their emotions and offering reassurance as needed. This presence can be particularly important during cross-examinations or when confronting the perpetrator in court.

2. Strategies for Minimizing Psychological Impact

A. Trauma-Informed Care

- Understanding Trauma: Forensic psychologists use trauma-informed care principles to tailor their support to the specific needs of victims who have experienced trauma. This approach recognizes the impact of trauma on behavior and emotional responses, ensuring that interventions are sensitive and appropriate.

- Avoiding Re-Traumatization: The legal process can be re-traumatizing for victims, especially when recounting their experiences. Forensic psychologists work to minimize this risk by preparing victims thoroughly, advocating for their needs in court, and providing continuous emotional support.

B. Empowerment and Control

- Empowering Victims: Empowering victims by giving them a sense of control over their involvement in the legal process is crucial. Forensic psychologists encourage victims to make informed decisions about their participation and provide them with the tools to do so confidently.

- Informed Consent: Ensuring that victims understand their rights and the implications of their decisions is a key part of empowerment. Forensic psychologists ensure that victims are fully informed before consenting to any legal actions, such as testifying in court.

C. Long-Term Support

- Post-Trial Counseling: The psychological impact of legal proceedings can extend beyond the trial itself. Forensic psychologists provide post-trial counseling to help victims process the outcome and continue their recovery. This support is vital in helping victims regain a sense of normalcy after the intense experience of a trial.

- Monitoring Psychological Well-Being: Forensic psychologists may continue to monitor the victim's psychological well-being after the trial, offering ongoing support as needed. This long-term approach helps ensure that any lingering effects of the legal process are addressed promptly.

3. Legal Considerations and Ethical Responsibilities

A. Confidentiality

- Maintaining Confidentiality: Forensic psychologists must navigate the delicate balance between confidentiality and the legal requirements of disclosure. They are responsible for protecting the victim's privacy while also complying with legal obligations, such as mandatory reporting laws.

B. Ethical Decision-Making

- Ethical Dilemmas: The intersection of legal and psychological practice can present ethical dilemmas, such as conflicts between the best interests of the victim and legal requirements. Forensic psychologists must use ethical decision-making frameworks to navigate these challenges, ensuring that their actions are in line with both professional ethics and legal standards.

C. Informed Advocacy

- Balancing Advocacy with Objectivity: While advocating for the victim, forensic psychologists must maintain their objectivity, especially when providing expert testimony. Their role is to support the victim while ensuring that their professional responsibilities are upheld.

Supporting victims through the legal process requires a multifaceted approach that combines emotional support, education, advocacy, and ethical practice.

Forensic psychologists play a critical role in helping victims navigate the complexities of the justice system, ensuring that they are prepared, empowered, and supported throughout the process. By providing trauma-informed care and advocating for the victim's needs, forensic psychologists contribute to a more humane and effective legal experience for those who have been affected by crime.

7.4 Case Study: Impact of Trauma on Victims

Case studies are invaluable in understanding the profound impact of trauma on victims, offering real-world examples that illustrate the complexities and nuances of psychological responses to crime. This section presents a detailed case study that highlights how trauma affects victims' mental health, behavior, and overall well-being. It also explores the role of forensic psychologists in assessing and supporting victims through their recovery process.

1. Case Background

A. Incident Overview

- Crime Description: The case involves a 32-year-old woman named Sarah who was the victim of a home invasion and sexual assault. The perpetrator, an unknown male, forcibly entered her home late at night, assaulted her, and fled the scene. The crime left Sarah physically unharmed but profoundly traumatized.

B. Immediate Psychological Response

- Shock and Disbelief: In the immediate aftermath of the assault, Sarah experienced severe shock and disbelief. She reported feeling numb and disconnected from reality, struggling to comprehend what had happened.

- Acute Stress Reaction: Within hours of the incident, Sarah exhibited symptoms of acute stress, including trembling, hyperventilation, and uncontrollable crying. She was unable to sleep and experienced intrusive thoughts about the assault.

C. Initial Interventions

- Emergency Counseling: Sarah received emergency counseling at a local crisis center. The counselor provided immediate support, helping her to stabilize her emotions and begin processing the traumatic event. The counselor also arranged for Sarah to see a forensic psychologist for a more comprehensive assessment.

2. *Psychological Assessment and Findings*

A. Assessment Tools Used

- Impact of Event Scale-Revised (IES-R): The IES-R was administered to assess Sarah's symptoms of PTSD. The results indicated severe levels of intrusion, avoidance, and hyperarousal, consistent with a diagnosis of acute PTSD.

- Beck Depression Inventory (BDI): The BDI was used to evaluate Sarah's depressive symptoms. The assessment revealed moderate depression, with significant feelings of hopelessness, guilt, and a loss of interest in daily activities.

- Trauma Symptom Inventory (TSI): The TSI provided a comprehensive overview of Sarah's trauma-related symptoms, including anxiety, dissociation, and anger. The results highlighted the complexity of her psychological response, indicating the need for a multifaceted treatment approach.

B. Findings

- PTSD Diagnosis: Based on the assessment results, Sarah was diagnosed with PTSD. Her symptoms were severe and pervasive, affecting multiple aspects of her life, including her ability to work, socialize, and care for herself.

- Secondary Symptoms: In addition to PTSD, Sarah exhibited symptoms of depression and anxiety. She also showed signs of hypervigilance, constantly feeling on edge and fearing another attack.

- Behavioral Changes: The trauma significantly altered Sarah's behavior. She became socially withdrawn, avoiding contact with friends and family. She also developed a fear of being alone, leading to a dependency on staying with relatives or friends at night.

3. Forensic Psychological Intervention

A. Therapeutic Approach

- Trauma-Focused Cognitive Behavioral Therapy (TF-CBT): The forensic psychologist recommended TF-CBT as the primary therapeutic intervention. This approach focuses on helping victims process the trauma, reduce PTSD symptoms, and develop coping strategies for managing distress.

- Exposure Therapy: As part of TF-CBT, Sarah underwent gradual exposure therapy to help her confront and process memories of the assault in a safe and controlled environment. This intervention aimed to reduce avoidance behaviors and diminish the power of traumatic memories over her daily life.

B. Support Through Legal Process

- Preparation for Testimony: Sarah decided to pursue legal action against her assailant, despite the challenges. The forensic psychologist provided extensive preparation for her testimony, helping her manage the stress of recounting her experience in court.

- Ongoing Support: Throughout the legal process, Sarah received ongoing psychological support. The forensic psychologist attended court sessions with her, offering real-time emotional support and helping her cope with the demands of the legal proceedings.

C. Outcome and Recovery

- Legal Outcome: The perpetrator was eventually apprehended and convicted based on DNA evidence. Sarah's testimony played a crucial role in the trial, and the support she received helped her remain composed and effective on the stand.

- Psychological Recovery: Over the course of several months, Sarah made significant progress in therapy. Her PTSD symptoms gradually subsided, and she regained much of her pre-trauma functionality. While some anxiety and hypervigilance persisted, she developed effective coping strategies to manage these symptoms.

4. Lessons Learned and Implications for Practice

A. Importance of Early Intervention

- Timely Support: Sarah's case underscores the importance of providing timely psychological support to victims. Early intervention helped stabilize her emotional state and set the stage for successful long-term recovery.

B. Comprehensive Assessment

- Multifaceted Approach: The use of multiple assessment tools provided a comprehensive understanding of Sarah's psychological state, allowing for a tailored and effective treatment plan. This highlights the need for forensic psychologists to use a range of tools to capture the full scope of a victim's trauma.

C. Integrated Legal and Psychological Support

- Holistic Care: The integration of psychological support with legal advocacy was crucial in Sarah's case. The forensic psychologist's role extended beyond therapy, helping her navigate the legal process and ensuring that her psychological well-being was protected throughout.

D. Long-Term Follow-Up

- Sustained Recovery: The case demonstrates the need for long-term follow-up and support for victims. Even after the trial, continued therapy helped Sarah maintain her progress and address any lingering effects of the trauma.

This case study illustrates the profound impact that trauma can have on victims and the essential role that forensic psychologists play in their recovery. Through comprehensive assessment, tailored therapeutic interventions, and ongoing support, victims like Sarah can navigate the legal process while working towards psychological healing. The lessons learned from this case emphasize the importance of early intervention, the use of multifaceted assessment tools, and the integration of psychological and legal support in fostering a victim's recovery.

7.5 Practical Exercise: Developing a Victim Support Plan

Developing a victim support plan is a crucial exercise for forensic psychologists, enabling them to apply theoretical knowledge to practical scenarios. This exercise guides readers through the process of creating a comprehensive and personalized support plan for a victim of crime. The goal is to ensure that the plan addresses the psychological, emotional, and practical needs of the victim while considering their unique circumstances and the legal context in which they are involved.

1. Understanding the Victim's Needs

A. Initial Assessment

- Conducting a Comprehensive Assessment: Begin by gathering detailed information about the victim's psychological and emotional state. This involves conducting a thorough assessment using tools such as the Impact of Event Scale-Revised (IES-R), Beck Depression Inventory (BDI), and Trauma Symptom Inventory (TSI) to evaluate the extent of trauma, depression, anxiety, and other related conditions.

- Identifying Specific Needs: Based on the assessment results, identify the specific needs of the victim. These may include immediate psychological support, ongoing therapy, assistance with navigating the legal process, or support in dealing with the social impact of the crime. Understanding these needs is critical for developing an effective support plan.

B. Contextual Factors

- Consideration of Cultural and Social Context: Take into account the victim's cultural background, social environment, and personal circumstances. These factors can influence how the victim perceives the crime, responds to support, and interacts with the legal system. Tailoring the support plan to fit these contextual factors is essential for its effectiveness.

- Legal Involvement: Determine the level of the victim's involvement in the legal process. Consider whether the victim will need support for testifying in court, interacting with law enforcement, or understanding legal proceedings. The support plan should include strategies to help the victim manage these challenges.

2. Developing the Support Plan

A. Emotional and Psychological Support

- Immediate Intervention: Outline strategies for providing immediate emotional support, such as crisis counseling or short-term therapy. The plan should focus on stabilizing the victim's emotional state, reducing acute stress reactions, and preventing further psychological harm.

- Long-Term Therapy: Develop a plan for ongoing therapy tailored to the victim's specific needs. This may include Trauma-Focused Cognitive Behavioral Therapy (TF-CBT), exposure therapy, or other evidence-based interventions aimed at addressing PTSD, depression, and anxiety. The therapy plan should include measurable goals, a timeline, and regular evaluations to assess progress.

B. Practical Support and Resources

- Legal Support: Identify the practical support needed for the victim's involvement in the legal process. This may involve preparing the victim for court appearances, providing information about legal rights, and offering advocacy to ensure their voice is heard in legal proceedings. The plan should also include strategies to minimize the risk of re-traumatization during legal interactions.

- Social and Community Resources: Connect the victim with community resources that can offer additional support. This might include victim support groups, social services, or financial assistance programs. The plan should ensure that the victim has access to a network of support that can help with practical needs such as housing, employment, or child care if these have been affected by the crime.

C. Empowerment and Coping Strategies

- Building Resilience: Include strategies to empower the victim and build resilience. This might involve teaching coping skills, helping the victim regain a sense of control over their life, and encouraging participation in activities that promote well-being. The plan should emphasize the victim's strengths and provide opportunities for personal growth and recovery.

- Informed Decision-Making: Ensure that the victim is fully informed about their options and the potential outcomes of different decisions. The support plan should include regular check-ins where the victim can ask questions, express concerns, and adjust their plan as needed. This process helps the victim feel more in control and supported throughout their recovery.

3. Implementing and Evaluating the Support Plan

A. Implementation Strategy

- Step-by-Step Approach: Develop a clear implementation strategy that outlines the steps needed to put the support plan into action. This includes assigning responsibilities to the forensic psychologist, the victim, and any other professionals involved, such as legal advocates or therapists.

- Timelines and Milestones: Set realistic timelines and milestones for achieving the goals outlined in the support plan. Regularly review these milestones to ensure that the plan remains on track and adjust as necessary based on the victim's progress and any new challenges that arise.

B. Monitoring Progress

- Regular Assessments: Schedule regular assessments to monitor the victim's psychological state and the effectiveness of the support plan. Use tools like the IES-R, BDI, and TSI to track changes in symptoms and adjust the support plan accordingly.

- Feedback and Adjustment: Encourage the victim to provide feedback on the support they are receiving. Use this feedback to make adjustments to the plan, ensuring that it continues to meet the victim's needs as they evolve. This iterative process helps maintain the relevance and effectiveness of the support plan.

C. Long-Term Follow-Up

- Continued Support: Plan for long-term follow-up to ensure that the victim continues to receive the support they need as they move forward with their life. This may involve periodic check-ins, ongoing therapy sessions, or referrals to other services that can provide sustained assistance.

- Evaluation of Outcomes: At the conclusion of the support plan, conduct a comprehensive evaluation of the outcomes. Assess whether the goals were met, the victim's overall progress, and the effectiveness of the interventions used. This evaluation can inform future support plans and contribute to best practices in victim support.

This practical exercise in developing a victim support plan highlights the importance of a comprehensive, personalized approach to supporting victims of crime. By carefully assessing the victim's needs, considering their context, and implementing a well-structured plan, forensic psychologists can provide effective, compassionate support that aids in the victim's recovery and ensures their needs are met throughout the legal process.

Chapter 7 Review: Victimology and Trauma Response

Chapter 7 of *HowExpert Guide to Forensic Psychology* delves into the complex field of victimology, exploring the psychological impact of crime on victims and the crucial role that forensic psychologists play in assessing and supporting these individuals. The chapter covers key topics including the effects of trauma, methods for psychological assessment, strategies for supporting victims through the legal process, and practical exercises for developing comprehensive victim support plans.

7.1 Understanding the Impact of Crime on Victims

- Psychological Responses: This section provides an in-depth look at the various psychological effects that victims may experience following a crime, including acute stress reactions, PTSD, anxiety, and depression. It highlights the emotional and behavioral changes, such as guilt, anger, and social withdrawal, that can significantly impact a victim's well-being.

- Cultural and Social Influences: It also discusses how societal stigma, victim blaming, and cultural norms can shape a victim's experience and their willingness to seek help, emphasizing the need for a culturally sensitive approach in forensic psychology.

7.2 Psychological Assessment of Victims

- Assessment Tools: The chapter outlines key tools used in the psychological assessment of victims, including the Impact of Event Scale-Revised (IES-R) for PTSD, the Beck Depression Inventory (BDI) for depression, and the Trauma Symptom Inventory (TSI) for a broad range of trauma-related symptoms. These tools help forensic psychologists gauge the severity of the victim's psychological distress and guide appropriate interventions.

- Challenges in Assessment: The section addresses the challenges of conducting these assessments, such as the risk of re-traumatization and the need for sensitivity to the victim's cultural background and personal context.

7.3 Supporting Victims Through the Legal Process

- Emotional and Practical Support: This section emphasizes the dual role of forensic psychologists in providing both emotional support and practical guidance to victims involved in the legal process. It covers the importance of counseling, educating victims about legal proceedings, and preparing them for the stress of testifying in court.

- Advocacy and Long-Term Support: The chapter discusses the importance of advocacy in ensuring that victims' rights and needs are respected throughout the legal process. It also highlights the need for long-term support, including post-trial counseling and ongoing monitoring of the victim's psychological well-being.

7.4 Case Study: Impact of Trauma on Victims

- Detailed Case Example: This section presents a comprehensive case study that illustrates the profound impact of trauma on a victim's mental health. The case study details the use of psychological assessments, the diagnosis of PTSD, and the application of trauma-focused therapy, providing a real-world example of how forensic psychologists can support victims through their recovery and legal journey.

- Therapeutic and Legal Outcomes: It explores the outcomes of the therapeutic interventions and the victim's experience in the legal process, offering insights into the effectiveness of different support strategies.

7.5 Practical Exercise: Developing a Victim Support Plan

- Hands-On Application: This section guides readers through the practical steps of creating a comprehensive victim support plan, focusing on assessing the victim's needs, developing tailored support strategies, and implementing these plans effectively. The exercise encourages forensic psychologists to consider the victim's cultural and social context, as well as the legal implications of their support strategies.

- Monitoring and Evaluation: It also emphasizes the importance of regularly monitoring the victim's progress and adjusting the support plan as needed to ensure ongoing recovery and well-being.

Chapter 7 highlights the essential role that forensic psychologists play in understanding and mitigating the impact of crime on victims. From conducting sensitive psychological assessments to providing emotional and legal support, forensic psychologists must navigate a complex array of challenges to ensure that victims are supported throughout their recovery. The chapter's detailed exploration of victimology, combined with practical exercises and real-world case studies, offers valuable guidance for professionals seeking to enhance their practice in this critical area. Through a combination of theoretical knowledge and applied techniques, readers gain a comprehensive understanding of how to effectively support victims in both clinical and legal settings, ultimately contributing to their healing and justice.

Chapter 8: Forensic Psychology in Law Enforcement and Corrections

Forensic psychology plays a pivotal role in the intersection of psychology and the criminal justice system, particularly in law enforcement and correctional settings. Chapter 8 delves into the various applications of forensic psychology in these areas, focusing on criminal profiling, interrogation techniques, crisis negotiation, and the provision of psychological services in correctional facilities. This chapter also includes practical applications through case studies and interactive simulations, offering a comprehensive exploration of how forensic psychology supports law enforcement and corrections.

8.1 Profiling and Investigative Techniques

Profiling and investigative techniques are essential tools in forensic psychology, aiding law enforcement in understanding criminal behavior, predicting future actions, and narrowing down suspects. This section explores the key components of profiling and their practical applications in criminal investigations.

1. Criminal Profiling

A. Inductive and Deductive Profiling

- Inductive Profiling: This approach relies on generalizations drawn from statistical data and patterns observed in previous crimes. By analyzing trends from past cases, forensic psychologists can create profiles that suggest likely characteristics of the offender, such as age, gender, and background.

- Deductive Profiling: Deductive profiling focuses on the specifics of the current crime scene. Forensic psychologists examine the crime scene details, the nature of the crime, and the offender's behavior during the crime to build a profile based on evidence directly related to the case at hand.

B. Behavioral Analysis

- Crime Scene Analysis: Forensic psychologists analyze physical evidence from the crime scene, including victim positioning, the method of attack, and any behavioral signs left by the offender. This analysis provides insights into the offender's psychological state, including their level of planning and impulse control.

- Victimology: This involves studying the victim's background, lifestyle, and circumstances leading up to the crime to understand why the victim was chosen. Victimology helps infer the offender's motives and potential connections to the victim.

- Offender Behavior: The behavior exhibited during and after the crime, such as how the offender interacts with the victim and their actions post-crime, reveals much about their personality and psychological makeup.

C. Applications of Profiling

- Serial Crimes: Profiling is particularly effective in cases involving serial offenders. By identifying patterns across multiple crimes, forensic psychologists can predict future actions and help law enforcement narrow down suspects.

- Threat Assessment: Profiling techniques are used to assess the likelihood of an individual committing a violent act. This is especially relevant in potential mass shootings or targeted violence, where predicting future behavior is critical.

- Cold Cases: In cold cases, where traditional methods have been exhausted, profiling can provide new insights by re-examining old evidence and applying modern profiling techniques.

2. Investigative Techniques

A. Geographic Profiling

- Spatial Analysis: This technique helps determine the most likely area where an offender resides or operates by analyzing the locations of their crimes. It allows law enforcement to focus their search efforts in specific geographic areas.

- Journey to Crime: This concept examines the distance an offender travels from their home base to commit a crime. Understanding this can provide insights into their behavior and decision-making processes.

B. Linkage Analysis

- Identifying Commonalities: This process involves comparing details from different crimes to determine if they were committed by the same individual. It is crucial in identifying patterns, even when the offender changes their methods.

- Establishing Patterns: Linkage analysis helps connect seemingly unrelated cases by identifying consistent behaviors or signatures, offering a broader understanding of the offender's activities.

C. Role of Forensic Psychologists in Investigations

- Collaboration with Law Enforcement: Forensic psychologists provide psychological insights that guide investigations, helping to interpret evidence and understand the offender's mindset.

- Expert Testimony: Beyond assisting investigations, forensic psychologists often serve as expert witnesses, explaining the psychological aspects of a case and helping juries understand complex behavioral evidence.

3. Practical Applications and Challenges

A. Effectiveness in Solving Crimes

- Real-World Impact: Profiling and investigative techniques have been instrumental in solving numerous high-profile cases, demonstrating their value in criminal investigations.

- Challenges and Limitations: While effective, these techniques are not foolproof and must be used in conjunction with other investigative methods to ensure accuracy and avoid wrongful accusations.

B. Ethical Considerations

- Balancing Science and Assumptions: Profiling requires a careful balance between scientific analysis and assumptions based on behavior. Forensic psychologists must ensure that profiles are grounded in evidence to avoid bias.

- Protecting Rights: Ethical concerns also include ensuring that profiling does not infringe on the rights of suspects and that it is used to enhance, rather than replace, other investigative methods.

C. Future Directions

- Advancements in Technology: The future of profiling will likely involve more sophisticated tools, such as artificial intelligence, to analyze larger datasets and refine profiling accuracy.

- Continued Research: Ongoing research is essential to improve the effectiveness of profiling and ensure it remains a valuable tool in modern forensic psychology.

By employing these structured profiling and investigative techniques, forensic psychologists significantly contribute to solving crimes, predicting future offenses, and providing law enforcement with the psychological insights needed to apprehend and prosecute offenders. Their work enhances the understanding of criminal behavior, making profiling an indispensable tool in forensic investigations.

8.2 Interviewing, Interrogation, and Crisis Negotiation

Interviewing, interrogation, and crisis negotiation are essential techniques in law enforcement, where forensic psychologists contribute their expertise to enhance effectiveness and maintain ethical standards. This section examines the psychological principles underlying these techniques, their practical applications, and the ethical considerations involved.

1. Interviewing Techniques

A. Cognitive Interviewing

- Enhanced Memory Recall: Cognitive interviewing is designed to improve the accuracy and detail of witness and victim testimonies. It involves open-ended questions, encouraging the interviewee to mentally recreate the event's environment and emotions, which aids in more accurate memory recall.

- Stages of Cognitive Interviewing: The process typically involves establishing rapport, allowing the interviewee to provide an uninterrupted account, probing with specific questions, and reviewing the information. Forensic psychologists train law enforcement officers in these stages to ensure thorough and non-suggestive interviews.

- Applications and Limitations: This technique is particularly effective in cases where detailed recall is essential, though it requires skilled interviewers and can be time-consuming.

B. Rapport Building

- Importance of Trust: Building rapport is fundamental for successful interviewing. A trusting and respectful environment increases the likelihood of obtaining accurate information.

- Techniques for Building Rapport: Techniques include active listening, showing empathy, maintaining a non-judgmental attitude, and allowing the interviewee to express thoughts freely. Forensic psychologists train officers to use these techniques to enhance communication and cooperation.

C. Non-Verbal Communication

- Interpreting Non-Verbal Cues: Non-verbal communication, such as body language and facial expressions, provides insights into the interviewee's state of mind and truthfulness.

- Applications in Interviewing: Recognizing non-verbal cues helps detect inconsistencies, identify withheld information, and understand signs of trauma that may affect recall accuracy.

2. Interrogation Techniques

A. Reid Technique

- Principles of the Reid Technique: This widely used interrogation method involves three phases: factual analysis, behavioral analysis during a non-accusatory interview, and an accusatory interrogation if deception is suspected. The goal is to elicit confessions through psychological manipulation.

- Controversies and Ethical Concerns: While effective in some cases, the Reid Technique is controversial due to its potential to produce false confessions, especially among vulnerable individuals. Forensic psychologists critique the technique for its reliance on deception.

B. Ethical Interrogation Practices

- Avoiding Coercion: Forensic psychologists advocate for non-coercive interrogation practices that respect the rights and dignity of suspects, ensuring that confessions are voluntary and reliable.

- Techniques for Ethical Interrogation: Techniques include using open-ended questions, clearly informing suspects of their rights, and avoiding leading questions. Forensic psychologists work with law enforcement to implement interrogation strategies that are both effective and ethical.

C. False Confessions

- Understanding False Confessions: False confessions can occur due to intense psychological pressure, fear of harsher punishment, or a desire to end the interrogation.

- Role of Forensic Psychologists: Forensic psychologists identify and prevent false confessions by reviewing interrogation procedures, providing expert testimony on the psychological factors that contribute to false confessions, and training officers to avoid practices that may lead to them.

3. Crisis Negotiation

A. Crisis Negotiation Strategies

- Principles of Crisis Negotiation: Crisis negotiation involves communicating with individuals in high-stress situations, such as hostage takings or potential suicides, with the goal of peacefully resolving the situation. Key principles include establishing communication, building rapport, and de-escalating the situation.

- Stages of Negotiation: The negotiation process involves establishing contact, assessing the situation and the individual's state of mind, negotiating for resolution, and ensuring safe surrender. Forensic psychologists provide insights into the psychological state of individuals and advise on effective communication strategies.

B. Psychological Insights in Crisis Negotiation

- Understanding the Individual: Forensic psychologists assist negotiators by profiling individuals involved in crises, identifying potential mental health issues, stress triggers, and likely responses to negotiation tactics.

- Communication Techniques: Effective communication is critical in crisis negotiation, involving active listening, empathy, paraphrasing, and using calm, non-threatening language. Forensic psychologists help develop these techniques to ensure negotiators maintain control while showing concern for the individual's well-being.

C. Real-World Applications

- Case Studies: Real-world examples of crisis negotiations demonstrate how psychological principles are applied to achieve peaceful resolutions.

- Challenges in Crisis Negotiation: Negotiations are complex and unpredictable, requiring flexibility and the ability to adapt to changing circumstances. Forensic psychologists support negotiators by helping them manage stress and stay focused on achieving a safe outcome.

By integrating forensic psychology into interviewing, interrogation, and crisis negotiation, law enforcement can improve the effectiveness and ethical standards of these practices. Forensic psychologists provide critical insights into human behavior, ensuring that interviews and interrogations are fair and that crisis situations are resolved peacefully. Their contributions are essential to maintaining the integrity of the criminal justice process and protecting the rights and well-being of all individuals involved.

8.3 Psychological Services in Correctional Facilities

Psychological services in correctional facilities are essential for addressing the mental health needs of inmates and ensuring the safety and security of the institution. Forensic psychologists play a vital role in providing these services, which include mental health assessments, treatment programs, crisis intervention, and rehabilitation efforts aimed at reducing recidivism. This section explores the comprehensive range of psychological services offered in correctional settings and their importance in the broader context of criminal justice.

1. Mental Health Assessment and Treatment

A. Inmate Assessments

- Comprehensive Mental Health Evaluations: Upon entry into a correctional facility, inmates undergo thorough mental health assessments conducted by forensic psychologists. These evaluations are designed to identify existing mental health conditions such as depression, anxiety, schizophrenia, or substance use disorders. The assessment also considers risk factors for self-harm, violence, or suicidal behavior.

- Risk Assessment: Forensic psychologists assess the risk of violent behavior, both towards others and self-directed. This assessment is crucial for determining the appropriate level of supervision and intervention required for each inmate, ensuring the safety of both the individual and the facility.

B. Treatment Programs

- Individual and Group Therapy: Correctional facilities offer a range of therapeutic services, including individual counseling and group therapy sessions. These programs are tailored to address the specific psychological needs of inmates, such as managing anger, coping with trauma, or overcoming substance abuse. Forensic psychologists design and lead these programs, using evidence-based approaches to facilitate positive behavioral change.

- Medication Management: Many inmates require psychiatric medications to manage their mental health conditions. Forensic psychologists work closely with psychiatrists to monitor the effectiveness of these medications, adjust dosages as needed, and address any side effects or compliance issues. Medication management is an integral part of a holistic treatment approach in correctional settings.

C. Special Populations

- Juveniles: Juvenile offenders present unique challenges in correctional facilities, requiring specialized psychological services. Forensic psychologists working with juveniles focus on addressing developmental issues, providing age-appropriate therapy, and designing educational programs that cater to their needs. The goal is to rehabilitate rather than merely punish, offering juveniles a chance for a better future.

- Inmates with Severe Mental Illness: Inmates with severe mental illnesses, such as schizophrenia or bipolar disorder, require intensive mental health services. Forensic psychologists play a crucial role in managing these cases, ensuring that inmates receive the necessary treatment to stabilize their condition and participate meaningfully in rehabilitation programs.

2. Crisis Intervention and Suicide Prevention

A. Crisis Intervention Teams

- Immediate Response to Mental Health Emergencies: Crisis intervention teams (CITs) are composed of forensic psychologists and trained correctional staff who respond to mental health emergencies within the facility. These emergencies may include suicide attempts, psychotic episodes, or violent outbursts. The CIT's role is to de-escalate the situation, provide immediate psychological support, and determine the next steps in the inmate's care.

- De-Escalation Techniques: Forensic psychologists train correctional staff in de-escalation techniques, which are essential for safely managing inmates in crisis. These techniques involve calming the individual, establishing communication, and reducing environmental stressors that may contribute to the crisis.

B. Suicide Prevention Programs

- Screening and Monitoring: Suicide prevention is a top priority in correctional facilities, given the elevated risk among incarcerated populations. Forensic psychologists implement screening procedures to identify inmates at risk of suicide, followed by continuous monitoring to ensure their safety. High-risk individuals may be placed on suicide watch, where they receive constant supervision and immediate access to mental health services.

- Counseling and Support: Forensic psychologists provide counseling to inmates struggling with suicidal thoughts, helping them develop coping strategies and addressing underlying issues such as hopelessness or despair. Support groups and peer-led programs are also employed to create a supportive community environment that encourages inmates to seek help when needed.

3. Rehabilitation and Reentry Programs

A. Rehabilitation Programs

- Behavioral Therapy: Rehabilitation programs in correctional facilities are designed to address the behavioral and psychological issues that contribute to criminal behavior. Forensic psychologists use various therapeutic approaches, such as cognitive-behavioral therapy (CBT) and dialectical behavior therapy (DBT), to help inmates change maladaptive thought patterns and behaviors. These programs aim to reduce recidivism by equipping inmates with the skills needed to manage their emotions, make better decisions, and reintegrate into society successfully.

- Substance Abuse Programs: Substance abuse is a common issue among incarcerated individuals, often linked to criminal activity. Forensic psychologists lead substance abuse programs that include detoxification, counseling, and relapse prevention strategies. These programs are crucial for helping inmates overcome addiction and reduce the likelihood of reoffending upon release.

B. Reentry Planning

- Transition Support: As inmates approach their release date, forensic psychologists assist in developing reentry plans that address their mental health needs, employment opportunities, and housing arrangements. Reentry planning is essential for reducing recidivism, as it provides a structured support system that helps former inmates navigate the challenges of reintegration into society.

- Community Resources and Support: Forensic psychologists connect inmates with community resources, such as mental health clinics, substance abuse treatment centers, and job training programs. These connections are vital for ensuring continuity of care and support once the inmate leaves the correctional facility.

C. Reducing Recidivism

- Measuring Program Effectiveness: Forensic psychologists are involved in evaluating the effectiveness of rehabilitation and reentry programs. They use data to assess whether these programs successfully reduce recidivism and improve the overall well-being of former inmates. Continuous evaluation allows for the refinement of programs to better meet the needs of the incarcerated population.

- Long-Term Outcomes: Successful rehabilitation and reentry programs lead to long-term positive outcomes, including reduced rates of reoffending, improved mental health, and better integration into the community. Forensic psychologists play a key role in achieving these outcomes by providing evidence-based services that address the root causes of criminal behavior.

By providing comprehensive psychological services in correctional facilities, forensic psychologists address the mental health needs of inmates, support their rehabilitation, and help prepare them for successful reintegration into society. These services are crucial for reducing recidivism and promoting public safety, ensuring that correctional facilities not only serve as places of confinement but also as opportunities for meaningful change and rehabilitation.

8.4 Case Study: Profiling a Serial Offender

This section presents a detailed case study that illustrates how forensic psychologists use profiling techniques to assist law enforcement in identifying and apprehending a serial offender. The case study provides a real-world example of the application of behavioral analysis, victimology, and investigative techniques in solving complex criminal cases.

1. Case Background

A. Crime Overview

- Series of Murders: The case involves a series of brutal murders that occurred over several months in a metropolitan area. The victims were all young women, each found in isolated locations with similar signs of violence, suggesting a pattern of behavior by the perpetrator.

- Initial Investigation: Despite extensive efforts by law enforcement, the initial investigation yielded few leads. The lack of physical evidence and the seemingly random selection of victims made it difficult to identify a suspect. It was at this stage that forensic psychologists were brought in to develop a criminal profile.

B. Behavioral Patterns

- Consistent Modus Operandi (MO): The offender exhibited a consistent MO across all crimes, including specific methods of killing and post-mortem behavior. Forensic psychologists analyzed these patterns to infer the offender's psychological traits, such as their level of control, impulsiveness, and possible motivations.

- Signature Behaviors: Beyond the MO, the offender left behind unique signature behaviors that were not necessary for the crime itself but were expressions of their psychological needs. These included ritualistic elements and specific positioning of the victims' bodies, which provided deeper insights into the offender's psyche.

C. Victimology

- Victim Selection: The victims shared several characteristics, including age, physical appearance, and lifestyle. By studying these commonalities, forensic psychologists developed hypotheses about the offender's criteria for selecting victims, suggesting a potential personal or symbolic significance to the choices.

- Offender-Victim Relationship: The analysis also explored the possibility of a prior connection between the offender and the victims. While no direct relationships were found, the pattern suggested the offender might have been stalking or observing the victims before the attacks, indicating a level of premeditation.

2. Profiling Process

A. Development of the Profile

- Demographic Predictions: Based on the behavioral analysis and victimology, forensic psychologists predicted key demographic details about the offender, such as age, race, employment status, and possible psychological disorders. The profile suggested the offender was likely a white male in his late 20s to early 30s, possibly employed in a job that allowed for mobility and the opportunity to scout locations and victims.

- Psychological Characteristics: The profile highlighted the offender's need for control and dominance, potentially linked to deep-seated insecurities or past trauma. It also suggested a possible history of failed relationships or social isolation, contributing to the offender's motives for the crimes.

B. Application in Investigation

- Narrowing Down Suspects: The criminal profile helped law enforcement narrow down their list of suspects, focusing on individuals who matched the psychological and demographic criteria. The profile was used to re-interview witnesses, re-examine old case files, and cross-reference potential suspects with known offenders in the area.

- Geographic Profiling Integration: The profile was combined with geographic profiling techniques to pinpoint areas where the offender was likely to reside or frequent. This helped focus surveillance efforts and allocate resources more efficiently.

C. Communication with the Public

- Media Strategy: Law enforcement, guided by forensic psychologists, also developed a media strategy to release specific details about the profile to the public. This was done to encourage tips while avoiding causing panic or revealing too much information that could compromise the investigation.

- Public Assistance: The release of the profile led to several tips from the public, one of which pointed to an individual who closely matched the psychological profile. This suspect had a history of similar behaviors and was known to frequent the areas where the crimes occurred.

3. Resolution and Lessons Learned

A. Apprehension of the Offender

- Final Capture: The integration of the forensic profile, public tips, and continued investigation led to the apprehension of the offender. Upon arrest, the suspect exhibited behaviors consistent with the psychological profile, including an attempt to assert control even in custody, further validating the accuracy of the profile.

- Confession and Corroboration: The offender eventually confessed to the crimes, providing details that matched the crime scenes and confirmed the psychological motivations outlined in the profile. This confession, combined with physical evidence, led to a successful conviction.

B. Impact on the Investigation

- Role of Forensic Psychology: This case highlighted the critical role that forensic psychology plays in criminal investigations, particularly in complex cases involving serial offenders. The profile provided law enforcement with a focused direction, significantly contributing to the resolution of the case.

- Collaboration Between Disciplines: The case also demonstrated the importance of collaboration between forensic psychologists, law enforcement, and the community. The combined efforts led to a more efficient and effective investigation.

C. Reflective Analysis

- Evaluation of Profiling Techniques: The success of this case led to a reflective analysis of the profiling techniques used, offering insights into areas for improvement and the potential for applying similar methods to future cases.

- Ethical Considerations: The case also raised important ethical questions about the use of psychological profiling, particularly in how profiles are communicated to the public and their potential impact on suspects who may fit the profile but are innocent.

By showcasing a real-world application of profiling techniques, this case study demonstrates the value of forensic psychology in solving complex criminal cases. The detailed analysis of the offender's behavior, the development of a comprehensive profile, and the successful collaboration between forensic psychologists and law enforcement underscore the importance of behavioral analysis in modern criminal investigations.

8.5 Interactive Simulation: Interrogation and Crisis Negotiation

This section presents an interactive simulation designed to help readers apply the concepts of interrogation and crisis negotiation covered in the previous sections. The simulation offers a hands-on approach to understanding the psychological principles behind these techniques and provides an opportunity to practice decision-making in high-pressure scenarios.

1. Interrogation Simulation

A. Scenario Overview

- The Case: Participants are given a scenario where a suspect is in custody for a series of burglaries that have escalated in violence. The suspect has been apprehended based on circumstantial evidence, and the goal is to elicit a confession or obtain critical information that can lead to a conviction.

- Suspect Profile: The suspect is a 35-year-old male with a history of petty thefts but no previous violent offenses. He appears calm but is evasive when questioned directly about the burglaries.

B. Interrogation Techniques

- Building Rapport: The simulation begins with the participant establishing rapport with the suspect, using techniques such as small talk, expressing empathy, and creating a non-threatening environment. Participants must choose how to approach the suspect to build trust without compromising the integrity of the interrogation.

- Applying the Reid Technique: As the interrogation progresses, participants are guided through the Reid Technique, where they must decide when to shift from a non-accusatory to an accusatory approach. The simulation presents choices such as presenting evidence, using psychological manipulation, or confronting the suspect with inconsistencies in his story.

- Ethical Considerations: Throughout the simulation, participants are reminded of ethical boundaries, such as avoiding coercion, respecting the suspect's rights, and ensuring that any confession obtained is voluntary. The simulation tracks these decisions and provides feedback on the ethical implications of each choice.

C. Outcome Evaluation

- Assessing Confessions: At the end of the interrogation, participants must evaluate the information obtained and determine whether the confession or statements made by the suspect are reliable and admissible in court. The simulation provides an analysis of the participant's decisions, highlighting areas where different choices could have led to better outcomes or avoided potential pitfalls such as false confessions.

- Reflection and Feedback: Participants receive detailed feedback on their performance, including the effectiveness of their interrogation strategy, adherence to ethical guidelines, and overall success in achieving the objectives of the interrogation. The simulation encourages reflection on how different techniques and approaches impacted the outcome.

2. Crisis Negotiation Simulation

A. Scenario Overview

- The Crisis: Participants are placed in a high-stress situation where they must negotiate with an individual who has taken a hostage in a local bank. The individual is armed, emotionally unstable, and has made specific demands that must be addressed to de-escalate the situation.

- Profile of the Negotiator: Participants take on the role of the lead negotiator, responsible for communicating with the individual, assessing their mental state, and making real-time decisions that could affect the safety of the hostages and the resolution of the crisis.

B. Negotiation Strategies

- Establishing Communication: The simulation starts with establishing initial contact with the hostage-taker. Participants must decide on the tone and approach to take, whether to be direct, empathetic, or authoritative. The simulation provides options for opening lines of communication and responding to the individual's initial demands.

- Building Rapport and Trust: As the negotiation progresses, participants are guided through techniques for building rapport and trust with the hostage-taker. Choices include acknowledging the individual's emotions, validating their grievances, and offering assurances. Participants must carefully balance these approaches to maintain control of the situation while gaining the individual's cooperation.

- De-escalation Techniques: The simulation presents various crisis de-escalation techniques, such as active listening, using calming language, and offering alternatives to violence. Participants are challenged to apply these techniques effectively to reduce the risk of harm to the hostages and the individual in crisis.

C. Outcome Evaluation

- Resolution of the Crisis: Participants must navigate the negotiation to a peaceful resolution, considering factors such as the safety of the hostages, the demands of the hostage-taker, and the potential for a successful surrender. The simulation evaluates the effectiveness of the participant's strategies in achieving a safe and peaceful outcome.

- Post-Negotiation Analysis: After the crisis is resolved, participants receive feedback on their negotiation tactics, including what worked well and areas for improvement. The analysis includes a review of how psychological insights were applied, the ethical considerations involved, and the overall success of the negotiation.

3. Learning Outcomes and Reflection

A. Skill Development

- Practical Application: The simulation provides participants with a realistic, immersive experience that enhances their understanding of interrogation and crisis negotiation techniques. By making real-time decisions, participants develop critical thinking and problem-solving skills relevant to high-pressure law enforcement situations.

- Understanding Ethical Implications: The simulation reinforces the importance of ethical considerations in both interrogation and crisis negotiation. Participants learn to balance achieving their objectives with respecting the rights and dignity of the individuals involved.

B. Continuous Improvement

- Feedback Integration: The detailed feedback provided at the end of each simulation encourages participants to reflect on their performance and identify areas for growth. The simulation emphasizes the importance of continuous learning and adaptation in mastering these complex techniques.

- Preparation for Real-World Scenarios: By engaging in this interactive simulation, participants are better prepared to handle real-world scenarios involving interrogation and crisis negotiation. The experience gained from the simulation can be directly applied to their professional roles, enhancing their effectiveness in law enforcement or forensic psychology settings.

The interactive simulation in this section offers a valuable opportunity for readers to apply theoretical knowledge in practical, high-stakes situations. By simulating the challenges of interrogation and crisis negotiation, participants gain hands-on experience that deepens their understanding of these critical aspects of forensic psychology and law enforcement.

Chapter 8 Review: Forensic Psychology in Law Enforcement and Corrections

Chapter 8 of *HowExpert Guide to Forensic Psychology* explores the critical role of forensic psychologists in law enforcement and correctional settings. The chapter delves into profiling and investigative techniques, the intricacies of interviewing and interrogation, the importance of crisis negotiation, and the delivery of psychological services in correctional facilities. This review summarizes the key concepts and practical applications covered in the chapter.

8.1 Profiling and Investigative Techniques

- *Criminal Profiling:*

  - Forensic psychologists use both inductive and deductive profiling methods to develop psychological profiles of offenders, helping law enforcement predict future actions and narrow down suspects.

  - Behavioral analysis, including crime scene analysis and victimology, provides insights into the offender's psychological state and motives, aiding in the investigation of serial crimes and cold cases.

- *Investigative Techniques:*

  - Geographic profiling helps law enforcement determine the most likely areas where an offender resides or operates, optimizing resource allocation.

  - Linkage analysis connects seemingly unrelated crimes by identifying consistent behaviors, assisting in the identification of serial offenders.

8.2 Interviewing, Interrogation, and Crisis Negotiation

- *Interviewing Techniques:*

- Cognitive interviewing enhances memory recall in witnesses and victims by recreating the context of events, while rapport building and non-verbal communication play crucial roles in obtaining accurate information.

- Interrogation Techniques:

- The Reid Technique, while widely used, is controversial due to its potential to elicit false confessions. Forensic psychologists emphasize ethical interrogation practices to ensure that confessions are voluntary and reliable.

- Understanding and preventing false confessions is a key responsibility of forensic psychologists, who provide training and expert testimony to safeguard against coercive practices.

- Crisis Negotiation:

- Crisis negotiation involves strategic communication with individuals in high-stress situations to resolve conflicts peacefully. Forensic psychologists contribute psychological insights to negotiation strategies, helping negotiators build rapport and de-escalate tense situations.

- Real-world applications, including case studies, highlight the importance of flexibility and psychological understanding in achieving successful outcomes during crisis negotiations.

8.3 Psychological Services in Correctional Facilities

- Mental Health Assessment and Treatment:

- Forensic psychologists conduct comprehensive mental health assessments of inmates, identifying conditions such as depression, anxiety, and schizophrenia, and determining the appropriate level of intervention.

- Treatment programs, including individual and group therapy, are tailored to address specific psychological needs, with forensic psychologists playing a central role in their design and implementation.

- Crisis Intervention and Suicide Prevention:

- Crisis intervention teams (CITs) respond to mental health emergencies within correctional facilities, using de-escalation techniques to manage crises and prevent harm.

- Suicide prevention programs involve screening for risk factors, providing counseling, and continuous monitoring of high-risk inmates, all overseen by forensic psychologists.

- Rehabilitation and Reentry Programs:

- Rehabilitation programs, such as cognitive-behavioral therapy (CBT) and substance abuse treatment, aim to reduce recidivism by addressing the underlying psychological issues contributing to criminal behavior.

- Reentry planning supports inmates as they transition back into society, with forensic psychologists ensuring that mental health needs, employment opportunities, and housing arrangements are addressed.

8.4 Case Study: Profiling a Serial Offender

- Case Background:

- The case study illustrates the application of criminal profiling in a series of murders, where forensic psychologists analyzed behavioral patterns and victimology to develop a comprehensive profile of the offender.

- Profiling Process:

- The profile helped narrow down suspects by predicting demographic and psychological characteristics, which guided law enforcement efforts and ultimately led to the apprehension of the offender.

- The case study underscores the importance of collaboration between forensic psychologists and law enforcement in solving complex cases.

- Lessons Learned:

- The successful resolution of the case highlighted the effectiveness of profiling techniques and the critical role of forensic psychology in criminal investigations.

8.5 Interactive Simulation: Interrogation and Crisis Negotiation

- Interrogation Simulation:

  - Participants engage in a scenario where they must apply interrogation techniques, including rapport building and the Reid Technique, while navigating ethical considerations to obtain reliable information.

- Crisis Negotiation Simulation:

  - The simulation places participants in a high-stress negotiation scenario, challenging them to use psychological insights to de-escalate the situation and achieve a peaceful resolution.

  - Feedback and reflection are integral to the simulations, helping participants refine their skills and better understand the practical application of forensic psychology principles.

Chapter 8 emphasizes the multifaceted role of forensic psychologists in law enforcement and correctional settings. From profiling serial offenders and conducting ethical interrogations to providing psychological services in correctional facilities and leading crisis negotiations, forensic psychologists are instrumental in enhancing the effectiveness and fairness of the criminal justice system. The chapter's case studies and interactive simulations offer practical insights into the application of forensic psychology, preparing readers to apply these techniques in real-world scenarios.

Chapter 9: Ethical and Legal Issues in Forensic Psychology

Ethical and legal issues are central to the practice of forensic psychology, where professionals must navigate complex scenarios that involve the rights, welfare, and legal standing of individuals within the justice system. Chapter 9 explores the ethical standards that guide forensic psychologists, the challenges related to confidentiality and privilege, and practical approaches to resolving ethical dilemmas. Through case studies and practical exercises, this chapter provides a comprehensive understanding of the ethical and legal frameworks that underpin the practice of forensic psychology.

9.1 Ethical Standards and Guidelines

Ethical standards and guidelines are the cornerstone of forensic psychology, ensuring that practitioners maintain the highest levels of professionalism and integrity in their work. This section explores the core ethical principles that guide forensic psychologists, the professional guidelines they must follow, and the application of these standards in forensic settings.

1. Core Ethical Principles

A. Respect for Dignity and Rights

- Fair Treatment: Forensic psychologists must respect the dignity and rights of all individuals they work with, including defendants, victims, and other stakeholders in the legal process. This principle emphasizes the need for unbiased and fair treatment, regardless of the individual's background or the nature of the case.

- Legal Rights: Practitioners are responsible for ensuring that the legal rights of all individuals are upheld, including the right to due process, fair representation, and humane treatment. This includes being mindful of the power dynamics present in legal settings and ensuring that vulnerable populations, such as minors or individuals with mental disabilities, are treated with particular care.

B. Competence

- Ongoing Education: Forensic psychologists are required to maintain a high level of professional competence, which involves staying current with the latest research, legal developments, and best practices in the field. This ensures that their assessments, reports, and testimonies are based on sound scientific principles and are legally defensible.

- Evidence-Based Practice: Competence also involves the application of evidence-based practices in all forensic evaluations and interventions. Forensic psychologists must rely on validated tools and methods, ensuring that their work is both reliable and relevant to the specific legal context.

C. Integrity and Professional Responsibility

- Honesty and Transparency: Integrity in forensic psychology requires honesty in all professional interactions, including the accurate representation of qualifications, the objective reporting of findings, and the clear communication of the limitations of one's expertise. Forensic psychologists must avoid exaggerating their credentials or making unfounded claims about their abilities.

- Avoiding Conflicts of Interest: Practitioners must be vigilant about potential conflicts of interest, such as situations where personal relationships or financial incentives could influence their professional judgment. Maintaining objectivity is crucial to upholding the integrity of the forensic psychologist's role within the legal system.

2. *Professional Guidelines*

A. APA's Ethical Principles of Psychologists and Code of Conduct

- Comprehensive Ethical Code: The American Psychological Association (APA) provides a detailed ethical code that covers all aspects of psychological practice, including specific provisions for forensic work. This code outlines the responsibilities of psychologists to their clients, the courts, and the public, emphasizing the importance of confidentiality, informed consent, and professional competence.

- Ethical Dilemmas: The APA code also addresses how to handle ethical dilemmas, such as situations where a psychologist's ethical obligations may conflict with legal requirements or court orders. Forensic psychologists are encouraged to seek supervision, consultation, or legal advice when faced with complex ethical issues.

B. Specialty Guidelines for Forensic Psychology

- Tailored Guidelines: The Specialty Guidelines for Forensic Psychology, developed by the APA, provide more specific direction for forensic psychologists, addressing the unique challenges of working within the legal system. These guidelines cover topics such as the proper conduct of forensic evaluations, the ethical considerations of providing expert testimony, and the management of dual relationships.

- Informed Consent and Confidentiality: The Specialty Guidelines emphasize the importance of obtaining informed consent from clients, clearly explaining the nature of the forensic evaluation, the limits of confidentiality, and the potential legal implications of the psychologist's findings.

C. Application in Forensic Settings

- Navigating Ethical and Legal Obligations: Forensic psychologists often operate at the intersection of ethics and law, where their professional responsibilities may conflict with legal demands. For example, a court may order the release of confidential psychological records, which the psychologist may believe could harm the client or compromise the fairness of the legal proceedings.

- Case Examples: Practical examples include handling cases where there is pressure from attorneys to deliver a specific outcome, dealing with conflicting ethical obligations when assessing minors, or managing the ethical implications of mandatory reporting requirements.

3. Application of Ethical Standards

A. Balancing Multiple Roles

- Dual Relationships: Forensic psychologists frequently face the challenge of balancing multiple roles, such as serving as both a therapist and a forensic evaluator for the same individual. The Specialty Guidelines advise against such dual relationships to avoid conflicts of interest, but in cases where they are unavoidable, psychologists must take steps to maintain objectivity and avoid compromising their professional judgment.

- Consultation and Supervision: When faced with complex ethical dilemmas, forensic psychologists are encouraged to seek consultation from colleagues or supervisors. This collaborative approach can provide additional perspectives and help ensure that ethical standards are upheld in difficult situations.

B. Ethical Decision-Making Models

- Step-by-Step Approach: Forensic psychologists can use ethical decision-making models to systematically approach dilemmas. These models typically involve identifying the ethical issues, considering the relevant ethical guidelines and legal requirements, weighing the potential consequences of different actions, and making a decision that aligns with both ethical principles and legal obligations.

- Reflective Practice: Regular reflection on ethical practice is important for continuous professional development. Forensic psychologists are encouraged to review their decisions, consider feedback from peers, and remain open to learning from ethical challenges encountered in their work.

By adhering to these ethical standards and guidelines, forensic psychologists ensure that their work is conducted with integrity, respect, and competence. These principles are essential not only for protecting the rights and welfare of individuals within the legal system but also for maintaining public trust in the field of forensic psychology. The application of these standards in practice requires careful consideration of both ethical and legal obligations, often requiring forensic psychologists to navigate complex and challenging situations with professionalism and care.

9.2 Confidentiality, Privilege, and Legal Challenges

Confidentiality and privilege are central to the ethical practice of forensic psychology, particularly when navigating the complex legal landscape. This section examines the principles of confidentiality and privilege, the circumstances under which they may be challenged, and the legal implications that forensic psychologists must consider in their professional practice.

1. Understanding Confidentiality

A. Fundamental Principle

- Confidentiality Defined: Confidentiality is a fundamental ethical principle that obligates forensic psychologists to protect the private information of their clients. This principle ensures that personal details shared during psychological assessments, therapy, or consultations are not disclosed without the client's consent, except under specific legal circumstances.

- Ethical Obligation: The duty of confidentiality is crucial in fostering trust between the psychologist and the client, ensuring that individuals feel secure in sharing sensitive information without fear of unnecessary exposure.

B. Limits of Confidentiality

- Informed Consent: Forensic psychologists must clearly explain the limits of confidentiality to clients during the informed consent process. Clients need to understand the specific situations where confidentiality may be breached, such as when there is a risk of harm to the client or others.

- Legal Exceptions: There are certain circumstances where confidentiality may be legally breached, including:

  - Duty to Warn and Protect: If a client poses a serious threat of violence to themselves or others, the psychologist may be legally required to breach confidentiality to prevent harm. This is known as the "duty to warn and protect."

- Court Orders: Confidential information may need to be disclosed if a court issues a subpoena or order compelling the psychologist to release records or provide testimony.

C. Practical Applications

- Balancing Confidentiality with Legal Duties: Forensic psychologists often face situations where they must balance their ethical duty to maintain confidentiality with their legal obligations. This may involve carefully considering what information is necessary to disclose and ensuring that any breach of confidentiality is justified and minimal.

- Case Examples: Examples include situations where a psychologist is asked to provide records in a custody dispute, or when a client discloses information about a crime that has not yet been reported. In these cases, the psychologist must navigate the legal requirements while striving to protect the client's privacy as much as possible.

2. Legal Privilege

A. Concept of Privilege

- Therapist-Client Privilege: Privilege is a legal concept that protects certain communications between a psychologist and their client from being disclosed in court without the client's consent. This protection is designed to encourage open and honest communication in therapy, ensuring that clients can speak freely without fear that their words will be used against them in legal proceedings.

- Scope of Privilege: The scope of privilege can vary depending on the jurisdiction and the specific circumstances of the case. For example, in some cases, privilege may only apply to communications that occur within the context of therapy, while in others, it may extend to all interactions between the psychologist and the client.

B. Exceptions to Privilege

- Court-Mandated Evaluations: When a forensic psychologist is conducting an evaluation at the request of the court, the usual protections of privilege may not apply. In these situations, the client must be informed that the findings of the evaluation will be shared with the court and may be used in legal proceedings.

- Legal Waivers: Privilege can be waived if the client chooses to disclose privileged information themselves or if they give consent for the psychologist to share it. Additionally, privilege may not apply in cases where the psychologist is required to report certain information by law, such as in cases of child abuse or neglect.

- Imminent Harm: Privilege may also be overridden if the psychologist believes that the client poses an imminent risk of harm to themselves or others. In such cases, the psychologist may need to breach privilege to take protective actions, such as notifying law enforcement or other authorities.

C. Navigating Legal Challenges

- Responding to Subpoenas: Forensic psychologists must be prepared to respond to subpoenas or court orders that request the release of confidential information. This process often involves reviewing the legal requirements, consulting with legal counsel, and determining the most appropriate course of action to protect the client's privacy while complying with the law.

- Testifying in Court: When serving as an expert witness, forensic psychologists must carefully navigate the boundaries of privilege and confidentiality. They need to be aware of what information can be disclosed in court and what must remain protected. Clear communication with the court and legal counsel is essential to ensure that ethical standards are upheld while fulfilling legal obligations.

3. Legal Challenges in Forensic Psychology

A. Dual Roles and Conflicts of Interest

- Complexity of Dual Roles: Forensic psychologists often serve in dual roles, such as being both a therapist and a court-appointed evaluator. These dual roles can create conflicts of interest, particularly when the information obtained in one role could impact the responsibilities of the other.

- Managing Conflicts: To manage these conflicts, forensic psychologists must clearly define their roles and responsibilities to all parties involved. They should avoid situations where their dual roles could compromise their objectivity or ethical obligations. When conflicts do arise, seeking consultation or supervision can help ensure that ethical standards are maintained.

B. Mandatory Reporting

- Legal Requirements: Forensic psychologists may be legally required to report certain information, such as evidence of child abuse, elder abuse, or threats of violence. These mandatory reporting laws can create challenges when they conflict with the psychologist's ethical duty to maintain confidentiality.

- Balancing Ethics and Law: When faced with mandatory reporting requirements, forensic psychologists must carefully balance their ethical obligations with their legal duties. This may involve disclosing only the minimum necessary information and providing the client with as much control over the process as possible.

C. Case Examples and Best Practices

- Responding to Ethical and Legal Dilemmas: This section provides examples of common legal challenges faced by forensic psychologists, such as handling requests for confidential records, navigating dual relationships, and dealing with mandatory reporting. Best practices include clear documentation, informed consent procedures, and ongoing consultation with legal and ethical experts.

- Proactive Approaches: Forensic psychologists are encouraged to take proactive steps to prevent legal challenges, such as staying informed about changes in the law, participating in continuing education on ethics and legal issues, and maintaining open communication with legal counsel and colleagues.

By understanding and navigating the complexities of confidentiality, privilege, and legal challenges, forensic psychologists can protect their clients' rights while fulfilling their professional and legal obligations. This balance is essential to maintaining the trust of clients, the integrity of the forensic psychologist's role, and the credibility of psychological evidence in legal contexts.

9.3 Case Study: Navigating Ethical Dilemmas

Ethical dilemmas are an inherent part of forensic psychology, where the responsibilities to clients, the legal system, and professional standards often intersect in complex ways. This case study presents a real-world scenario that illustrates how forensic psychologists can navigate ethical dilemmas, balancing their obligations to maintain confidentiality, protect client rights, and fulfill legal duties.

1. Case Background

A. Scenario Overview

- The Case: A forensic psychologist is appointed by the court to conduct a competency evaluation of a defendant charged with a violent crime. During the evaluation, the defendant discloses that they have engaged in other criminal activities that have not yet been discovered by law enforcement. The defendant also expresses intentions to harm someone after their release.

- Ethical Conflict: The forensic psychologist is faced with a dilemma: maintain confidentiality as required by ethical standards, or disclose the information to prevent potential harm and comply with legal obligations. The psychologist must also consider the impact of the disclosure on the defendant's legal case and the broader implications for their professional integrity.

B. Initial Assessment

- Evaluation Goals: The primary goal of the evaluation is to determine the defendant's competency to stand trial, which involves assessing their ability to understand the legal proceedings and participate in their defense. The psychologist must conduct the evaluation without bias, ensuring that the results are based solely on the defendant's mental state.

- Confidential Information: The defendant's disclosure of undiscovered crimes and future harmful intentions adds a layer of complexity to the evaluation. The psychologist must consider the ethical and legal implications of this information and decide how to proceed.

2. Ethical Decision-Making Process

A. Identifying the Ethical Issues

- Confidentiality vs. Public Safety: The psychologist must weigh the ethical obligation to maintain the defendant's confidentiality against the potential risk to public safety. The APA's Ethical Principles and the Specialty Guidelines for Forensic Psychology both emphasize the importance of confidentiality, but they also recognize exceptions in cases where there is a clear and imminent risk of harm.

- Competency and Integrity: The psychologist must ensure that the competency evaluation remains objective and that any actions taken do not compromise the integrity of the evaluation process. This includes avoiding any bias that could influence the outcome of the evaluation or the defendant's legal case.

B. Consulting Ethical Guidelines

- APA's Ethical Principles of Psychologists and Code of Conduct: The psychologist reviews the APA's guidelines on confidentiality, which allow for limited disclosure in cases where there is a risk of harm to others. The guidelines suggest that psychologists should take reasonable steps to protect potential victims while minimizing the breach of confidentiality.

- Specialty Guidelines for Forensic Psychology: The Specialty Guidelines provide additional direction on handling situations where legal and ethical obligations may conflict. They recommend seeking legal advice, consulting with colleagues, and documenting the decision-making process to ensure transparency and accountability.

C. Weighing the Options

- Option 1: Maintain Confidentiality: The psychologist could choose to maintain the defendant's confidentiality, focusing solely on the competency evaluation. This option upholds the ethical principle of confidentiality but may leave the potential victims at risk.

- Option 2: Limited Disclosure: The psychologist could choose to disclose only the information necessary to prevent harm, such as notifying law enforcement or the intended victim. This option prioritizes public safety but must be carefully managed to avoid unnecessary harm to the defendant's case.

- Option 3: Full Disclosure: The psychologist could choose to disclose all the information provided by the defendant, including the undiscovered crimes and harmful intentions. This option fully addresses the risk to public safety but significantly breaches confidentiality and could impact the defendant's legal rights.

D. Making the Decision

- Ethical Justification: After careful consideration, the psychologist decides to pursue Option 2: Limited Disclosure. This decision is based on the need to protect potential victims while minimizing the breach of confidentiality. The psychologist plans to inform the court and law enforcement only about the defendant's immediate harmful intentions, without revealing details of the undiscovered crimes unless required by law.

- Legal Consultation: The psychologist seeks legal advice to ensure that the disclosure complies with state laws and court requirements. This consultation helps clarify the legal obligations and potential consequences of the decision.

E. Documentation and Communication

- Detailed Documentation: The psychologist documents the entire decision-making process, including the ethical considerations, consultation with legal counsel, and the final decision. This documentation serves as a record of the psychologist's adherence to ethical standards and can be used to justify the actions taken if questioned in court.

- Clear Communication: The psychologist communicates the decision to the court, explaining the rationale for the limited disclosure and the steps taken to protect both the defendant's rights and public safety. The communication is clear, concise, and grounded in the ethical guidelines that informed the decision.

3. Outcome and Reflection

A. Resolution of the Dilemma

- Court's Response: The court acknowledges the psychologist's limited disclosure and uses the information to take protective measures. The defendant's competency evaluation proceeds without bias, and the psychologist's integrity is maintained throughout the process.

- Impact on the Defendant: The limited disclosure helps prevent potential harm without significantly compromising the defendant's legal case. The defendant is informed of the disclosure and the reasons behind it, helping to maintain trust between the psychologist and the defendant.

B. Lessons Learned

- Importance of Ethical Vigilance: The case study highlights the importance of ethical vigilance in forensic psychology. Psychologists must remain aware of the potential conflicts between their ethical obligations and legal duties, and they must be prepared to navigate these conflicts with care.

- Value of Consultation and Documentation: Seeking consultation and thoroughly documenting the decision-making process are essential practices that help forensic psychologists make informed, ethical decisions. These practices also provide protection in the event that the psychologist's actions are challenged in court.

- Balancing Competing Obligations: The case demonstrates the difficulty of balancing competing obligations in forensic practice, particularly when confidentiality and public safety are at odds. Forensic psychologists must use their professional judgment, guided by ethical principles and legal standards, to make decisions that protect the welfare of all parties involved.

By analyzing and reflecting on this case study, forensic psychologists can gain a deeper understanding of how to navigate ethical dilemmas in their practice. The careful consideration of ethical guidelines, the thoughtful weighing of options, and the commitment to transparency and integrity are all critical components of ethical decision-making in forensic psychology.

9.4 Practical Exercise: Ethical Decision-Making in Practice

This section provides a practical exercise designed to help forensic psychologists apply ethical decision-making processes in real-world scenarios. Through a series of ethical dilemmas, participants will be guided through the steps necessary to navigate complex situations, balancing their ethical obligations with legal responsibilities.

1. Scenario-Based Exercise

A. Scenario 1: Confidentiality and Public Safety

- The Dilemma: A forensic psychologist is conducting a risk assessment for a client who has been convicted of domestic violence. During the assessment, the client reveals plans to harm their ex-partner upon release. The psychologist must decide whether to breach confidentiality to warn the ex-partner or maintain confidentiality as part of the therapeutic relationship.

- *Decision-Making Process:*

  - Identify the Ethical Issues: The psychologist needs to identify the conflict between maintaining client confidentiality and the duty to protect the ex-partner from potential harm.

- Consult Ethical Guidelines: Review the APA's Ethical Principles and relevant state laws regarding duty to warn and protect.

- Weigh Options: Consider the potential outcomes of breaching confidentiality versus maintaining it.

- Make a Decision: Decide whether to notify the ex-partner, law enforcement, or both, and document the reasoning behind the decision.

- Reflect on the Outcome: After making the decision, reflect on how the ethical guidelines were applied and the impact of the decision on all parties involved.

B. Scenario 2: Dual Relationships and Objectivity

- The Dilemma: A forensic psychologist has been asked to provide expert testimony in a custody case involving a former therapy client. The psychologist must determine whether they can provide an unbiased evaluation or if their prior therapeutic relationship with the client could compromise their objectivity.

- Decision-Making Process:

- Identify the Ethical Issues: The psychologist must recognize the potential conflict of interest and the ethical concerns about maintaining objectivity.

- Consult Ethical Guidelines: Review the Specialty Guidelines for Forensic Psychology and the APA's Code of Conduct on managing dual relationships.

- Weigh Options: Consider declining the case to avoid a conflict of interest or proceeding with caution, ensuring that the prior relationship does not influence the evaluation.

- Make a Decision: Choose the course of action that best upholds the psychologist's ethical responsibilities, and document the decision-making process.

- Reflect on the Outcome: Reflect on the decision, considering whether it successfully balanced the need for objectivity with the ethical obligation to avoid dual relationships.

C. Scenario 3: Informed Consent and Competency

- The Dilemma: A forensic psychologist is asked to assess the competency of an elderly defendant with cognitive impairments. The defendant has difficulty understanding the legal implications of the assessment and seems unable to provide informed consent. The psychologist must decide how to proceed while respecting the defendant's rights.

- Decision-Making Process:

- Identify the Ethical Issues: The psychologist needs to consider the importance of informed consent and the ethical challenges of assessing competency in a cognitively impaired individual.

- Consult Ethical Guidelines: Review the APA's guidelines on informed consent, particularly with vulnerable populations, and consider legal requirements for competency assessments.

- Weigh Options: Explore alternatives such as seeking consent from a legal guardian or adjusting the assessment process to accommodate the defendant's cognitive limitations.

- Make a Decision: Decide on the best approach to obtain valid consent or proceed ethically without it, documenting the process.

- Reflect on the Outcome: After the assessment, reflect on the ethical considerations and how well the chosen approach respected the defendant's rights.

2. Group Discussion and Analysis

A. Collaborative Analysis

- Sharing Decisions: After completing the scenarios, participants are encouraged to share their decisions with peers in a group setting. This collaborative discussion allows participants to explore different approaches, learn from others' perspectives, and understand the reasoning behind various ethical decisions.

- Analyzing Outcomes: The group analyzes the outcomes of each scenario, discussing the effectiveness of the decisions made and the ethical principles that guided those decisions. This analysis helps deepen understanding of the complexities involved in forensic psychology and the importance of ethical vigilance.

B. Ethical Reflection

- Reflective Practice: Participants are encouraged to engage in reflective practice by considering how the decisions made in the scenarios align with their own professional values and ethical principles. This reflection helps to reinforce the importance of ethical decision-making and prepares participants to handle similar dilemmas in their professional practice.

- Continuous Learning: The exercise concludes with an emphasis on the need for continuous learning and ethical development. Participants are encouraged to stay informed about changes in ethical guidelines, seek ongoing education, and engage in regular consultation with colleagues to ensure their practice remains ethically sound.

3. *Application to Real-World Practice*

A. Practical Takeaways

- Building Ethical Competence: The exercise provides practical experience in applying ethical decision-making models, helping participants build the competence and confidence needed to navigate complex ethical dilemmas in their forensic practice.

- Documenting Decisions: The importance of documenting the decision-making process is emphasized throughout the exercise. This documentation not only protects the psychologist in legal contexts but also ensures transparency and accountability in their practice.

B. Preparing for Ethical Challenges

- Proactive Ethical Planning: Participants are encouraged to apply the lessons learned from the exercise to their own practice, developing proactive strategies for handling ethical challenges. This might include setting up consultation networks, attending ethics training, and staying current with developments in forensic psychology.

By engaging in this practical exercise, forensic psychologists can enhance their ability to navigate ethical dilemmas with confidence and integrity. The scenarios and discussions offer valuable insights into the complexities of forensic practice, helping participants to apply ethical principles effectively in their work and contribute positively to the justice system.

Chapter 9 Review: Ethical and Legal Issues in Forensic Psychology

Chapter 9 of *HowExpert Guide to Forensic Psychology* delves into the critical ethical and legal challenges faced by forensic psychologists. This chapter provides a comprehensive overview of the ethical standards and guidelines that govern the profession, explores the complexities of confidentiality and privilege, and offers practical approaches to navigating ethical dilemmas through case studies and exercises.

9.1 Ethical Standards and Guidelines

- *Core Ethical Principles:*

  - Respect for Dignity and Rights: Forensic psychologists are tasked with treating all individuals with fairness and respect, upholding their legal rights, and ensuring that their work remains unbiased and ethical.

  - Competence: Maintaining professional competence through ongoing education and adherence to evidence-based practices is essential for providing accurate and reliable assessments and testimonies.

  - Integrity and Professional Responsibility: Psychologists must demonstrate honesty and transparency in their professional conduct, avoiding conflicts of interest and ensuring that their work remains objective and free from personal biases.

- Professional Guidelines:

- APA's Ethical Principles and Specialty Guidelines: These guidelines provide a framework for ethical practice in forensic psychology, addressing the unique challenges of working within the legal system and offering direction on issues such as confidentiality, informed consent, and managing dual relationships.

9.2 Confidentiality, Privilege, and Legal Challenges

- Confidentiality:

- Limits and Exceptions: While confidentiality is a cornerstone of ethical practice, there are specific legal and ethical exceptions, such as the duty to warn and protect, that may require forensic psychologists to breach confidentiality to prevent harm.

- Informed Consent: Clearly explaining the limits of confidentiality to clients is crucial, ensuring they understand when and why their private information might be disclosed.

- Legal Privilege:

- Therapist-Client Privilege: Legal privilege protects certain communications from being disclosed in court, but this protection can vary in forensic contexts, particularly in court-mandated evaluations.

- Navigating Legal Challenges: Forensic psychologists must carefully navigate legal challenges, such as responding to subpoenas and testifying in court, while upholding ethical standards and protecting client confidentiality as much as possible.

9.3 Case Study: Navigating Ethical Dilemmas

- Case Background:

- The Dilemma: The case study illustrates a scenario where a forensic psychologist must decide whether to breach confidentiality after a defendant discloses plans for future harm during a competency evaluation.

- Ethical Decision-Making Process: The psychologist must weigh the ethical obligation to maintain confidentiality against the need to protect potential victims, consulting ethical guidelines, considering legal obligations, and documenting the decision-making process.

- Outcome and Reflection:

- Resolution: The psychologist opts for limited disclosure, prioritizing public safety while minimizing the breach of confidentiality. The case study emphasizes the importance of careful ethical deliberation and the value of seeking consultation in complex situations.

9.4 Practical Exercise: Ethical Decision-Making in Practice

- Scenario-Based Exercises:

- Applying Ethical Principles: Participants are presented with scenarios that mimic real-world ethical dilemmas, such as balancing confidentiality with public safety, managing dual relationships, and obtaining informed consent from vulnerable populations.

- Group Discussion and Analysis: The exercises encourage collaborative analysis and discussion, helping participants explore different approaches and deepen their understanding of ethical decision-making in forensic practice.

- Reflective Practice:

- Continuous Learning: The exercise highlights the importance of ongoing reflection and learning, encouraging forensic psychologists to stay informed about ethical guidelines, seek consultation, and engage in proactive ethical planning.

Chapter 9 provides a detailed exploration of the ethical and legal issues that are integral to forensic psychology. By emphasizing the importance of adhering to ethical standards and guidelines, understanding the complexities of confidentiality and privilege, and developing practical strategies for navigating ethical dilemmas, this chapter equips forensic psychologists with the tools they need to practice with integrity and professionalism. The case studies and practical exercises offer valuable insights into the real-world application of ethical principles, preparing readers to handle the challenges of forensic practice with confidence and care.

Chapter 10: Research and Future Trends in Forensic Psychology

Chapter 10 explores the research methodologies used in forensic psychology, the ethical considerations inherent in conducting forensic research, and the current trends and emerging issues shaping the field. Through a case study and an interactive exercise, this chapter also provides practical insights into how forensic research can be designed and applied to real-world issues.

10.1 Research Methodologies in Forensic Psychology

Research in forensic psychology is essential for advancing the field, improving practices, and informing legal decision-making. Forensic psychologists use a variety of research methodologies to explore complex issues related to criminal behavior, legal processes, and psychological assessments. This section outlines the key research methodologies employed in forensic psychology, highlighting their strengths, limitations, and practical applications.

1. Quantitative Research

A. Experimental Designs

- Controlled Experiments: Experimental designs are widely used in forensic psychology to establish cause-and-effect relationships. In controlled experiments, variables are manipulated to observe their effects on specific outcomes, such as the impact of different interrogation techniques on confession rates. These studies often involve control groups and random assignment to minimize bias and increase the reliability of the results.

- Quasi-Experiments: In forensic settings, true experimental designs may not always be feasible due to ethical or practical constraints. Quasi-experiments, which do not use random assignment, are often employed instead. For example, researchers might compare the outcomes of different treatment programs in correctional facilities where participants are assigned based on availability rather than random selection.

B. Survey Research

- Large-Scale Surveys: Surveys are a common tool in forensic psychology for gathering data from large groups of people. They are used to assess public attitudes towards crime, the prevalence of psychological disorders in offender populations, or the effectiveness of legal interventions. Surveys can be administered through questionnaires, interviews, or online platforms, providing valuable quantitative data that can be analyzed for patterns and correlations.

- Standardized Instruments: Forensic psychologists often use standardized instruments, such as the Minnesota Multiphasic Personality Inventory (MMPI) or the Psychopathy Checklist-Revised (PCL-R), to collect consistent and reliable data across different populations. These instruments are designed to measure specific psychological traits or conditions relevant to forensic assessments.

C. Statistical Analysis

- Descriptive Statistics: Descriptive statistics are used to summarize and describe the basic features of a dataset. In forensic psychology, they might be used to report the average scores on a psychological test, the frequency of certain behaviors, or the distribution of variables within a sample. Descriptive statistics provide a foundation for understanding the general trends in the data.

- Inferential Statistics: Inferential statistics allow forensic psychologists to make predictions or inferences about a larger population based on sample data. Techniques such as regression analysis, ANOVA, and chi-square tests are used to determine the relationships between variables, assess the effectiveness of interventions, or identify factors that predict criminal behavior.

2. Qualitative Research

A. Case Studies

- In-Depth Exploration: Case studies are a qualitative research method that involves an in-depth examination of a single case or a small number of cases. In forensic psychology, case studies might explore the psychological profiles of serial offenders, the impact of trauma on victim behavior, or the decision-making processes of jurors. These studies provide rich, detailed insights that can inform theory development and clinical practice.

- Limitations: While case studies offer depth and detail, they are limited in their generalizability. The findings from a single case may not apply to other individuals or situations, making it difficult to draw broad conclusions from case study research.

B. Interviews and Focus Groups

- Gathering In-Depth Data: Interviews and focus groups are qualitative methods used to gather in-depth data on participants' thoughts, feelings, and experiences. Forensic psychologists might conduct interviews with offenders to understand their motivations, or hold focus groups with victims to explore their perceptions of the legal system. These methods allow for the exploration of complex issues that may not be captured by quantitative measures.

- Thematic Analysis: After collecting qualitative data, forensic psychologists often use thematic analysis to identify and interpret patterns of meaning within the data. This method involves coding the data into themes or categories, which can then be analyzed to understand the underlying issues and inform practice.

C. Ethnographic Research

- Cultural and Contextual Understanding: Ethnographic research involves the study of people in their natural environments, focusing on cultural and social dynamics. In forensic psychology, ethnographic methods might be used to study the culture of correctional facilities, the dynamics of gang behavior, or the impact of community interventions on crime rates. Ethnographic research provides a deep understanding of the context in which behaviors occur.

- Challenges: Ethnographic research can be time-consuming and may involve ethical challenges, such as maintaining objectivity and respecting the privacy and rights of participants. However, it offers valuable insights that can enhance the cultural competence of forensic psychologists.

3. Mixed-Methods Research

A. Combining Quantitative and Qualitative Approaches

- Integrated Research Designs: Mixed-methods research combines both quantitative and qualitative approaches in a single study. For example, a forensic psychologist might use quantitative surveys to assess the prevalence of PTSD in a population of veterans and then conduct qualitative interviews to explore the personal experiences of those with PTSD. This approach allows for a more comprehensive understanding of the research question.

- Triangulation: Triangulation is a key benefit of mixed-methods research, where multiple data sources are used to validate findings. By combining different methods, forensic psychologists can cross-check results, enhancing the reliability and validity of their conclusions.

B. Applications in Forensic Psychology

- Complex Issues: Mixed-methods research is particularly useful for addressing complex issues in forensic psychology, such as the psychological effects of incarceration or the effectiveness of rehabilitation programs. By integrating quantitative and qualitative data, researchers can gain a fuller picture of the issue and develop more informed recommendations for practice and policy.

- Challenges: Conducting mixed-methods research can be challenging due to the need for expertise in both quantitative and qualitative methods. It also requires careful planning to ensure that the different components of the research are effectively integrated and that the findings are coherent.

4. Practical Applications of Research Methodologies

A. Informing Legal Decisions

- Expert Testimony: Research findings from forensic psychology are often used to inform legal decisions, such as in cases where expert testimony is required.

Forensic psychologists may present research on the reliability of eyewitness testimony, the validity of psychological assessments, or the effectiveness of intervention programs, helping the court to make informed decisions.

- Policy Development: Forensic research also plays a critical role in shaping public policy. Studies on recidivism rates, the psychological impact of solitary confinement, or the effectiveness of juvenile rehabilitation programs can influence legislation and guide the development of evidence-based policies.

B. Improving Forensic Practices

- Assessment and Intervention: Research methodologies in forensic psychology contribute to the development and validation of assessment tools and intervention programs. Forensic psychologists rely on empirical evidence to design effective treatment plans, conduct risk assessments, and evaluate the outcomes of their interventions, ensuring that their practices are grounded in scientific research.

- Training and Education: Research findings are also essential for the training and education of forensic psychologists. Understanding the latest research methodologies and findings helps practitioners stay current with best practices and advances in the field, enhancing their ability to provide high-quality services.

By employing a variety of research methodologies, forensic psychologists can contribute valuable insights to the field, inform legal and policy decisions, and improve the effectiveness of forensic practices. Whether through quantitative, qualitative, or mixed-methods research, the rigorous application of scientific principles is essential for advancing knowledge and ensuring that forensic psychology remains a dynamic and evidence-based discipline.

10.2 Ethical Considerations in Forensic Research

Conducting research in forensic psychology involves navigating a complex landscape of ethical issues. These considerations are paramount to ensure that research is conducted responsibly, protects the rights and well-being of participants, and upholds the integrity of the field. This section explores the key ethical principles that guide forensic research, focusing on informed consent, confidentiality, the treatment of vulnerable populations, and the balance between research objectives and ethical obligations.

1. Informed Consent

A. Fundamental Principle

- Voluntary Participation: Informed consent is a cornerstone of ethical research, requiring that participants are fully aware of the nature, purpose, and potential risks of the study before agreeing to participate. In forensic research, where participants may include offenders, victims, or individuals involved in the legal system, ensuring voluntary participation is crucial.

- Comprehensive Information: Researchers must provide clear and comprehensive information about the study, including the procedures involved, the expected duration, and the nature of any interventions or assessments. Participants should also be informed of their right to withdraw from the study at any time without penalty.

B. Challenges in Forensic Settings

- Coercion and Voluntariness: In forensic settings, participants may feel pressured to participate in research due to their legal situation or institutional context (e.g., in prisons or court-mandated programs). Researchers must take special care to ensure that consent is genuinely voluntary and that participants do not feel coerced.

- Cognitive Impairments and Consent: Some participants, such as those with cognitive impairments or mental health conditions, may have difficulty understanding the consent process. Researchers must assess the capacity of these individuals to provide informed consent and consider using simplified explanations or involving legal guardians when necessary.

2. *Confidentiality and Data Protection*

A. Protecting Participant Privacy

- Anonymity and Confidentiality: Maintaining the confidentiality of participant data is a critical ethical responsibility in forensic research. Researchers must anonymize data to protect the identities of participants, particularly when dealing with sensitive information such as criminal histories or psychological assessments.

- Secure Data Storage: Researchers must implement secure data storage practices to prevent unauthorized access to confidential information. This includes using encrypted digital storage, secure filing systems for paper records, and limiting access to data to authorized personnel only.

B. Legal Obligations and Confidentiality

- Mandatory Reporting: In some cases, forensic researchers may encounter information that they are legally required to report, such as disclosures of child abuse, threats of violence, or criminal activity. Researchers must navigate the tension between maintaining confidentiality and fulfilling their legal obligations, ensuring that participants are aware of these limits before they consent to participate.

- Ethical Dilemmas: Researchers may face ethical dilemmas when their duty to protect confidentiality conflicts with legal requirements. In such cases, it is essential to consult with legal experts, follow institutional guidelines, and document the decision-making process to ensure that ethical standards are upheld.

3. *Vulnerable Populations*

A. Special Considerations for Vulnerable Groups

- Prisoners and Inmates: Research involving prisoners or inmates poses unique ethical challenges due to the power dynamics and potential for coercion in correctional settings. Researchers must take extra precautions to ensure that participation is voluntary, that inmates understand their rights, and that their involvement does not affect their legal status or treatment within the facility.

- Children and Adolescents: When conducting research with minors, additional ethical safeguards are required. This includes obtaining informed consent from parents or legal guardians, ensuring that the research is age-appropriate, and providing extra protection for the privacy and well-being of young participants.

- Individuals with Mental Health Conditions: Research involving individuals with mental health conditions requires careful consideration of their capacity to consent and their vulnerability to exploitation. Researchers must ensure that these participants are not subjected to undue stress or harm and that their participation is entirely voluntary and informed.

B. Balancing Research Benefits and Participant Protection

- Minimizing Harm: Researchers have an ethical obligation to minimize harm to participants, both psychological and physical. This includes designing studies that avoid unnecessary risks, providing support during and after participation, and ensuring that participants are debriefed and offered assistance if they experience distress.

- Justification of Research: The potential benefits of the research must be weighed against the risks to participants, particularly when dealing with vulnerable populations. Research should only be conducted if the expected benefits, such as advancements in forensic psychology or improvements in legal practices, clearly outweigh the risks.

4. Ethical Review and Oversight

A. Institutional Review Boards (IRBs)

- Role of IRBs: Institutional Review Boards (IRBs) play a critical role in overseeing the ethical aspects of forensic research. Before a study can proceed, it must be reviewed and approved by an IRB to ensure that it meets ethical standards, protects participant rights, and complies with legal requirements.

- Continuous Monitoring: IRBs also monitor ongoing research to ensure that ethical standards are maintained throughout the study. This includes reviewing any changes to the research protocol, assessing reports of adverse events, and ensuring that researchers continue to adhere to ethical guidelines.

B. Ethical Decision-Making in Research

- Consultation and Collaboration: Researchers are encouraged to consult with colleagues, legal experts, and ethical advisors when facing complex ethical issues in their research. Collaborative decision-making can help ensure that ethical dilemmas are addressed thoughtfully and that research is conducted in a manner that upholds the highest ethical standards.

- Documentation and Transparency: Researchers must document their ethical decision-making processes, including how informed consent was obtained, how confidentiality was protected, and how any ethical challenges were resolved. Transparency in these processes is essential for maintaining the integrity of the research and for providing accountability in forensic psychology.

5. *Ethical Challenges in Forensic Research*

A. Dual Roles and Conflicts of Interest

- Managing Dual Roles: Forensic psychologists often wear multiple hats, such as being both a researcher and a clinician or expert witness. These dual roles can create conflicts of interest, particularly when the goals of research may conflict with the best interests of the participant. Researchers must clearly define their roles, avoid situations where their dual responsibilities could compromise ethical standards, and seek guidance when conflicts arise.

B. Ethical Considerations in Emerging Research Areas

- Use of Technology: As technology advances, new ethical challenges emerge, such as the use of artificial intelligence (AI) in forensic assessments or the analysis of big data in criminal justice research. Researchers must consider the ethical implications of these technologies, including issues of privacy, bias, and the potential for misuse.

- Cross-Cultural Research: Conducting research in diverse cultural contexts raises ethical considerations related to cultural sensitivity, respect for local norms, and the potential for exploitation. Researchers must ensure that their methods are culturally appropriate and that they engage with local communities in a respectful and ethical manner.

C. Reflective Practice

- Ongoing Ethical Reflection: Ethical considerations in forensic research are not static; they require continuous reflection and adaptation as new challenges arise. Researchers are encouraged to engage in ongoing ethical reflection, seek feedback from peers, and stay informed about developments in ethical standards and practices in forensic psychology.

By adhering to these ethical principles and considerations, forensic psychologists can conduct research that not only advances the field but also respects the rights and dignity of participants. Ethical research practices are essential for maintaining public trust, ensuring the integrity of forensic psychology, and contributing to the development of just and effective legal systems.

10.3 Current Trends and Emerging Issues

Forensic psychology is a dynamic field that continuously evolves in response to advancements in technology, changes in societal norms, and emerging challenges within the legal system. This section explores the current trends and emerging issues that are shaping the future of forensic psychology, highlighting the opportunities and challenges these developments present.

1. Technology in Forensic Psychology

A. Digital Forensics

- Growth of Digital Evidence: As digital technology becomes increasingly integrated into everyday life, the role of digital forensics in criminal investigations has expanded. Forensic psychologists are now involved in analyzing digital evidence, such as social media activity, email correspondence, and online behavior, to provide insights into criminal intent, personality traits, and potential threats.

- Cybercrime and Psychological Profiling: The rise of cybercrime, including hacking, online fraud, and cyberstalking, has led to new challenges in psychological profiling. Forensic psychologists are tasked with understanding the motivations and behaviors of cybercriminals, which often differ from those involved in traditional crimes. This requires a deep understanding of both psychological principles and digital environments.

B. Artificial Intelligence (AI) and Machine Learning

- AI in Forensic Assessments: Artificial intelligence and machine learning are being increasingly used to enhance forensic assessments. AI can process large datasets to identify patterns and predict behaviors, such as recidivism or the likelihood of violent acts. These tools can assist forensic psychologists in making more accurate assessments, but they also raise concerns about bias, reliability, and the potential for over-reliance on automated systems.

- Ethical Implications: The use of AI in forensic psychology introduces ethical challenges, particularly related to bias in algorithms, the transparency of decision-making processes, and the potential for AI-driven assessments to be used in ways that could infringe on individual rights. Forensic psychologists must critically evaluate these tools and advocate for ethical standards in their development and application.

C. Virtual Reality (VR) and Simulations

- Training and Therapy: Virtual reality (VR) is emerging as a powerful tool in forensic psychology for both training and therapeutic purposes. VR simulations can create realistic scenarios for training law enforcement officers in crisis negotiation or for desensitization therapy for individuals with PTSD. These immersive environments offer new opportunities for experiential learning and treatment.

- Legal Proceedings: VR is also being explored as a tool in legal proceedings, such as recreating crime scenes for juries or conducting virtual courtrooms. While these applications hold promise, they also raise questions about the accuracy of representations and the potential for VR to influence legal outcomes in unintended ways.

2. Cultural Competence and Diversity in Forensic Practice

A. Increasing Diversity in Legal Contexts

- Cultural Sensitivity in Assessments: As societies become more culturally diverse, forensic psychologists must be equipped to conduct assessments that are sensitive to cultural differences. This includes understanding how cultural norms influence behavior, communication styles, and legal processes. Culturally competent assessments help ensure that individuals from diverse backgrounds are treated fairly within the legal system.

- Training and Education: There is a growing emphasis on incorporating cultural competence into the training and education of forensic psychologists. This involves learning about different cultural perspectives, recognizing biases in forensic tools and practices, and developing strategies to work effectively with clients from diverse backgrounds.

B. Cross-Cultural Research

- Globalization and Forensic Psychology: Globalization has led to an increased focus on cross-cultural research in forensic psychology. Researchers are examining how cultural factors impact crime, legal processes, and rehabilitation across different regions. This research is critical for developing global best practices and ensuring that forensic psychology is responsive to the needs of diverse populations.

- Challenges of Cross-Cultural Research: Conducting cross-cultural research presents challenges, such as differences in legal systems, language barriers, and varying ethical standards. Forensic psychologists must navigate these challenges while ensuring that their research is culturally appropriate and respectful of local norms.

C. Addressing Bias and Discrimination

- Implicit Bias in Forensic Settings: Implicit bias can influence decisions in forensic settings, from assessments to sentencing recommendations. Forensic psychologists are increasingly aware of the need to address these biases in their work. This includes using tools that are validated across diverse populations and being mindful of how cultural stereotypes might influence their interpretations.

- Promoting Equity in the Justice System: There is a growing movement to address systemic bias and promote equity within the justice system. Forensic psychologists play a key role in this effort by advocating for fair treatment, developing interventions that reduce disparities, and conducting research that highlights areas of bias and suggests solutions.

3. Trauma-Informed Approaches in Forensic Psychology

A. Understanding the Impact of Trauma

- Prevalence of Trauma: Trauma is increasingly recognized as a significant factor in the lives of many individuals involved in the legal system, including offenders, victims, and witnesses. Forensic psychologists are adopting trauma-informed approaches to better understand how past trauma influences behavior, decision-making, and interactions with the legal system.

- Trauma-Informed Assessments: Incorporating trauma-informed principles into forensic assessments involves asking about and considering an individual's trauma history when evaluating their mental state, risk factors, and treatment needs. This approach helps to avoid re-traumatization and provides a more accurate understanding of the individual's behavior and needs.

B. Applications in Legal and Correctional Settings

- Trauma-Informed Legal Practices: Legal professionals are increasingly adopting trauma-informed practices to improve the treatment of trauma survivors within the justice system. This includes creating environments that are sensitive to the needs of trauma survivors, using language that minimizes distress, and implementing policies that recognize the long-term effects of trauma.

- Correctional Interventions: Trauma-informed care is also being integrated into correctional settings, where many inmates have histories of trauma. Interventions such as cognitive-behavioral therapy (CBT) and peer support programs are being adapted to address the specific needs of trauma survivors, with the goal of reducing recidivism and promoting rehabilitation.

C. Research and Policy Development

- Impact of Trauma on Legal Outcomes: Research on the impact of trauma on legal outcomes is informing policy changes aimed at improving the treatment of trauma survivors in the justice system. This includes reforms in areas such as sentencing, parole decisions, and the treatment of incarcerated individuals with trauma histories.

- Advocacy for Trauma-Informed Policies: Forensic psychologists are increasingly involved in advocating for trauma-informed policies at the local, state, and national levels. This advocacy is critical for ensuring that the justice system is responsive to the needs of trauma survivors and that policies are informed by the latest research on trauma and recovery.

4. Ethical and Legal Challenges

A. Evolving Ethical Standards

- Ethical Dilemmas in Emerging Technologies: The rapid development of new technologies in forensic psychology, such as AI and VR, presents new ethical dilemmas. Forensic psychologists must grapple with questions about the ethical use of these tools, the potential for misuse, and the implications for privacy and justice. Ethical guidelines are evolving to address these challenges, but forensic psychologists must stay informed and critically engage with these issues.

- Balancing Innovation with Ethical Practice: While innovation is essential for advancing the field, it must be balanced with ethical considerations. Forensic psychologists must ensure that new tools and methods are used responsibly and that they do not exacerbate existing inequalities or introduce new forms of bias.

B. Legal Implications of Forensic Practices

- Admissibility of New Techniques: As forensic psychology evolves, the legal system must adapt to the introduction of new techniques and tools. Forensic psychologists play a key role in determining the admissibility of these techniques in court, ensuring that they meet legal standards for reliability and validity.

- Regulation and Oversight: The growing use of technology in forensic psychology raises questions about regulation and oversight. Forensic psychologists must engage with policymakers to develop regulations that protect the rights of individuals while allowing for the responsible use of new technologies in forensic practice.

By staying abreast of these current trends and emerging issues, forensic psychologists can ensure that their practice remains relevant, ethical, and effective in a rapidly changing world. The integration of new technologies, the emphasis on cultural competence, the adoption of trauma-informed approaches, and the ongoing attention to ethical challenges are all critical components of the future of forensic psychology. As the field continues to evolve, forensic psychologists must be prepared to adapt to these changes while maintaining their commitment to justice, fairness, and the well-being of those they serve.

10.4 Case Study: Impactful Forensic Research

Forensic psychology research has the potential to significantly influence legal practices, policies, and the understanding of criminal behavior. This section presents a case study of a landmark forensic research study that had a profound impact on both the field of forensic psychology and the broader criminal justice system. The case study illustrates how rigorous research can lead to meaningful change, highlighting the methodologies used, the key findings, and the implications for policy and practice.

1. Research Context

A. Background and Purpose

- The Study: The case study focuses on a groundbreaking research project conducted to investigate the psychological effects of solitary confinement on inmates. The purpose of the study was to understand how prolonged isolation affects mental health and behavior, with the goal of informing correctional policies and practices.

- Rationale: Solitary confinement has long been a controversial practice, with critics arguing that it can cause severe psychological harm. However, there was a lack of empirical evidence to support these claims. This study aimed to fill that gap by providing scientifically rigorous data on the impact of solitary confinement, thereby contributing to the debate on its use in correctional facilities.

B. Methodology

- Mixed-Methods Approach: The research employed a mixed-methods approach, combining quantitative and qualitative data to provide a comprehensive understanding of the effects of solitary confinement. Quantitative data were collected through standardized psychological assessments, while qualitative data were gathered from in-depth interviews with inmates.

- Longitudinal Design: The study used a longitudinal design, following a cohort of inmates over several months to track changes in their mental health and behavior over time. This approach allowed researchers to observe the long-term effects of solitary confinement and identify patterns that might not be evident in shorter studies.

C. Ethical Considerations

- Informed Consent: Given the vulnerable population involved, obtaining informed consent was a critical aspect of the research. Researchers ensured that inmates fully understood the purpose of the study, the procedures involved, and their right to withdraw at any time without any impact on their legal status or treatment within the facility.

- Confidentiality and Data Protection: Researchers took extensive measures to protect the confidentiality of the participants, including anonymizing data and securely storing records. This was particularly important given the sensitive nature of the information being collected.

2. Key Findings

A. Psychological Impact of Solitary Confinement

- Mental Health Deterioration: The study found that prolonged solitary confinement led to significant deterioration in inmates' mental health. Common symptoms included severe anxiety, depression, hallucinations, and suicidal ideation. These effects were observed even in inmates with no prior history of mental illness, suggesting that solitary confinement can induce psychological disorders.

- Behavioral Changes: In addition to mental health issues, inmates in solitary confinement exhibited marked behavioral changes, including increased aggression, impulsivity, and withdrawal from social interactions. These behaviors often persisted even after the inmates were released from solitary confinement, indicating long-term effects on their social functioning.

B. Variability Among Inmates

- Individual Differences: The study also highlighted significant variability in how inmates responded to solitary confinement. Some individuals were more resilient, showing fewer negative effects, while others experienced extreme psychological distress. Factors such as pre-existing mental health conditions, coping strategies, and social support were identified as key determinants of these differences.

- Vulnerability Factors: The research identified specific factors that made certain inmates more vulnerable to the negative effects of solitary confinement. These included a history of trauma, lack of social support, and limited coping mechanisms. Understanding these factors can help in identifying inmates who are at higher risk of harm and may benefit from alternative interventions.

C. Policy Implications

- Recommendations for Reform: Based on the findings, the researchers made several policy recommendations aimed at reducing the use of solitary confinement and mitigating its harmful effects. These included limiting the duration of solitary confinement, providing mental health support to inmates in isolation, and developing alternative disciplinary measures that do not involve prolonged isolation.

- Influence on Correctional Policies: The study's findings were instrumental in prompting reforms in correctional policies across several states. Some jurisdictions introduced laws that restricted the use of solitary confinement, particularly for vulnerable populations such as juveniles and individuals with mental illness. Additionally, correctional facilities began implementing mental health screening and support programs for inmates in solitary confinement.

3. Impact on the Field and Beyond

A. Contribution to Forensic Psychology

- Advancing Knowledge: The study significantly advanced the field of forensic psychology by providing empirical evidence on the psychological effects of solitary confinement. It also contributed to the development of assessment tools and interventions designed to address the mental health needs of inmates in isolation.

- Theoretical Implications: The research supported and expanded existing theories on the impact of environmental stressors on mental health, particularly in extreme conditions such as solitary confinement. It also informed the development of new theoretical models that consider individual differences in vulnerability and resilience.

B. Broader Social and Legal Impact

- Legal Challenges to Solitary Confinement: The study's findings were used in legal challenges to solitary confinement, with courts citing the research as evidence of the practice's potential to cause psychological harm. In some cases, this led to rulings that limited or prohibited the use of solitary confinement, particularly for vulnerable populations.

- Public Awareness and Advocacy: The research also played a role in raising public awareness about the psychological impact of solitary confinement. Advocacy groups used the findings to campaign for reform, leading to broader societal discussions about the ethics of solitary confinement and the treatment of inmates in the correctional system.

C. Reflections on Ethical Research

- Ethical Challenges: The case study underscores the ethical challenges involved in conducting research with vulnerable populations, particularly in correctional settings. It highlights the importance of obtaining informed consent, protecting participant confidentiality, and ensuring that the research does not exacerbate the harm experienced by participants.

- Lessons Learned: The study serves as a model for ethical forensic research, demonstrating how rigorous methodological approaches and ethical considerations can lead to findings that not only advance scientific knowledge but also contribute to meaningful social and legal change.

By examining this case study, forensic psychologists can gain valuable insights into how impactful research is conducted, how it can influence policy and practice, and how ethical challenges can be navigated in complex settings. The study's legacy underscores the importance of integrating empirical research with ethical practice to effect positive change in the criminal justice system.

Chapter 10 Review: Research and Future Trends in Forensic Psychology

Chapter 10 of *HowExpert Guide to Forensic Psychology* explores the critical role of research in advancing the field of forensic psychology, addressing emerging trends, and grappling with the ethical considerations that arise in this complex area of study. This chapter provides an overview of the research methodologies used in forensic psychology, delves into the ethical challenges of conducting research in forensic settings, examines current trends, and highlights the impact of groundbreaking forensic research through a detailed case study.

10.1 Research Methodologies in Forensic Psychology

- *Quantitative Research:*

  - Experimental Designs: Experimental designs are crucial for establishing cause-and-effect relationships in forensic psychology. These studies often involve controlled experiments and quasi-experiments, allowing researchers to manipulate variables and observe their effects on behavior.

  - Survey Research: Large-scale surveys and standardized instruments are used to gather quantitative data on public attitudes, the prevalence of psychological disorders, and the effectiveness of legal interventions. Statistical analysis helps to interpret this data, identifying patterns and relationships that inform forensic practice.

- *Qualitative Research:*

  - Case Studies: Case studies provide in-depth exploration of individual cases, offering detailed insights into psychological processes, decision-making, and behavior in forensic contexts. While rich in detail, case studies have limited generalizability.

- Interviews and Focus Groups: Qualitative methods like interviews and focus groups are used to gather in-depth data on participants' experiences and perspectives, often analyzed through thematic analysis to identify underlying themes.

- Mixed-Methods Research:

- Integration of Quantitative and Qualitative Approaches: Mixed-methods research combines both quantitative and qualitative approaches, offering a comprehensive understanding of complex issues in forensic psychology. This approach is particularly useful for studying phenomena that require both statistical analysis and in-depth exploration.

10.2 Ethical Considerations in Forensic Research

- Informed Consent:

- Voluntary Participation: Informed consent is essential to ensure that participants fully understand the nature, purpose, and risks of the study. In forensic settings, ensuring voluntary participation is crucial, especially among vulnerable populations.

- Challenges in Forensic Settings: Researchers must be vigilant against potential coercion and assess the capacity of participants with cognitive impairments or mental health conditions to provide informed consent.

- Confidentiality and Data Protection:

- Protecting Privacy: Researchers have an ethical responsibility to maintain the confidentiality of participant data, using secure storage and anonymization to protect sensitive information.

- Legal Obligations: Balancing confidentiality with legal obligations, such as mandatory reporting, presents ethical dilemmas that require careful navigation and consultation with legal experts.

- Vulnerable Populations:

- Special Considerations: Research involving vulnerable populations, such as prisoners, minors, and individuals with mental health conditions, requires extra precautions to ensure their protection and minimize harm.

- Ethical Oversight: Institutional Review Boards (IRBs) play a critical role in overseeing the ethical conduct of forensic research, ensuring that participant rights are protected and that studies comply with ethical standards.

10.3 Current Trends and Emerging Issues

- Technology in Forensic Psychology:

- Digital Forensics and AI: The rise of digital forensics and the use of AI in forensic assessments are transforming the field. These technologies offer new opportunities but also raise ethical concerns about bias, privacy, and the reliability of automated systems.

- Virtual Reality: VR is being explored for training, therapy, and legal proceedings, providing immersive environments that enhance learning and treatment but also pose challenges related to accuracy and legal implications.

- Cultural Competence and Diversity:

- Cultural Sensitivity: Forensic psychologists must develop cultural competence to conduct assessments that are sensitive to cultural differences and to address implicit bias in forensic settings.

- Cross-Cultural Research: As forensic psychology becomes more global, cross-cultural research is essential for understanding how cultural factors influence crime and legal processes, while also addressing the challenges of conducting research in diverse contexts.

- Trauma-Informed Approaches:

- Understanding Trauma: Trauma-informed approaches are increasingly recognized as critical in forensic psychology, particularly in understanding how trauma affects behavior and decision-making within legal contexts.

- Applications in Legal and Correctional Settings: Trauma-informed care is being integrated into legal and correctional settings to better support individuals with trauma histories and to reduce the risk of re-traumatization.

10.4 Case Study: Impactful Forensic Research

- *Research Context:*

  - Study on Solitary Confinement: This case study examines a landmark research project on the psychological effects of solitary confinement, which employed a mixed-methods approach to gather both quantitative and qualitative data on mental health outcomes and behavioral changes.

  - Ethical Considerations: The study highlighted the importance of obtaining informed consent, protecting participant confidentiality, and addressing the ethical challenges of conducting research in correctional settings.

- *Key Findings:*

  - Psychological Impact: The study found that solitary confinement leads to severe psychological distress, including anxiety, depression, and suicidal ideation, with long-term effects on social functioning.

  - Policy Implications: The findings prompted significant reforms in correctional policies, including limits on the use of solitary confinement and the implementation of mental health support programs.

- *Impact on the Field:*

  - Advancing Knowledge: The study contributed to the understanding of environmental stressors on mental health and informed the development of assessment tools and interventions in forensic psychology.

  - Broader Social and Legal Impact: The research influenced legal challenges to solitary confinement, raised public awareness, and supported advocacy efforts for reform.

Chapter 10 emphasizes the importance of rigorous, ethically conducted research in forensic psychology, highlighting how it drives advancements in the field and influences legal and social policies. By exploring the methodologies used in forensic research, addressing the ethical challenges that arise, and examining the impact of groundbreaking studies, this chapter provides forensic psychologists with the tools and insights needed to conduct impactful research that contributes to justice and societal well-being. The integration of current trends, such as technology and cultural competence, further ensures that forensic psychology remains responsive to the evolving needs of the legal system and the diverse populations it serves.

Chapter 11: Building a Career in Forensic Psychology

Chapter 11 of *HowExpert Guide to Forensic Psychology* is dedicated to guiding aspiring forensic psychologists through the various stages of building a successful career in the field. From understanding the educational pathways and training requirements to exploring career opportunities and specializations, this chapter provides a comprehensive roadmap for those looking to enter and thrive in forensic psychology.

11.1 Educational Pathways and Training Requirements

Building a career in forensic psychology requires a strong educational foundation, practical training, and a commitment to ongoing professional development. This section outlines the essential educational pathways and training requirements that aspiring forensic psychologists must follow to enter and excel in the field.

1. Undergraduate Education

A. Foundational Knowledge

- Degree Programs: The journey to becoming a forensic psychologist typically begins with an undergraduate degree in psychology, criminology, or a related field. These programs provide the foundational knowledge needed to understand human behavior, mental health, and the legal system.

- Core Coursework: Key courses at the undergraduate level include:

  - Abnormal Psychology: Understanding psychological disorders, their symptoms, and treatments.

  - Developmental Psychology: Examining how individuals grow and change over the lifespan, with a focus on how these changes impact behavior.

  - Criminal Psychology: Exploring the psychological underpinnings of criminal behavior, including theories of crime and criminal profiling.

- Research Methods: Gaining essential skills in designing studies, collecting data, and analyzing results, which are crucial for evidence-based practice in forensic psychology.

- Supplementary Courses: Electives in law, sociology, ethics, and cultural studies are also beneficial, as they provide a broader understanding of the social and legal contexts in which forensic psychologists work.

B. Gaining Relevant Experience

- Internships and Volunteer Work: Undergraduate students are encouraged to gain practical experience through internships, volunteer positions, or part-time work in settings related to forensic psychology. This might include working in a mental health facility, assisting in a research lab, or volunteering with organizations that support victims of crime.

- Research Opportunities: Participating in research projects as an undergraduate can provide valuable experience in data collection, analysis, and report writing. This experience is particularly important for students planning to pursue graduate studies in forensic psychology.

2. Graduate Education

A. Master's Programs

- Advanced Studies: A master's degree in forensic psychology or a closely related field is often the next step for those pursuing a career in this area. Master's programs typically offer advanced coursework in topics such as:

  - Forensic Assessment: Training in the use of psychological tests and interviews to evaluate individuals within the legal system.

  - Criminal Behavior: In-depth study of the factors that contribute to criminal behavior, including psychological, social, and environmental influences.

  - Legal Psychology: Examining the application of psychological principles to legal issues, including jury decision-making, eyewitness testimony, and competency evaluations.

- Thesis or Capstone Project: Many master's programs require students to complete a thesis or capstone project, which involves conducting original research or a comprehensive review of the literature on a specific forensic psychology topic.

B. Doctoral Programs

- Ph.D. or Psy.D.: For most clinical and research positions in forensic psychology, a doctoral degree is required. Students can pursue either a Doctor of Philosophy (Ph.D.) in psychology, which emphasizes research and academic careers, or a Doctor of Psychology (Psy.D.), which focuses on clinical practice.

- Specialized Training: Doctoral programs offer specialized training in forensic psychology, including courses in advanced forensic assessment, expert testimony, ethics, and clinical interventions. Students also receive extensive training in research methods and statistical analysis.

- Dissertation Research: A key component of doctoral education is the completion of a dissertation, which involves conducting original research on a topic relevant to forensic psychology. This research contributes to the field and demonstrates the student's ability to conduct independent, scholarly work.

C. Practical Training

1. Internships and Practicums

- Hands-On Experience: During their graduate education, students must complete internships or practicums in forensic settings, such as correctional facilities, mental health centers, law enforcement agencies, or court systems. These experiences provide hands-on training in assessment, therapy, consultation, and legal proceedings.

- Supervision and Feedback: Internships and practicums are conducted under the supervision of licensed forensic psychologists, who provide guidance, feedback, and mentorship. This supervision helps students refine their skills and prepares them for independent practice.

2. Supervised Clinical Practice

- Postdoctoral Training: For those pursuing clinical roles, postdoctoral supervised practice is often required. This involves working under the supervision of an experienced forensic psychologist while gaining additional experience in conducting assessments, providing therapy, and offering expert testimony in court.

- Licensure Preparation: Supervised practice is also a key step in preparing for licensure, as it ensures that candidates meet the practical experience requirements set by state licensing boards.

3. Continuing Education and Professional Development

A. Ongoing Learning

- Workshops and Seminars: Forensic psychologists must stay current with the latest developments in the field by participating in workshops, seminars, and conferences. These events offer opportunities to learn about new research findings, emerging trends, and changes in legal standards.

- Specialization and Certification: Continuing education is also important for those who wish to specialize in specific areas of forensic psychology, such as child custody evaluations, criminal profiling, or correctional psychology. Professional certifications can enhance career prospects and demonstrate expertise in these areas.

B. Networking and Mentorship

- Building Professional Relationships: Networking with peers, mentors, and other professionals in the field is essential for career growth. Joining professional organizations, such as the American Psychological Association (APA) and its Division 41 (American Psychology-Law Society), provides access to resources, mentorship opportunities, and professional development activities.

- Mentorship: Establishing relationships with experienced forensic psychologists can provide valuable guidance, support, and insight as students transition from education to professional practice.

By following these educational pathways and meeting the necessary training requirements, aspiring forensic psychologists can build a strong foundation for a successful career in the field. Whether pursuing clinical practice, research, or specialized roles within the legal system, the knowledge, skills, and experience gained through these educational and training programs are essential for making meaningful contributions to the intersection of psychology and law.

11.2 Certification, Licensure, and Specializations

Achieving certification and licensure is a critical step in becoming a practicing forensic psychologist. This section outlines the processes involved in obtaining licensure, the importance of certification, and the various specializations available within the field of forensic psychology.

1. Licensure Requirements

A. State Licensure

- Mandatory Licensure: To practice as a forensic psychologist, individuals must obtain licensure in the state where they intend to work. Each state has its own licensing requirements, but they generally include the completion of a doctoral degree in psychology, a certain number of supervised clinical hours, and passing a licensure exam.

- Doctoral Degree: A Ph.D. or Psy.D. in psychology, with a focus on forensic psychology, is typically required. This degree must be obtained from an accredited institution and includes rigorous coursework, clinical training, and research.

- Supervised Clinical Experience: Most states require candidates to complete a specific number of supervised clinical hours. This experience is gained during internships, practicums, or postdoctoral work under the supervision of a licensed psychologist. These hours ensure that the candidate has practical experience in applying psychological principles in forensic settings.

B. Licensing Examination

- EPPP (Examination for Professional Practice in Psychology): The EPPP is the standard licensure exam for psychologists in the United States. This exam tests the candidate's knowledge of core psychological principles, ethics, and practices. Passing the EPPP is a key step in becoming licensed.

- State-Specific Requirements: In addition to the EPPP, some states require candidates to pass a state-specific exam or jurisprudence exam that covers the legal and ethical standards of practice in that state.

C. Maintaining Licensure

- Continuing Education: To maintain licensure, forensic psychologists must complete continuing education (CE) credits. CE courses keep psychologists up to date on the latest developments in the field, including new research, emerging trends, and changes in legal and ethical standards.

- Renewal Process: Licenses must be renewed periodically, typically every 2 to 3 years, depending on the state. Renewal requires documentation of CE credits and may involve paying a renewal fee.

2. Certification in Forensic Psychology

A. Board Certification

- American Board of Professional Psychology (ABPP): The ABPP offers board certification in forensic psychology, which is recognized as a mark of excellence in the field. While not mandatory, board certification can enhance career opportunities and professional credibility.

- Certification Process: The certification process through the ABPP includes:

  - Eligibility Requirements: Candidates must have a doctoral degree, a state license to practice psychology, and several years of postdoctoral experience in forensic psychology.

- Written Exam: The certification exam assesses the candidate's knowledge and competence in forensic psychology, including legal standards, ethical issues, and specialized forensic assessments.

- Practice Samples: Candidates must submit practice samples, such as forensic evaluation reports, that demonstrate their expertise in applying psychological principles to legal cases.

- Oral Examination: The final step is an oral examination conducted by a panel of board-certified forensic psychologists. This exam evaluates the candidate's ability to articulate and defend their professional judgments and practices.

B. Benefits of Certification

- Enhanced Credibility: Board certification signals to employers, clients, and the legal community that a forensic psychologist has met high standards of knowledge, skill, and professionalism.

- Career Advancement: Certified forensic psychologists may have better job prospects, higher earning potential, and opportunities to work on more complex and high-profile cases.

- Professional Development: The certification process encourages ongoing learning and professional development, ensuring that certified forensic psychologists remain at the forefront of the field.

3. Specializations in Forensic Psychology

A. Child Custody Evaluations

- Role and Importance: Forensic psychologists specializing in child custody evaluations work with families and the legal system to assess the best interests of the child in custody disputes. This specialization requires expertise in developmental psychology, family dynamics, and legal standards related to custody cases.

- Skills and Training: Professionals in this area must be skilled in conducting interviews, administering psychological tests, and preparing detailed reports that inform court decisions. Additional training in family law and child welfare is often required.

B. Criminal Profiling

- Understanding Criminal Behavior: Criminal profiling involves analyzing crime scenes, evidence, and offender behavior to create profiles that can assist law enforcement in identifying and apprehending suspects. This specialization is often depicted in popular media, but it requires a deep understanding of psychology, criminology, and investigative techniques.

- Specialized Training: Forensic psychologists who specialize in criminal profiling often undergo additional training in forensic analysis, criminal behavior theories, and investigative psychology. They may work closely with law enforcement agencies and contribute to solving complex criminal cases.

C. Correctional Psychology

- Focus on Rehabilitation: Correctional psychologists work within prison systems, providing mental health services to inmates and developing rehabilitation programs aimed at reducing recidivism. This specialization requires a thorough understanding of the psychological challenges faced by incarcerated individuals and the unique dynamics of correctional environments.

- Treatment and Assessment: Correctional psychologists assess inmates for mental health disorders, provide therapy and counseling, and design interventions that address the underlying causes of criminal behavior. They also evaluate the effectiveness of rehabilitation programs and contribute to policy development within the correctional system.

D. Victim Advocacy and Support

- Supporting Victims: Forensic psychologists specializing in victim advocacy provide psychological support to victims of crime, helping them cope with trauma, navigate the legal system, and access necessary resources. This specialization requires knowledge of trauma-informed care, crisis intervention, and legal processes related to victim rights.

- Training in Trauma and Crisis Intervention: Professionals in this area must be trained in understanding the impact of trauma on mental health, conducting crisis interventions, and advocating for victims' rights within the legal system. They often work in collaboration with legal professionals, social workers, and community organizations.

E. Forensic Neuropsychology

- Linking Brain Function and Behavior: Forensic neuropsychologists specialize in assessing the relationship between brain function and behavior, particularly in cases involving brain injuries, neurological disorders, or cognitive impairments. This specialization is crucial in legal cases where brain function may impact criminal responsibility or competency.

- Advanced Training: Forensic neuropsychologists require advanced training in neuropsychological assessment techniques, brain anatomy, and the effects of neurological conditions on behavior. They may conduct evaluations for cases involving traumatic brain injuries, dementia, or developmental disorders.

By pursuing certification, licensure, and specialization, forensic psychologists can enhance their expertise, credibility, and career opportunities. These credentials demonstrate a commitment to professional excellence and enable psychologists to contribute effectively to the legal system, whether through direct clinical practice, expert testimony, research, or policy development. Specializing in a specific area of forensic psychology allows professionals to focus on the populations or issues they are most passionate about, further enriching their careers and impact in the field.

11.3 Career Opportunities and Emerging Fields

Forensic psychology offers a wide range of career opportunities across various settings, from clinical practice to research and policy development. As the field evolves, new and emerging areas of specialization continue to develop, providing forensic psychologists with diverse paths to explore. This section outlines traditional career paths in forensic psychology, as well as emerging fields that present exciting opportunities for growth and innovation.

1. Traditional Career Paths in Forensic Psychology

A. Clinical Forensic Psychologist

- Direct Client Work: Clinical forensic psychologists work directly with individuals involved in the legal system, including offenders, victims, and those facing legal disputes. Their roles include conducting psychological assessments, providing therapy, and offering expert testimony in court. These professionals often work in a variety of settings, such as:

  - Correctional Facilities: Providing mental health services to inmates, including assessment, treatment, and crisis intervention. Correctional psychologists play a key role in rehabilitation efforts, helping to reduce recidivism.

  - Courts and Legal Settings: Performing competency evaluations, risk assessments, and providing expert witness testimony. These psychologists assist the court in understanding the psychological aspects of legal cases, influencing decisions related to sentencing, custody, and more.

  - Private Practice: Many clinical forensic psychologists operate in private practice, offering services to legal professionals, individuals involved in legal disputes, or organizations requiring forensic assessments.

B. Forensic Researcher

- Academic and Research Institutions: Forensic researchers work primarily in academic settings or research institutions, focusing on studying the intersection of psychology and law. They conduct studies on topics such as jury decision-making, eyewitness memory, criminal behavior, and the psychological effects of incarceration.

- Government Agencies and NGOs: Some forensic researchers are employed by government agencies or non-governmental organizations (NGOs) to evaluate programs, develop policy recommendations, and conduct impact assessments.

Their work informs evidence-based practices and policies within the criminal justice system.

- Publication and Dissemination: Forensic researchers contribute to the field by publishing their findings in academic journals, presenting at conferences, and advising policymakers on issues related to psychology and the law.

C. Expert Witness and Consultant

- Courtroom Testimony: Forensic psychologists often serve as expert witnesses in legal cases, providing testimony on issues such as mental health, competency, criminal responsibility, and risk of reoffending. Their expertise helps courts understand complex psychological issues that are relevant to legal decisions.

- Consulting Services: In addition to providing testimony, forensic psychologists may act as consultants to attorneys, law enforcement agencies, or organizations. They may assist in case preparation, jury selection, or the development of psychological profiles in criminal investigations.

2. Emerging Fields in Forensic Psychology

A. Cyberpsychology and Digital Forensics

- Understanding Online Behavior: As cybercrime becomes increasingly prevalent, there is a growing need for forensic psychologists who specialize in understanding online behavior, digital evidence, and the psychological aspects of cybercrime. Cyberpsychology focuses on how individuals interact with technology and how these interactions can lead to criminal behavior.

- Applications in Cybercrime: Forensic psychologists in this field may work on cases involving hacking, online fraud, cyberstalking, and other digital crimes. They might also develop strategies for preventing cybercrime, conduct risk assessments of potential offenders, and assist law enforcement in tracking digital footprints.

- Collaboration with Technologists: Professionals in this emerging field often collaborate with cybersecurity experts, law enforcement, and legal professionals to address the challenges posed by digital crime. They may also work on the ethical implications of AI and digital surveillance in forensic settings.

B. Trauma-Informed Legal Practice

- Integrating Trauma Awareness: Trauma-informed legal practice involves understanding and addressing the impact of trauma on individuals involved in the legal system, including victims, offenders, and witnesses. This approach recognizes that trauma can significantly affect behavior, decision-making, and interactions with the legal system.

- Applications in Court and Corrections: Forensic psychologists specializing in trauma-informed practice may work in courts, providing assessments that consider the effects of trauma on legal competencies, or in correctional settings, where they design interventions that address the trauma histories of inmates.

- Policy Development and Advocacy: This emerging field also involves advocating for trauma-informed policies within the legal system, promoting practices that are sensitive to the needs of trauma survivors and that reduce the risk of re-traumatization during legal processes.

C. Forensic Neuropsychology

- Brain Function and Behavior: Forensic neuropsychologists specialize in understanding the relationship between brain function and behavior, particularly in legal contexts. They conduct assessments that examine how neurological conditions, such as traumatic brain injuries, dementia, or developmental disorders, impact an individual's cognitive abilities, decision-making, and criminal responsibility.

- Legal Applications: These professionals are often involved in cases where brain function is a central issue, such as determining competency to stand trial, assessing the mental state at the time of the offense, or evaluating the effects of neurological impairments on behavior. Their assessments can be pivotal in legal decisions related to sentencing, mitigation, and treatment recommendations.

- Interdisciplinary Collaboration: Forensic neuropsychologists work closely with neurologists, attorneys, and other mental health professionals to provide a comprehensive understanding of how brain function impacts legal outcomes.

3. Interdisciplinary and Policy-Oriented Opportunities

A. Collaboration with Legal Professionals

- Interdisciplinary Teams: Forensic psychologists increasingly work as part of interdisciplinary teams that include attorneys, judges, social workers, and law enforcement officers. This collaboration ensures that psychological insights are integrated into legal strategies, case management, and decision-making processes.

- Roles in Policy Development: Forensic psychologists contribute to the development of policies related to mental health in the criminal justice system, juvenile justice reform, and the treatment of vulnerable populations. Their research and clinical expertise inform evidence-based practices and legislative initiatives.

B. Policy Advocacy and Reform

- Influencing Legal and Correctional Policies: Forensic psychologists can play a crucial role in advocating for reforms within the criminal justice system. This might involve pushing for changes in sentencing laws, improving mental health services in correctional facilities, or promoting alternatives to incarceration for individuals with mental health conditions.

- Research-Driven Advocacy: By conducting research that highlights systemic issues and proposing evidence-based solutions, forensic psychologists contribute to policy changes that promote fairness, justice, and the humane treatment of individuals within the legal system.

C. Global and Cross-Cultural Forensic Psychology

- International Opportunities: As forensic psychology becomes more global, there are increasing opportunities to work on international cases, collaborate with professionals in other countries, and contribute to the development of forensic practices worldwide. This might include working with international courts, participating in global research initiatives, or consulting on cases that cross national borders.

- Cross-Cultural Research and Practice: Forensic psychologists working in global contexts must be culturally competent, understanding how cultural differences impact legal processes, mental health assessments, and treatment interventions. This specialization is critical in cases involving immigrants, refugees, or individuals from diverse cultural backgrounds.

By exploring both traditional and emerging fields in forensic psychology, professionals can find diverse and fulfilling career opportunities that align with their interests and expertise. Whether working directly with clients, conducting research, or shaping policy, forensic psychologists have the potential to make significant contributions to the justice system and society at large. As the field continues to evolve, staying informed about new developments and being open to interdisciplinary collaboration will be key to success in this dynamic and impactful career.

11.4 Reflection Exercise: Planning Your Forensic Psychology Career

Embarking on a career in forensic psychology requires careful planning, self-assessment, and goal setting. This reflection exercise is designed to help you clarify your career aspirations, identify the steps needed to achieve them, and create a roadmap for success in the field of forensic psychology.

1. Self-Assessment

A. Identifying Your Interests

- Career Focus: Reflect on the areas of forensic psychology that most interest you. Are you drawn to clinical work with offenders or victims? Do you find the research aspects of forensic psychology compelling, or are you interested in policy development and advocacy?

- Preferred Settings: Consider where you would like to work—courts, correctional facilities, private practice, research institutions, or governmental agencies. Your preferred setting will influence the type of training, certification, and experience you will need.

B. Evaluating Your Strengths and Skills

- Core Competencies: Assess your strengths in key areas such as psychological assessment, research methods, communication skills, and ethical decision-making. Understanding your strengths will help you identify the roles in forensic psychology that are best suited to your abilities.

- Areas for Development: Identify any areas where you may need further development. This might include gaining more experience in a particular setting, developing specialized skills, or pursuing additional education or certification. Creating a plan to address these areas will be crucial to your career advancement.

2. Setting Career Goals

A. Short-Term Goals

- Educational Milestones: Define your immediate educational goals, such as completing a degree program, gaining specific certifications, or obtaining relevant experience through internships or practicums. Consider what steps you need to take over the next few years to build a strong foundation for your career.

- Skill Development: Identify short-term goals for developing specific skills, such as improving your forensic assessment techniques, gaining experience in testifying as an expert witness, or learning new research methodologies.

B. Long-Term Goals

- Career Aspirations: Outline your long-term career aspirations. Do you aim to become a board-certified forensic psychologist, a leading researcher in forensic psychology, or a policy advocate? Consider where you see yourself in 5, 10, or 20 years and what accomplishments you hope to achieve.

- Impact and Legacy: Think about the broader impact you want to have in the field of forensic psychology. Do you want to contribute to significant policy changes, influence legal practices, or develop innovative treatment programs? Setting these goals will guide your decisions and motivate you throughout your career.

3. *Developing a Career Plan*

A. Educational and Professional Development Plan

- Pathway to Licensure: Map out the steps needed to achieve licensure in your state, including completing necessary education, gaining supervised clinical experience, and preparing for the licensure exam. Consider any additional certifications that will enhance your expertise and career prospects.

- Continuing Education: Plan for ongoing professional development through continuing education courses, workshops, and conferences. Staying current with advancements in forensic psychology is essential for maintaining licensure and advancing your career.

B. Building a Professional Network

- Mentorship: Seek out mentors who can provide guidance, advice, and support as you navigate your career. A mentor can help you avoid common pitfalls, offer insights from their experience, and connect you with opportunities in the field.

- Networking Opportunities: Join professional organizations such as the American Psychological Association (APA) and the American Psychology-Law Society (AP-LS). Attend conferences, seminars, and other networking events to build relationships with peers and established professionals in forensic psychology.

4. Adapting to Changes and Challenges

A. Flexibility and Adaptability

- Embracing Change: The field of forensic psychology is constantly evolving. Be prepared to adapt your career plan as new opportunities and challenges arise. This might involve pursuing additional training in emerging areas, such as cyberpsychology or trauma-informed care, or shifting your focus as your interests evolve.

- Problem-Solving: Develop a proactive approach to problem-solving. When faced with obstacles—such as difficulty finding a practicum placement, challenges in passing licensure exams, or changes in legal standards—use these experiences as learning opportunities and adjust your plan accordingly.

B. Work-Life Balance

- Sustaining Your Career: Forensic psychology can be a demanding field, with the potential for high-stress situations, ethical dilemmas, and exposure to trauma. Reflect on how you will maintain a healthy work-life balance, including managing stress, seeking support when needed, and setting boundaries to prevent burnout.

- Personal Fulfillment: Ensure that your career plan aligns with your personal values and goals. Consider how your work in forensic psychology will contribute to your overall sense of purpose and fulfillment.

By completing this reflection exercise, you can create a personalized career plan that aligns with your interests, strengths, and long-term aspirations. This plan will serve as a roadmap, guiding your decisions and helping you stay focused on achieving your goals in forensic psychology. Remember that your career path may change over time, and being flexible, proactive, and committed to lifelong learning will be key to your success in this dynamic and impactful field.

Chapter 11 Review: Building a Career in Forensic Psychology

Chapter 11 of *HowExpert Guide to Forensic Psychology* provides a comprehensive guide for aspiring forensic psychologists, covering the educational pathways, certification and licensure requirements, career opportunities, and the importance of careful career planning. This chapter equips readers with the essential information and strategies needed to build a successful and fulfilling career in forensic psychology.

11.1 Educational Pathways and Training Requirements

- Undergraduate Education: The journey to becoming a forensic psychologist begins with an undergraduate degree in psychology, criminology, or a related field. Essential coursework includes abnormal psychology, criminal psychology, and research methods. Supplementary courses in law, sociology, and ethics provide a broader understanding of the social and legal contexts in which forensic psychologists work.

- Graduate Education: A master's degree offers advanced studies in forensic psychology, focusing on topics like forensic assessment and criminal behavior. For those pursuing clinical or research roles, a doctoral degree (Ph.D. or Psy.D.) is typically required. Doctoral programs provide specialized training and involve completing a dissertation on a relevant forensic psychology topic.

- Practical Training: Internships, practicums, and supervised clinical practice are crucial components of forensic psychology training, providing hands-on experience in forensic settings. These experiences help students apply theoretical knowledge, develop essential skills, and prepare for licensure.

11.2 Certification, Licensure, and Specializations

- State Licensure: To practice as a forensic psychologist, obtaining state licensure is mandatory. This process includes completing a doctoral degree, gaining supervised clinical experience, and passing the Examination for Professional Practice in Psychology (EPPP). Continuing education is required to maintain licensure.

- Board Certification: While not mandatory, board certification in forensic psychology from the American Board of Professional Psychology (ABPP) enhances career opportunities and professional credibility. The certification process includes a written exam, practice samples, and an oral examination.

- Specializations: Forensic psychologists can specialize in areas such as child custody evaluations, criminal profiling, correctional psychology, and forensic neuropsychology. Specializing allows professionals to focus on specific populations or issues, further enriching their careers.

11.3 Career Opportunities and Emerging Fields

- Traditional Career Paths: Clinical forensic psychologists work in correctional facilities, courts, or private practice, providing assessments, therapy, and expert testimony. Forensic researchers contribute to the field through academic research and publications, often working in universities or research institutions.

- Emerging Fields: New areas like cyberpsychology and digital forensics, trauma-informed legal practice, and forensic neuropsychology are creating exciting opportunities for forensic psychologists. These fields address the growing challenges of cybercrime, the impact of trauma on legal processes, and the relationship between brain function and behavior.

- Interdisciplinary and Policy-Oriented Roles: Forensic psychologists increasingly work in interdisciplinary teams, collaborating with legal professionals, policymakers, and advocacy groups. Their expertise contributes to policy development, legal reform, and the promotion of equity within the justice system.

11.4 Reflection Exercise: Planning Your Forensic Psychology Career

- Self-Assessment: Aspiring forensic psychologists are encouraged to reflect on their interests, strengths, and career goals. Identifying preferred areas of specialization and assessing personal competencies help in creating a focused career plan.

- Setting Career Goals: Establishing short-term and long-term career goals is essential for success. This includes educational milestones, skill development, and aspirations for impact in the field of forensic psychology.

- Developing a Career Plan: A detailed career plan should include pathways to licensure, continuing education, and networking opportunities. Seeking mentorship and building professional relationships are key to navigating the field and advancing one's career.

- Adapting to Changes: Flexibility and adaptability are crucial as the field of forensic psychology evolves. Professionals must be prepared to embrace new opportunities, overcome challenges, and maintain a healthy work-life balance.

Chapter 11 emphasizes the importance of a well-planned approach to building a career in forensic psychology. By understanding the educational and training requirements, obtaining necessary certifications, exploring various career opportunities, and engaging in thoughtful career planning, aspiring forensic psychologists can set themselves on a path to success. The chapter also highlights the dynamic nature of the field, encouraging professionals to stay adaptable, pursue lifelong learning, and remain committed to their personal and professional growth. Through careful planning and dedication, forensic psychologists can make meaningful contributions to the justice system and positively impact the lives of those they serve.

Chapter 12: Case Studies and Real-World Applications

Chapter 12 of *HowExpert Guide to Forensic Psychology* takes a practical approach by examining real-world applications of forensic psychology through detailed case studies, lessons from successful interventions, and the exploration of best practices. This chapter provides readers with the opportunity to apply theoretical knowledge to real-life scenarios, enhancing their understanding of how forensic psychology operates within the justice system.

12.1 Analyzing High-Profile Criminal Cases

High-profile criminal cases offer a unique opportunity to explore the application of forensic psychology in real-world scenarios. These cases often involve complex psychological evaluations, ethical dilemmas, and significant legal outcomes that can influence public perception and legal practices. This section delves into several notable cases, providing a detailed analysis of the forensic psychology techniques used, the challenges faced, and the impact on the field.

1. Case Selection Criteria

A. Complexity and Influence

- Legal and Psychological Complexity: The selected cases are chosen for their complexity, both legally and psychologically. These cases often involve multiple psychological assessments, conflicting expert testimonies, and intricate legal arguments that require a deep understanding of forensic psychology.

- Impact on Forensic Psychology: Each case has had a significant impact on the field, either by setting legal precedents, influencing public policy, or advancing the understanding of psychological concepts within the legal system.

B. Public and Media Attention

- Media Coverage: High-profile cases often attract extensive media coverage, which can shape public opinion and influence the judicial process. The role of forensic psychologists in these cases is critical, as their assessments and testimony are scrutinized by both the legal community and the public.

- Ethical Implications: The media attention surrounding these cases also raises ethical considerations, such as the psychologist's responsibility to maintain confidentiality, avoid bias, and present their findings objectively despite public pressure.

2. Detailed Case Analysis

A. Psychological Assessment and Techniques

- Assessment Tools: In each case, forensic psychologists utilized various psychological assessment tools to evaluate the mental state, personality traits, and cognitive abilities of the defendants. Common tools include the Minnesota Multiphasic Personality Inventory (MMPI-2), the Hare Psychopathy Checklist, and the Wechsler Adult Intelligence Scale (WAIS).

  - Example: In the case of [specific case], the forensic psychologist used the MMPI-2 to assess the defendant's personality structure and potential mental disorders, which played a crucial role in the defense strategy.

- Diagnostic Challenges: The psychologists faced challenges in diagnosing mental health conditions, particularly when defendants exhibited symptoms that could be attributed to multiple disorders or when malingering was suspected. The accuracy of these assessments was critical in determining legal outcomes such as competency to stand trial and criminal responsibility.

B. Legal Outcomes and Testimony

- Expert Testimony: Forensic psychologists often provided expert testimony in court, explaining their findings and how these findings related to the defendant's mental state during the crime. This testimony was used to support or challenge claims of insanity, diminished capacity, or competency to stand trial.

- Example: In [specific case], the psychologist's testimony regarding the defendant's lack of criminal responsibility due to a severe mental disorder was pivotal in the jury's decision to deliver a verdict of Not Guilty by Reason of Insanity (NGRI).

- Influence on Verdicts: The psychologists' assessments and testimonies significantly influenced the verdicts in these cases, often determining whether defendants were found guilty, received lesser sentences, or were referred to mental health facilities instead of prison.

C. Ethical Dilemmas and Considerations

- Dual Roles and Conflicts of Interest: In high-profile cases, forensic psychologists may face ethical dilemmas related to their dual roles as evaluators and expert witnesses. Balancing objectivity with the expectations of the legal teams that hire them can be challenging, particularly in cases with intense public and media scrutiny.

  - Example: In [specific case], the psychologist had to navigate the ethical challenge of maintaining impartiality while being under pressure from the defense team to provide a favorable evaluation.

- Confidentiality and Public Disclosure: Protecting the confidentiality of psychological assessments is particularly challenging in high-profile cases, where information leaks can occur, and media outlets may sensationalize details. Forensic psychologists must adhere to ethical guidelines while managing the potential impact of public disclosure on the legal process.

3. Broader Impact on the Field

A. Setting Legal Precedents

- Influence on Future Cases: The outcomes of these high-profile cases often set legal precedents that influence future cases, particularly in areas such as the admissibility of psychological evidence, the standards for insanity defenses, and the evaluation of competency.

- Example: The ruling in [specific case] established new criteria for evaluating competency to stand trial, which has since been referenced in subsequent cases across multiple jurisdictions.

- Policy Changes: In some cases, the findings and recommendations of forensic psychologists have led to changes in public policy, such as reforms in how the legal system handles defendants with mental health issues or the implementation of new protocols for psychological assessments in criminal cases.

B. Advancement of Forensic Psychology

- Contributions to Research and Practice: Analyzing high-profile cases contributes to the advancement of forensic psychology by highlighting the effectiveness of various assessment tools, identifying areas where further research is needed, and refining best practices for psychological evaluations in legal contexts.

 - Example: The analysis of [specific case] led to new research on the psychological impact of prolonged isolation on defendants and the development of guidelines for assessing the mental health of individuals in solitary confinement.

- Public Perception and Education: High-profile cases also play a role in shaping public perception of forensic psychology. These cases educate the public about the complexities of mental health in the legal system and the critical role that forensic psychologists play in ensuring justice is served.

By examining these high-profile criminal cases, forensic psychologists can gain valuable insights into the practical application of their skills, the challenges they may face in high-stakes legal environments, and the broader impact of their work on the legal system and society. These cases serve as powerful examples of how forensic psychology can influence legal outcomes, shape public policy, and contribute to the ongoing development of the field.

12.2 Lessons from Successful Interventions

Successful interventions in forensic psychology provide valuable insights into effective strategies for rehabilitation, risk management, and therapeutic support within the legal and correctional systems. By examining these interventions, forensic psychologists can learn from the approaches that have yielded positive outcomes, understand the factors that contributed to their success, and apply these lessons to future cases.

1. Intervention Strategies

A. Rehabilitation Programs in Correctional Facilities

- Cognitive Behavioral Therapy (CBT): CBT has been widely used in correctional settings to address cognitive distortions and maladaptive behaviors in offenders. This approach helps individuals develop healthier thinking patterns and coping strategies, reducing the likelihood of reoffending.

  - Example: In [specific correctional program], CBT was implemented to help inmates recognize and change harmful thought patterns that contributed to criminal behavior. The program reported significant reductions in recidivism rates among participants.

- Anger Management and Emotional Regulation: Programs focused on anger management and emotional regulation have proven effective in helping offenders control impulsive behaviors and reactions to stressors. These interventions often include techniques such as mindfulness, relaxation exercises, and conflict resolution skills.

  - Example: [Specific program] utilized anger management workshops that combined group therapy with individual counseling, leading to a measurable decrease in violent incidents within the facility.

B. Therapeutic Support for Trauma Survivors

- Trauma-Informed Care: Trauma-informed care is an approach that recognizes the pervasive impact of trauma on individuals' lives and integrates this understanding into all aspects of service delivery. It emphasizes safety, trustworthiness, and empowerment for trauma survivors.

- Example: A trauma-informed program in [specific setting] provided specialized therapy for victims of domestic violence, focusing on rebuilding trust, enhancing resilience, and fostering recovery. The program's success was reflected in the participants' improved mental health and reduced PTSD symptoms.

- Support Groups and Peer Counseling: Support groups and peer counseling have been effective in helping trauma survivors share their experiences, gain support from others who have gone through similar situations, and develop coping strategies.

- Example: In [specific program], a peer-led support group for sexual assault survivors provided a safe space for participants to process their trauma and work towards healing. The program reported high levels of participant satisfaction and positive mental health outcomes.

C. Risk Assessment and Management

- Structured Professional Judgment (SPJ): SPJ combines actuarial data with clinical judgment to assess an individual's risk of future offending. This approach is particularly useful in cases where the risk factors are complex or dynamic.

- Example: In [specific jurisdiction], SPJ was used to assess the risk of violent reoffending among parolees. The intervention involved regular assessments, targeted interventions based on risk level, and close monitoring. This approach led to a significant decrease in violent reoffenses among the population.

- Early Intervention Programs: Early intervention programs target at-risk individuals, often juveniles, before they engage in serious criminal behavior. These programs focus on addressing the underlying issues that contribute to delinquency, such as substance abuse, family dysfunction, or academic problems.

- Example: The [specific early intervention program] targeted youth with behavioral issues and provided comprehensive services, including family therapy, academic support, and substance abuse treatment. The program achieved notable success in reducing juvenile delinquency rates in the community.

2. Outcome Evaluation

A. Measuring Success

- Quantitative Metrics: Success in forensic interventions is often measured using quantitative metrics such as recidivism rates, psychological assessments, and behavioral improvements. These metrics provide objective data that can be used to evaluate the effectiveness of an intervention.

  - Example: The effectiveness of a substance abuse treatment program in a correctional facility was evaluated by tracking relapse rates and re-incarceration rates among participants. The program showed a significant reduction in both metrics compared to a control group.

- Qualitative Feedback: In addition to quantitative data, qualitative feedback from participants, staff, and stakeholders provides valuable insights into the perceived effectiveness of an intervention. This feedback can highlight areas of success as well as areas needing improvement.

  - Example: A qualitative evaluation of a restorative justice program included interviews with offenders, victims, and facilitators. Participants reported high levels of satisfaction with the process, particularly in terms of the emotional healing and sense of closure it provided.

B. Long-Term Impact

- Sustained Behavioral Change: One of the key indicators of a successful intervention is whether it leads to sustained behavioral change over time. This is particularly important in correctional settings, where the goal is often to reduce reoffending and promote reintegration into society.

  - Example: A long-term study of a vocational training program in a prison setting found that participants were significantly more likely to secure employment and less likely to reoffend after release, demonstrating the program's lasting impact.

- Influence on Policy and Practice: Successful interventions can also have a broader impact by influencing policy changes or serving as models for other programs. When an intervention demonstrates clear benefits, it can lead to the adoption of similar approaches in other settings.

- Example: The success of a mental health court in [specific location] led to the expansion of mental health courts across the state, with similar programs being implemented to address the needs of individuals with mental health issues in the criminal justice system.

3. Replication and Adaptation

A. Adapting Strategies to New Contexts

- Tailoring Interventions: While successful interventions provide valuable models, they must often be adapted to fit different contexts, populations, or legal frameworks. This involves considering cultural, demographic, and systemic differences that may affect the implementation and outcomes of the intervention.

  - Example: A restorative justice program originally designed for adult offenders was adapted for use with juvenile offenders in a different region. The program was modified to include age-appropriate activities and involved families more directly in the process, resulting in positive outcomes.

- Overcoming Barriers: Adapting successful interventions can also involve overcoming barriers such as resource limitations, resistance from stakeholders, or logistical challenges. These obstacles must be carefully navigated to ensure that the adapted intervention remains effective.

  - Example: When implementing a cognitive-behavioral therapy program in a rural correctional facility, the program faced challenges related to staffing shortages and limited access to training. By securing funding for remote training and utilizing telehealth services, the program was successfully adapted and delivered.

B. Scaling Up Successful Programs

- Expansion and Scaling: Once an intervention has been proven successful in a pilot or limited setting, there may be opportunities to scale it up to reach a larger population. This requires careful planning to maintain the quality and effectiveness of the intervention as it expands.

- Example: A community-based reentry program that showed success in reducing recidivism among a small group of former inmates was expanded to serve a broader population across multiple counties. The expansion included additional staff training and the development of partnerships with local employers to support job placement.

- Ensuring Fidelity: When scaling up, it is essential to maintain the fidelity of the intervention, ensuring that the core components that contributed to its success are preserved. This may involve developing standardized training materials, conducting regular evaluations, and providing ongoing support to staff.

- Example: The scaling up of a trauma-informed care program in correctional facilities included the creation of a detailed implementation guide and regular fidelity checks to ensure that the program's principles were consistently applied across different locations.

By examining the lessons learned from successful interventions in forensic psychology, professionals can gain valuable insights into the factors that contribute to positive outcomes. These lessons can inform the development of new interventions, guide the adaptation of existing programs to different contexts, and support the scaling up of effective approaches to reach a broader population. Ultimately, these interventions help to improve the lives of individuals within the justice system and contribute to a more just and effective legal process.

12.3 Best Practices in Forensic Psychology

Best practices in forensic psychology are essential for ensuring that assessments, interventions, and ethical standards are consistently applied in a manner that upholds the integrity of the field and contributes to fair and just legal outcomes. This section explores the core components of best practices, how they are applied across various settings, and the challenges associated with maintaining these standards.

1. Defining Best Practices

A. Evidence-Based Practice

- Foundation in Research: Best practices in forensic psychology are grounded in evidence-based approaches that have been rigorously tested and validated through research. This ensures that the methods used are reliable, effective, and applicable to diverse forensic contexts.

  - Example: The use of actuarial risk assessment tools in predicting recidivism is an evidence-based practice that has been supported by extensive research. These tools provide a structured approach to evaluating the likelihood of reoffending, contributing to more accurate and consistent decision-making in legal settings.

- Continuous Evaluation: To maintain best practices, forensic psychologists must engage in continuous evaluation of their methods, incorporating the latest research findings and adapting to new developments in the field. This commitment to ongoing learning helps ensure that practices remain relevant and effective.

  - Example: Forensic psychologists regularly update their knowledge of new assessment tools, therapeutic techniques, and legal precedents by attending conferences, participating in workshops, and reviewing current literature.

B. Core Components of Best Practices

- Comprehensive Assessments: Conducting thorough and unbiased assessments is a fundamental best practice in forensic psychology. This involves using a combination of standardized tools, clinical interviews, and collateral information to develop a complete understanding of the individual being assessed.

  - Example: A comprehensive forensic assessment for a competency evaluation might include psychological testing, interviews with the defendant, and a review of legal and medical records to provide a well-rounded picture of the individual's mental state.

- Ethical Standards: Adhering to strict ethical standards is crucial in maintaining best practices. Forensic psychologists must navigate complex ethical dilemmas, such as issues of confidentiality, dual relationships, and informed consent, with a strong commitment to professional integrity.

- Example: Ensuring that clients fully understand the limits of confidentiality in a forensic evaluation is an ethical requirement that helps protect the client's rights while maintaining the psychologist's professional responsibilities.

- Effective Communication: Clear and accurate communication of findings is another key component of best practices. This includes writing detailed reports, providing testimony that is understandable to non-experts, and engaging in collaborative discussions with legal professionals.

- Example: Forensic psychologists must present their findings in court in a manner that is both scientifically sound and accessible to judges, juries, and attorneys, ensuring that their testimony contributes meaningfully to the legal process.

2. Application Across Settings

A. Clinical Practice in Forensic Settings

- Standardized Protocols: In clinical practice, best practices involve using standardized protocols for conducting assessments and delivering interventions. This ensures that all individuals receive the same level of care and that the results are reliable and comparable across cases.

- Example: A forensic psychologist conducting a risk assessment for a parole hearing would follow a standardized protocol that includes the use of validated assessment tools, interviews, and a review of the individual's criminal history.

- Trauma-Informed Approaches: Incorporating trauma-informed approaches into clinical practice is increasingly recognized as a best practice in forensic psychology. This involves recognizing the impact of trauma on behavior and ensuring that the treatment environment is safe, supportive, and empowering.

- Example: In correctional facilities, trauma-informed care might include training staff to recognize signs of trauma in inmates and adapting therapeutic approaches to be sensitive to the needs of trauma survivors.

B. Research and Academic Settings

- Rigorous Methodology: Best practices in forensic research require the use of rigorous methodologies, including well-designed studies, appropriate sampling methods, and the use of reliable and valid measurement tools. This ensures that the research findings are robust and contribute meaningfully to the field.

  - Example: A study examining the effects of solitary confinement on mental health would be designed with a control group, longitudinal data collection, and the use of validated psychological assessments to ensure the accuracy and reliability of the findings.

- Ethical Research Conduct: Ethical considerations are paramount in forensic research, particularly when working with vulnerable populations. Researchers must obtain informed consent, protect participant confidentiality, and minimize potential harm to participants.

  - Example: When conducting research in a correctional setting, researchers must ensure that inmates understand their rights as participants, that participation is voluntary, and that their decision to participate or not will not affect their legal status or treatment.

C. Policy Development and Advocacy

- Evidence-Informed Policy: Forensic psychologists contribute to policy development by advocating for evidence-informed policies that reflect current research and best practices. This can involve working with lawmakers, contributing to policy discussions, and providing expert testimony on the psychological aspects of legal issues.

  - Example: Forensic psychologists might advocate for policies that limit the use of solitary confinement, based on research showing its detrimental effects on mental health, or support the development of diversion programs for individuals with mental health issues.

- Interdisciplinary Collaboration: Effective policy development often requires collaboration between forensic psychologists, legal professionals, social workers, and other stakeholders. By working together, these professionals can develop comprehensive policies that address the complex needs of individuals within the legal system.

- Example: Developing a mental health court program might involve collaboration between forensic psychologists, judges, attorneys, and mental health providers to create a system that diverts individuals with mental health issues from traditional criminal proceedings to treatment-focused alternatives.

3. Challenges and Considerations

A. Barriers to Implementation

- Resource Limitations: One of the main challenges in implementing best practices is the availability of resources, including funding, staffing, and access to training. These limitations can make it difficult to consistently apply best practices across all cases and settings.

  - Example: In underfunded correctional facilities, implementing trauma-informed care might be challenging due to a lack of trained staff and resources for therapeutic interventions. Forensic psychologists must find creative solutions, such as training existing staff or seeking external funding, to overcome these barriers.

- Resistance to Change: Another challenge is resistance to change, both within organizations and from individual practitioners. Implementing new practices often requires a cultural shift, which can be difficult to achieve, particularly in established systems like the criminal justice system.

  - Example: Introducing evidence-based risk assessment tools in a parole board setting might face resistance from decision-makers who are accustomed to relying on their own judgment. Forensic psychologists may need to provide education and demonstrate the effectiveness of these tools to gain acceptance.

B. Continuous Improvement

- Ongoing Evaluation: Best practices are not static; they require ongoing evaluation and adaptation to ensure they remain relevant and effective. This involves regularly reviewing practices, seeking feedback from clients and stakeholders, and staying informed about new research and developments in the field.

- Example: A forensic psychologist might regularly review their assessment protocols to incorporate new research findings, update their training based on emerging best practices, and seek peer feedback to refine their approach.

- Adapting to New Challenges: The field of forensic psychology is continually evolving, with new challenges emerging as legal standards change, new psychological disorders are recognized, and societal attitudes shift. Best practices must be flexible enough to adapt to these changes while maintaining their core principles.

- Example: As digital evidence becomes more prevalent in legal cases, forensic psychologists may need to develop new best practices for assessing the psychological impact of cybercrime, adapting existing assessment tools to address the unique challenges posed by digital environments.

By adhering to best practices in forensic psychology, professionals can ensure that their work is of the highest quality, ethically sound, and effective in achieving positive legal and psychological outcomes. Whether working in clinical practice, research, or policy development, forensic psychologists play a critical role in upholding the standards of the field and contributing to a fair and just legal system. Continuous evaluation, adaptation, and commitment to ethical principles are essential for maintaining these standards and advancing the practice of forensic psychology.

12.4 Reflection Questions

Reflection questions are a powerful tool for deepening understanding, encouraging critical thinking, and fostering personal and professional growth. In the context of forensic psychology, these questions help practitioners, students, and researchers to reflect on their experiences, evaluate their practices, and consider how they can improve their work within the field. This section provides a series of reflection questions designed to provoke thoughtful consideration of the topics covered in this chapter and to support ongoing development in forensic psychology.

1. Analyzing High-Profile Criminal Cases

A. What are the key psychological factors that contributed to the outcomes in the high-profile cases you studied? How did the forensic psychologists involved influence these outcomes?

- Consider the role of psychological assessments, expert testimony, and ethical decision-making in shaping the legal conclusions of these cases.

B. How did media coverage of these cases impact the legal process and the work of forensic psychologists?

- Reflect on the challenges of maintaining objectivity and ethical standards in cases that receive intense public and media scrutiny.

C. What lessons can be learned from the ethical dilemmas faced by forensic psychologists in these high-profile cases? How would you handle similar situations?

- Think about how you would navigate dual roles, confidentiality issues, and potential conflicts of interest in high-stakes legal environments.

2. Lessons from Successful Interventions

A. Which intervention strategies discussed in this chapter do you find most compelling, and why? How could these strategies be applied to the populations you work with or plan to work with?

- Reflect on the specific elements of successful interventions, such as cognitive-behavioral therapy, trauma-informed care, or early intervention programs, and how they might be adapted to different settings.

B. What challenges might arise when adapting a successful intervention to a new context, and how could these challenges be addressed?

- Consider factors such as resource limitations, cultural differences, and resistance to change, and how you would overcome these barriers to implement effective interventions.

C. How do you measure the success of an intervention? What metrics or feedback mechanisms would you use to evaluate the long-term impact of your work?

- Think about both quantitative and qualitative measures of success, including recidivism rates, participant feedback, and long-term behavioral changes.

3. Best Practices in Forensic Psychology

A. What does it mean to practice forensic psychology according to best practices? How do you ensure that your work meets these standards?

- Reflect on the importance of evidence-based practice, ethical conduct, and effective communication in your role as a forensic psychologist.

B. What are the main challenges you anticipate in implementing best practices in your professional work? How can you prepare to address these challenges?

- Consider the specific barriers you might face, such as limited resources, organizational resistance, or the need for continuous learning, and how you would overcome them.

C. How can interdisciplinary collaboration enhance the implementation of best practices in forensic psychology?

- Reflect on the benefits of working with legal professionals, social workers, and other stakeholders to develop and maintain best practices in your work.

4. Personal and Professional Growth

A. What areas of forensic psychology do you feel most confident in, and where do you see the need for further development?

- Reflect on your strengths and areas for growth, and consider how you can build on your existing skills while seeking opportunities for further education and training.

B. How has studying high-profile cases, successful interventions, and best practices influenced your understanding of your role as a forensic psychologist?

- Consider how your perspective on forensic psychology has evolved and how this knowledge will influence your future work.

C. What steps will you take to ensure that you stay current with developments in forensic psychology and continue to practice at the highest standard?

- Reflect on your commitment to lifelong learning, professional development, and the continuous improvement of your skills and knowledge in the field.

These reflection questions are designed to help you critically engage with the material covered in this chapter, deepen your understanding of forensic psychology, and identify areas for personal and professional growth. By regularly reflecting on your experiences and practices, you can ensure that you continue to develop as a competent, ethical, and effective forensic psychologist, contributing to the advancement of the field and the pursuit of justice.

12.5 Practical Exercise: Applying Lessons to Case Studies

The practical application of theoretical knowledge is essential for mastering the complexities of forensic psychology. This exercise is designed to help you apply the lessons learned from previous sections, particularly those related to high-profile criminal cases, successful interventions, and best practices, to new case studies. By engaging in this exercise, you will develop critical thinking skills, refine your assessment techniques, and enhance your ability to address real-world challenges in forensic psychology.

1. Case Study Analysis

A. Selecting a Case Study

- Variety of Scenarios: Choose a case study that reflects the types of scenarios commonly encountered in forensic psychology. This could include cases involving criminal behavior, mental health assessments, risk evaluations, or legal competencies.

  - Example: You might select a case study involving a defendant with a history of trauma who is facing criminal charges, requiring both psychological assessment and consideration of mitigating factors.

B. Analyzing the Psychological Factors

- Comprehensive Assessment: Conduct a thorough analysis of the psychological factors at play in the case study. Consider the individual's mental health history, personality traits, cognitive abilities, and any relevant social or environmental influences.

- Example: In the case of a defendant with a history of substance abuse, you would analyze how their addiction has influenced their behavior and decision-making processes, and how this might affect their legal responsibility.

C. Ethical Considerations

- Identifying Ethical Dilemmas: Reflect on any ethical dilemmas that may arise during the assessment or intervention process. Consider how you would navigate issues such as confidentiality, informed consent, and potential conflicts of interest.

- Example: If the case study involves a dual relationship where the psychologist has previously treated the individual, you would need to consider how to maintain objectivity and avoid any conflicts of interest.

2. Developing an Action Plan

A. Designing an Intervention Strategy

- Tailored Interventions: Based on your analysis, develop a targeted intervention strategy that addresses the psychological needs identified in the case study. This might include therapeutic approaches, risk management plans, or recommendations for legal outcomes.

- Example: For a case involving a juvenile offender, you might design an intervention that includes cognitive-behavioral therapy, family counseling, and educational support to address both the psychological and social factors contributing to their behavior.

B. Implementing Best Practices

- Incorporating Evidence-Based Methods: Ensure that your intervention strategy incorporates best practices in forensic psychology, including the use of evidence-based assessment tools, adherence to ethical standards, and effective communication with legal professionals.

- Example: When conducting a risk assessment, you would use validated tools like the HCR-20 to evaluate the likelihood of future offending, and present your findings in a clear, accessible report for the court.

C. Preparing for Potential Challenges

- Anticipating Obstacles: Consider potential challenges or obstacles that may arise during the implementation of your intervention strategy. Develop contingency plans to address these challenges effectively.

- Example: If the case study involves a defendant who is resistant to treatment, you might plan for additional motivational interviewing sessions or explore alternative therapeutic approaches to engage the individual.

3. Collaborative Review and Feedback

A. Engaging in Peer Review

- Collaborative Discussion: If working in a group or classroom setting, share your case study analysis and action plan with peers. Engage in collaborative discussions to provide and receive feedback, considering alternative perspectives and approaches.

- Example: During peer review, you might receive feedback on the feasibility of your intervention strategy, prompting you to refine your approach or consider additional factors.

B. Incorporating Feedback

- Refining Your Plan: Use the feedback received from peers or instructors to refine your action plan. This iterative process helps ensure that your intervention is well-rounded, practical, and aligned with best practices.

- Example: After receiving feedback, you might adjust your intervention to include more community-based resources or modify your assessment approach to better address the client's cultural background.

C. Reflecting on the Learning Process

- Personal Reflection: Take time to reflect on what you have learned through this exercise. Consider how the process of analyzing the case study, developing an intervention, and receiving feedback has enhanced your understanding of forensic psychology.

  - Example: Reflect on how this exercise has improved your ability to apply theoretical knowledge to practical scenarios, and identify areas where you might need further study or experience.

This practical exercise provides an opportunity to apply the lessons learned in forensic psychology to real-world scenarios. By analyzing case studies, developing intervention strategies, and engaging in collaborative review, you will refine your skills and deepen your understanding of the complexities involved in forensic psychology. This hands-on approach prepares you to effectively address the challenges you will encounter in your professional practice, ensuring that your work is grounded in evidence-based methods, ethical standards, and a commitment to achieving just outcomes.

Chapter 12 Review: Case Studies and Real-World Applications

Chapter 12 of *HowExpert Guide to Forensic Psychology* offers a practical exploration of forensic psychology through the lens of real-world case studies, successful interventions, and the establishment of best practices. This chapter is designed to bridge the gap between theory and practice, providing readers with insights into how forensic psychology is applied in various legal and correctional settings.

12.1 Analyzing High-Profile Criminal Cases

- Psychological Assessments: This section highlights the role of psychological assessments in high-profile criminal cases, focusing on tools like the Minnesota

Multiphasic Personality Inventory (MMPI-2) and the Hare Psychopathy Checklist. These assessments provide critical insights into the mental state, personality traits, and cognitive abilities of defendants, influencing legal outcomes such as competency determinations and insanity defenses.

- Legal and Ethical Challenges: The analysis of high-profile cases also delves into the ethical dilemmas faced by forensic psychologists, including issues of confidentiality, media influence, and maintaining objectivity under public scrutiny. The section emphasizes the importance of adhering to ethical standards while providing testimony that withstands legal challenges.

- Impact on Legal Precedents: The outcomes of these cases often set legal precedents that shape future practices in forensic psychology. The section discusses how these cases contribute to the development of the field and influence the way psychological evidence is presented and evaluated in court.

12.2 Lessons from Successful Interventions

- Effective Intervention Strategies: This section explores various intervention strategies that have proven successful in forensic settings, such as Cognitive Behavioral Therapy (CBT) and trauma-informed care. These approaches are shown to reduce recidivism, improve mental health outcomes, and facilitate the rehabilitation of offenders.

- Outcome Evaluation: The success of these interventions is measured through both quantitative metrics, like recidivism rates, and qualitative feedback from participants. The section highlights the importance of long-term follow-up and continuous evaluation to ensure that interventions remain effective over time.

- Replication and Adaptation: The section also discusses how successful interventions can be adapted to different contexts and populations. It emphasizes the need for flexibility and creativity in overcoming barriers such as resource limitations and resistance to change, ensuring that best practices can be implemented across diverse settings.

12.3 Best Practices in Forensic Psychology

- Evidence-Based Approaches: Best practices in forensic psychology are grounded in evidence-based methods that have been rigorously tested and validated. This section underscores the importance of using standardized protocols, maintaining ethical standards, and engaging in continuous professional development to ensure the highest quality of practice.

- Application Across Settings: The section explores how best practices are applied in various forensic settings, from clinical practice to research and policy development. It highlights the role of interdisciplinary collaboration in maintaining these standards and the challenges associated with implementing best practices in resource-limited environments.

- Continuous Improvement: Best practices are not static; they require ongoing evaluation and adaptation to stay relevant. This section discusses the importance of staying informed about new research, seeking peer feedback, and being open to change to maintain excellence in forensic psychology.

12.4 Reflection Questions

- Critical Thinking: Reflection questions in this section encourage readers to critically analyze the case studies and interventions discussed in the chapter. These questions prompt consideration of the psychological factors, ethical dilemmas, and legal implications involved in each case.

- Personal Reflection: Readers are also encouraged to reflect on their own strengths, areas for growth, and career aspirations in forensic psychology. This self-assessment is aimed at helping readers identify opportunities for further development and aligning their professional goals with the lessons learned in the chapter.

12.5 Practical Exercise: Applying Lessons to Case Studies

- Case Study Analysis: The practical exercise involves analyzing a new case study using the concepts and strategies discussed in the chapter. Readers are tasked with developing an intervention strategy that addresses the psychological needs of the case, while also considering ethical challenges and best practices.

- Collaborative Review: The exercise encourages collaborative discussions with peers, allowing readers to refine their action plans and consider alternative perspectives. This process helps reinforce the application of theoretical knowledge to real-world scenarios and prepares readers for the challenges they will face in professional practice.

- Reflective Practice: The section concludes with an emphasis on reflective practice, encouraging readers to continuously assess their work, seek feedback, and stay committed to ongoing learning and improvement in forensic psychology.

Chapter 12 emphasizes the practical application of forensic psychology through detailed case studies, successful interventions, and the establishment of best practices. By analyzing real-world scenarios, reflecting on ethical and professional challenges, and engaging in hands-on exercises, readers gain a deeper understanding of how forensic psychology operates within the legal system. This chapter equips readers with the skills and knowledge needed to apply forensic psychology principles effectively, ensuring that their work contributes to fair and just legal outcomes.

Chapter 13: Conclusion

Chapter 13 brings *HowExpert Guide to Forensic Psychology* to a thoughtful close, offering a comprehensive summary of the key concepts and lessons explored throughout the book. This chapter reflects on the essential insights gained, discusses the future trajectory of forensic psychology, and encourages personal reflection on the knowledge acquired. It also provides a self-assessment quiz to help consolidate learning and identify areas for further growth. This concluding chapter aims to reinforce the reader's understanding of forensic psychology and inspire ongoing development in this dynamic field.

13.1 Summary of Key Takeaways

As we conclude *HowExpert Guide to Forensic Psychology*, it's crucial to take a deep dive into the core insights and lessons that have been woven throughout the book. These takeaways not only encapsulate the foundational knowledge and skills that forensic psychologists need but also emphasize the intricacies of applying psychological principles within the complex framework of the legal system.

1. The Foundation of Forensic Psychology

A. Historical and Theoretical Foundations

- Historical Evolution: The journey through the history of forensic psychology revealed how the field has evolved from its early intersections with law and psychiatry into a distinct discipline that plays a critical role in modern legal systems. This historical perspective is essential for understanding the current practices and future directions of the field.

- Theoretical Underpinnings: The exploration of key psychological theories—ranging from biological and psychological explanations of criminal behavior to sociological perspectives—provided a comprehensive framework for understanding the multifaceted nature of criminality. These theories form the backbone of forensic psychology, guiding practitioners in their assessments, interventions, and contributions to legal processes.

B. Integration with Legal Processes

- Role in the Justice System: Forensic psychology's integration into the legal system is multifaceted, involving everything from criminal profiling and risk assessments to competency evaluations and expert testimony. The book highlighted the critical ways in which forensic psychologists contribute to legal outcomes, emphasizing their role as both scientists and practitioners who bridge the gap between psychology and law.

- Impact on Legal Decisions: Through detailed case studies and real-world examples, the book demonstrated how forensic psychologists influence legal decisions at various stages of the judicial process. Whether assessing a defendant's mental state or providing insights into the psychological dynamics of a case, forensic psychologists have a profound impact on the administration of justice.

2. Ethical Considerations in Forensic Psychology

A. Navigating Complex Ethical Dilemmas

- Confidentiality and Objectivity: One of the most challenging aspects of forensic psychology is navigating ethical dilemmas, particularly those related to confidentiality and objectivity. The book emphasized the importance of maintaining ethical integrity while managing the dual roles that forensic psychologists often find themselves in—such as being both a therapist and an expert witness.

- Balancing Dual Relationships: The discussions on dual relationships were particularly critical, as they highlighted the potential conflicts that can arise when forensic psychologists are involved in multiple roles with the same client or case. Understanding these dynamics is essential for preventing ethical breaches and ensuring that the psychologist's contributions are fair and unbiased.

B. Ethical Standards and Best Practices

- Adherence to Ethical Guidelines: The book underscored the necessity of adhering to established ethical guidelines, such as those set forth by the American Psychological Association (APA). These guidelines provide a framework for making ethical decisions in complex situations, ensuring that the work of forensic psychologists remains within the bounds of professional conduct.

- Continuous Ethical Training: The need for continuous ethical training and education was also emphasized. As the field evolves, so do the ethical challenges that forensic psychologists face. Ongoing education and reflection are necessary to stay current with ethical standards and to adapt to new situations that may arise in practice.

3. Practical Applications and Real-World Impact

A. Case Studies and Applied Practice

- Real-World Case Studies: The inclusion of real-world case studies throughout the book served to ground theoretical knowledge in practical application. These case studies illustrated the complexities of forensic psychological assessments and interventions, providing readers with a clear understanding of how theory translates into practice.

- Impact on Individuals and Communities: The analysis of how forensic psychological practices affect individuals—whether they are defendants, victims, or members of the community—was a critical aspect of the book. These discussions highlighted the broader social implications of forensic psychology, emphasizing the responsibility of psychologists to contribute to fair and just legal processes.

B. Interventions and Outcomes

- Successful Interventions: The book detailed various intervention strategies that have been successful in forensic settings, such as cognitive-behavioral therapy (CBT) for offenders and trauma-informed care for victims. These examples demonstrated the importance of using evidence-based practices to achieve positive outcomes in legal and correctional settings.

- Evaluation of Outcomes: Measuring the success of these interventions was another key takeaway. The book emphasized the need for forensic psychologists to be diligent in evaluating the outcomes of their interventions, using both qualitative and quantitative data to assess effectiveness and make necessary adjustments.

4. Building a Career in Forensic Psychology

A. Educational Pathways and Professional Development

- Comprehensive Education: The book provided a roadmap for aspiring forensic psychologists, outlining the necessary educational pathways—from undergraduate studies to doctoral training. This structured approach ensures that individuals entering the field are well-prepared to meet the demands of forensic practice.

- Certification and Specialization: The importance of certification, licensure, and specialization was also discussed, with an emphasis on how these credentials enhance credibility and open up opportunities for career advancement. Specialized training in areas such as forensic neuropsychology or criminal profiling can position psychologists as experts in niche areas of the field.

B. Continuous Learning and Adaptation

- Lifelong Learning: A recurring theme was the importance of lifelong learning and professional development. Forensic psychology is a dynamic field that constantly evolves in response to new research, legal precedents, and societal changes. Staying current with these developments is essential for maintaining professional competence and delivering the highest quality of service.

- Adapting to Emerging Trends: The ability to adapt to emerging trends—such as the integration of technology in assessments or the increasing emphasis on trauma-informed practices—was highlighted as a critical skill for forensic psychologists. Embracing these changes ensures that practitioners remain relevant and effective in a rapidly changing field.

By revisiting these key takeaways, readers are reminded of the depth and breadth of forensic psychology as a discipline. The insights gained from this book are not just theoretical but are intended to be applied in real-world contexts, guiding forensic psychologists in their daily practice and contributing to the advancement of justice. As the field continues to evolve, these foundational principles will remain critical to the ongoing development and success of forensic psychology.

13.2 The Future of Forensic Psychology

As we look ahead to the future of forensic psychology, it's essential to consider how the field will evolve in response to emerging challenges, technological advancements, and shifting societal dynamics. The future of forensic psychology is not just about continuing established practices but about innovating and adapting to ensure that the discipline remains relevant and effective in an ever-changing world.

1. Technological Advancements and Their Impact

A. The Role of Artificial Intelligence and Machine Learning

- AI in Criminal Profiling: The integration of artificial intelligence (AI) and machine learning into forensic psychology promises to revolutionize the way criminal behavior is analyzed and predicted. AI tools can process vast amounts of data to identify patterns and correlations that may not be immediately apparent to human analysts. This technology could lead to more accurate criminal profiles and improve the effectiveness of law enforcement strategies.

- Virtual Reality in Psychological Assessments: Virtual reality (VR) technology is another frontier that could transform forensic psychological assessments. VR can create immersive environments that simulate real-world scenarios, allowing psychologists to observe behavior and responses in a controlled yet dynamic setting. This innovation has the potential to enhance the accuracy and depth of psychological evaluations, particularly in high-stakes legal contexts.

B. Digital Forensics and Cyberpsychology

- Rise of Digital Evidence: As digital technology becomes more pervasive, forensic psychologists will increasingly need to engage with digital forensics. This includes understanding the psychological implications of online behavior, cybercrimes, and the use of digital evidence in legal cases. The ability to analyze digital interactions and their psychological impacts will be crucial as the boundaries between physical and digital environments continue to blur.

- Cyberpsychology and Virtual Offenses: The emergence of cyberpsychology—a field that explores the psychological aspects of digital interactions—will play a significant role in the future of forensic psychology. As crimes increasingly occur in virtual spaces, forensic psychologists will need to develop new frameworks for understanding and addressing behaviors such as cyberbullying, online fraud, and digital harassment.

2. Evolving Legal and Ethical Considerations

A. Ethical Challenges in a Digital World

- Confidentiality in the Age of Data Breaches: The increasing digitization of psychological records and legal documents raises new ethical concerns, particularly regarding confidentiality and data security. Forensic psychologists will need to navigate the complexities of protecting sensitive information in an era where data breaches are common. Developing robust cybersecurity measures and ethical guidelines will be essential to maintaining trust and integrity in the profession.

- Bias in AI and Algorithmic Decision-Making: As AI becomes more integrated into forensic psychology, concerns about bias in algorithmic decision-making will come to the forefront. Forensic psychologists must ensure that these tools are used ethically, avoiding the perpetuation of biases related to race, gender, or socioeconomic status. This will require ongoing evaluation and refinement of AI systems to ensure fairness and accuracy in their applications.

B. Legal Reforms and Forensic Psychology

- Impact of Legal Precedents on Practice: Future legal reforms and court rulings will continue to shape the practice of forensic psychology. Forensic psychologists must stay informed about changes in laws and legal precedents that affect their work, particularly in areas such as competency evaluations, the insanity defense, and the admissibility of psychological evidence. Being proactive in understanding these changes will ensure that forensic psychologists remain effective and compliant with the law.

- Globalization and International Standards: As forensic psychology becomes more globalized, there will be a need for international standards and practices. Forensic psychologists will need to collaborate across borders, sharing knowledge and developing universal guidelines that can be applied in diverse legal contexts. This globalization will also necessitate an understanding of cultural differences and their impact on psychological assessments and legal outcomes.

3. Emerging Trends and Innovations

A. Trauma-Informed Practices and Victim Support

- Advances in Trauma-Informed Care: The growing recognition of the long-term psychological impacts of trauma will drive the development of more advanced trauma-informed practices in forensic psychology. This approach emphasizes understanding, recognizing, and responding to the effects of trauma, particularly in legal settings. Forensic psychologists will need to integrate these practices into their work with both victims and offenders, ensuring that trauma is appropriately addressed in all aspects of the legal process.

- Victim-Centered Approaches: There will be a continued shift towards victim-centered approaches in forensic psychology, focusing on the needs and rights of victims throughout the legal process. This trend will require forensic psychologists to develop new methods for assessing and supporting victims, particularly in cases involving severe trauma or long-term psychological harm.

B. Sustainability and Environmental Forensics

- Environmental Impact of Forensic Practices: As concerns about environmental sustainability grow, forensic psychologists will need to consider the environmental impact of their practices. This includes minimizing waste, reducing energy consumption, and adopting sustainable practices in forensic laboratories and offices. The field may also see the rise of environmental forensics, where psychologists play a role in addressing crimes related to environmental harm and advocating for policies that protect both human and environmental health.

- Psychological Impacts of Climate Change: The psychological impacts of climate change—such as eco-anxiety, trauma from natural disasters, and displacement—are emerging areas of concern that forensic psychologists will need to address. Developing expertise in these areas will be crucial as the global population faces increasing environmental challenges.

By exploring these potential developments, readers are encouraged to consider how the field of forensic psychology will continue to evolve and the opportunities that lie ahead. Embracing innovation, addressing emerging challenges, and maintaining ethical integrity will be key to the future success of forensic psychologists as they navigate the complexities of the legal and psychological landscapes.

13.3 Reflection on Learning and Personal Growth

As you reach the conclusion of *HowExpert Guide to Forensic Psychology*, it's important to take a moment to reflect on both the knowledge you've gained and the personal growth you've experienced throughout this journey. Forensic psychology is not just a field of study—it's a vocation that challenges you to think critically, act ethically, and engage deeply with complex human behaviors within the legal system.

1. Personal Insights and Self-Awareness

A. Deepening Understanding of Human Behavior

- Exploring the Criminal Mind: Throughout this book, you've delved into the intricacies of the criminal mind, gaining insights into the psychological disorders, environmental influences, and sociological factors that contribute to criminal behavior. This exploration not only broadens your understanding of others but also prompts you to reflect on your perceptions of morality, justice, and human nature.

- Self-Reflection on Bias and Judgment: The study of forensic psychology often reveals the biases and preconceived notions we hold about crime and criminality. Reflecting on these biases—whether they relate to race, gender, socioeconomic status, or mental health—allows you to grow both as a professional and as an individual. Recognizing and addressing these biases is crucial for developing a fair and ethical approach to forensic psychology.

B. Ethical Growth and Professional Integrity

- Navigating Ethical Dilemmas: Engaging with the ethical challenges presented in forensic psychology has likely enhanced your ability to navigate complex moral situations. This book has equipped you with the tools to make informed, ethical decisions, balancing the demands of the legal system with the principles of psychological care. Reflecting on how you've grown in your ability to handle these dilemmas is key to your ongoing development in the field.

- Commitment to Lifelong Learning: The dynamic nature of forensic psychology requires a commitment to continuous learning and ethical vigilance. As you reflect on your journey through this book, consider how you've embraced the need for ongoing education and how you plan to continue growing in knowledge and expertise as you move forward in your career.

2. Practical Skills and Application

A. Application of Theoretical Knowledge

- Bridging Theory and Practice: One of the most significant aspects of your learning journey has been the application of theoretical knowledge to real-world situations. Reflect on how you've integrated theories of criminal behavior, psychological assessment, and legal processes into practical strategies that can be used in forensic settings. This ability to bridge theory and practice is a critical skill that will serve you well as you advance in your career.

- Building Competence through Case Studies: The case studies presented in this book have offered you a glimpse into the practical challenges and complexities of forensic psychology. Reflect on how these case studies have enhanced your competence and confidence in dealing with similar scenarios in the future. Consider how you might apply the lessons learned to your own practice or studies.

B. Developing Professional Skills

- Mastering Assessment Techniques: The comprehensive coverage of psychological assessments and legal implications in this book has provided you with a solid foundation in the techniques and tools essential for forensic practice. Reflect on how your skills in conducting assessments, preparing reports, and presenting findings have improved, and how you can continue to refine these skills in your professional life.

- Enhancing Communication and Testimony Skills: Forensic psychology often requires clear and effective communication, especially in legal settings. Reflect on how you've grown in your ability to articulate complex psychological concepts to non-experts, whether through expert testimony or written reports. Developing these communication skills is vital for making a meaningful impact in the courtroom and beyond.

3. Personal Growth and Future Aspirations

A. Embracing Challenges and Overcoming Obstacles

- Resilience in the Face of Challenges: Forensic psychology is a demanding field that often involves dealing with difficult and emotionally charged situations. Reflect on how you've developed resilience and the ability to remain composed under pressure. Consider the personal challenges you've faced during this learning journey and how overcoming them has strengthened your resolve to succeed in this field.

- Growth through Reflection and Feedback: Personal growth often comes from reflecting on past experiences and learning from feedback. Consider how you've incorporated feedback—whether from peers, mentors, or self-assessments—into your professional development. Reflecting on these experiences can provide valuable insights into your strengths and areas for improvement.

B. Setting Future Goals

- Defining Your Career Path: As you look ahead, reflect on how this book has influenced your career aspirations in forensic psychology. Whether you're considering a specific specialization, further education, or a particular career path, take time to set clear, actionable goals that align with your interests and strengths. Defining these goals will help you navigate the next steps in your professional journey.

- Commitment to Personal and Professional Excellence: Finally, reflect on your commitment to personal and professional excellence. Forensic psychology is a field that requires dedication, empathy, and a passion for justice. Consider how you plan to embody these qualities in your future work, contributing positively to the field and making a meaningful impact on the lives of others.

By engaging in this reflection on learning and personal growth, you are not only solidifying the knowledge you've gained but also preparing yourself for the challenges and opportunities that lie ahead in the field of forensic psychology. This reflection serves as a reminder that the journey of learning and growth is ongoing, and that each step forward brings you closer to mastering the art and science of forensic psychology.

13.4 Comprehensive Self-Assessment Quiz

As you near the end of *HowExpert Guide to Forensic Psychology*, it's time to assess your understanding and application of the material covered. This comprehensive self-assessment quiz is designed to help you reflect on what you've learned, identify areas where you excel, and recognize opportunities for further study and improvement. Answer the questions thoughtfully and use them as a tool to gauge your readiness to apply forensic psychology concepts in real-world scenarios.

Section 1: Foundations of Forensic Psychology

1. Historical and Theoretical Foundations

A. What are the key historical milestones that have shaped the development of forensic psychology?

B. How do biological, psychological, and sociological theories of criminal behavior differ, and how can they be integrated to provide a comprehensive understanding of criminality?

2. Role of Forensic Psychologists in the Legal System

A. Describe the various roles that forensic psychologists play in the criminal justice system.

B. How does the work of a forensic psychologist impact legal outcomes, particularly in areas such as competency evaluations and expert testimony?

Section 2: The Criminal Mind and Psychological Assessments

3. Psychopathy and Sociopathy

A. What are the defining characteristics of psychopathy and sociopathy, and how do they influence criminal behavior?

B. Provide an example of how understanding these disorders can aid in criminal profiling and risk assessment.

4. Psychological Assessments in Legal Contexts

A. What are the different types of psychological assessments used in forensic psychology, and what are their purposes?

B. Describe a scenario where a risk assessment or competency evaluation would be crucial to a legal case.

Section 3: Juvenile and Developmental Forensic Psychology

5. Juvenile Delinquency

A. What factors contribute to juvenile delinquency, and how can developmental psychology be used to assess and rehabilitate young offenders?

B. Discuss a case study where a developmental assessment significantly influenced the outcome of a juvenile case.

6. Rehabilitation Approaches

A. What are some effective rehabilitation strategies for juvenile offenders, and how do they differ from those used with adult offenders?

B. How can forensic psychologists design and implement a rehabilitation program tailored to the needs of a juvenile offender?

Section 4: Victimology and Trauma Response

7. Impact of Crime on Victims

A. What psychological effects do crime victims commonly experience, and how can forensic psychologists support them through the legal process?

B. Provide an example of a victim support plan that addresses trauma and facilitates recovery.

8. Trauma-Informed Care

A. How does trauma-informed care differ from traditional psychological interventions, and why is it important in forensic settings?

B. Describe a case where trauma-informed care made a significant difference in the treatment and recovery of a victim.

Section 5: Ethical and Legal Considerations

9. Ethical Dilemmas in Forensic Psychology

A. What are some common ethical dilemmas that forensic psychologists face, and how should they navigate these challenges?

B. Discuss the importance of maintaining confidentiality and objectivity in forensic psychological practice.

10. Legal and Ethical Standards

A. How do legal precedents and ethical guidelines influence the practice of forensic psychology?

B. Provide an example of a legal case where ethical standards played a critical role in the outcome.

Section 6: Research and Future Trends

11. Emerging Trends in Forensic Psychology

A. What are some of the current trends in forensic psychology research, and how might they shape the future of the field?

B. How can forensic psychologists stay informed about and contribute to these emerging trends?

12. Technological Advancements

A. How might artificial intelligence and virtual reality technologies impact forensic psychological assessments and interventions in the future?

B. Discuss the ethical considerations that arise with the integration of new technologies into forensic psychology.

Section 7: Practical Application and Career Development

13. Case Study Analysis

A. Choose a case study from this book and summarize the key forensic psychological concepts applied.

B. Reflect on how you would approach a similar case in your practice or studies, considering the knowledge and skills you've acquired.

14. Career Planning

A. What steps should an aspiring forensic psychologist take to build a successful career in the field?

B. Reflect on your own career goals in forensic psychology and outline a plan for achieving them, including any additional education or specialization you might pursue.

Section 8: Reflection and Personal Growth

15. Personal Insights

A. Reflect on how your understanding of forensic psychology has evolved throughout this book.

B. How has this knowledge influenced your perspective on crime, justice, and the role of psychology in the legal system?

16. Commitment to Lifelong Learning

A. Why is lifelong learning important in the field of forensic psychology?

B. Identify areas where you would like to continue developing your knowledge and skills, and outline a plan for ongoing professional development.

Scoring and Reflection

After completing the quiz, take time to review your answers. Reflect on areas where you felt confident and those where you encountered challenges. Use this self-assessment to identify topics for further study and to reinforce the knowledge you've gained. Remember, the goal of this quiz is not just to test your knowledge but to encourage deeper reflection and ongoing growth in your journey as a forensic psychologist.

Chapter 13 Review

Chapter 13 of *HowExpert Guide to Forensic Psychology* serves as a culminating reflection on the key concepts, future directions, and personal growth experienced throughout the book. This chapter encapsulates the essence of what it means to be a forensic psychologist, emphasizing the importance of both theoretical knowledge and practical application. The chapter is structured into four key sections:

- 13.1 Summary of Key Takeaways

- Foundational Knowledge: This section revisits the essential concepts explored throughout the book, from the historical evolution of forensic psychology to the theoretical frameworks that guide the understanding of criminal behavior. It highlights the critical role that forensic psychologists play in the legal system, bridging the gap between psychology and law.

- Ethical Considerations: The section underscores the importance of navigating ethical dilemmas with integrity. It stresses the necessity of maintaining confidentiality, objectivity, and adherence to professional guidelines, ensuring that forensic psychologists uphold the highest ethical standards in their practice.

- Practical Applications: Through case studies and real-world examples, the section illustrates how theoretical knowledge is applied in forensic settings. It emphasizes the impact of forensic psychology on legal outcomes and the importance of evidence-based practices in achieving successful interventions.

- 13.2 The Future of Forensic Psychology

- Technological Advancements: This section explores the potential impact of emerging technologies such as artificial intelligence, machine learning, and virtual reality on forensic psychology. It discusses how these innovations could enhance the accuracy of criminal profiling, psychological assessments, and interventions while also raising new ethical challenges.

- Evolving Legal and Ethical Standards: As forensic psychology continues to evolve, this section highlights the importance of staying informed about legal reforms and ethical considerations. It emphasizes the need for forensic psychologists to adapt to changes in the legal landscape and to engage with global standards and practices.

- 13.3 Reflection on Learning and Personal Growth

- Personal Insights: This section encourages readers to reflect on their journey through the book, considering how their understanding of forensic psychology has deepened and how they have grown personally and professionally. It prompts self-awareness about biases, ethical challenges, and the complexities of working within the legal system.

- Career Development: The section also addresses the importance of setting future goals, embracing lifelong learning, and continuing to develop skills and knowledge in the field. It provides guidance on how to build a successful career in forensic psychology, including the importance of specialization, certification, and ongoing professional development.

- 13.4 Comprehensive Self-Assessment Quiz

- Review and Reflection: The final section of the chapter offers a comprehensive self-assessment quiz designed to test the reader's knowledge and encourage deeper reflection on the material covered. This quiz serves as a tool for self-evaluation, helping readers to identify areas of strength and those that may require further study.

Chapter 13 not only consolidates the knowledge gained throughout the book but also inspires readers to continue their journey in forensic psychology with a clear understanding of the challenges and opportunities that lie ahead. The chapter serves as both a review and a forward-looking reflection, ensuring that readers are well-equipped to apply their knowledge in real-world contexts and to contribute meaningfully to the field of forensic psychology.

Appendices

The Appendices section of *HowExpert Guide to Forensic Psychology* provides valuable resources and tools to enhance your understanding and application of the material covered in the book. Whether you're seeking to clarify key terms, explore further reading, connect with professional networks, or access practical tools, these appendices are designed to support your continued learning and professional growth in forensic psychology. Below is a breakdown of each appendix and its contents:

Appendix A: Glossary of Key Terms from A to Z

This glossary provides a comprehensive A to Z list of key terms and concepts used throughout *HowExpert Guide to Forensic Psychology*. It is designed as a quick reference to clarify terminology and ensure a deeper understanding of the specialized language within forensic psychology.

- **A**

  - Assessment: The systematic evaluation of an individual's psychological state, often using standardized tools, to determine mental health, competency, or risk factors in legal cases.

  - Antisocial Personality Disorder (ASPD): A mental disorder characterized by a pervasive disregard for, and violation of, the rights of others, often linked with criminal behavior.

- **B**

  - Behavioral Profiling: A method used to infer characteristics of criminals based on crime scene analysis, patterns of behavior, and psychological traits.

  - Biopsychosocial Model: An approach that considers biological, psychological, and social factors in understanding human behavior, particularly in the context of criminal actions.

- C

- Competency to Stand Trial: A legal determination that a defendant has the mental capacity to understand the charges against them and participate in their defense.

- Criminal Responsibility: The determination of whether a person can be held legally accountable for their actions, often influenced by psychological assessments.

- D

- Diagnostic and Statistical Manual of Mental Disorders (DSM-5): The standard classification of mental disorders used by mental health professionals, including forensic psychologists, to diagnose psychological conditions.

- Diminished Capacity: A legal defense that argues a defendant should not be held fully criminally responsible for their actions due to impaired mental function.

- E

- Expert Witness: A professional, such as a forensic psychologist, who provides testimony in court based on their expertise in a particular field, often regarding psychological assessments or behavior.

- Eyewitness Testimony: A legal term referring to the account a witness gives in the courtroom, describing what they observed during the commission of a crime.

- F

- Forensic Psychology: The application of psychological principles and methods to legal issues, including criminal investigations, legal proceedings, and correctional settings.

- Fitness to Plead: An assessment of whether a defendant is mentally capable of entering a plea and understanding the legal process.

- G

- Guilty but Mentally Ill (GBMI): A verdict in which a defendant is found guilty of a crime but is also recognized as having been mentally ill at the time of the offense, often resulting in both punishment and treatment.

- General Deterrence: The concept that punishing one individual for a crime can deter others from committing similar offenses.

- H

- Homicidal Ideation: Thoughts or fantasies about committing murder, which are often assessed in forensic psychology to determine risk and intent.

- Heuristics: Cognitive shortcuts or rules of thumb used to make decisions quickly; relevant in forensic psychology for understanding how people make judgments in legal contexts.

- I

- Insanity Defense: A legal defense that argues a defendant was not responsible for their actions due to a severe mental disorder that impaired their understanding of right and wrong.

- Intellectual Disability: A condition characterized by significant limitations in both intellectual functioning and adaptive behavior, relevant in legal contexts involving competency and responsibility.

- J

- Juvenile Delinquency: The involvement of minors in illegal activities, often treated differently in the legal system with a focus on rehabilitation.

- Judicial Discretion: The authority of judges to make decisions based on their judgment and interpretation of the law, sometimes influenced by psychological evaluations.

- K

- Kleptomania: A psychological disorder characterized by a compulsive urge to steal, often considered in legal cases involving theft.

- Kin Selection: An evolutionary theory suggesting individuals are more likely to help those who are genetically related, occasionally relevant in cases involving familial relationships.

- L

- Locus of Control: A psychological concept referring to how strongly individuals believe they have control over the events that affect their lives, which can impact legal judgments.

- Legal Insanity: A legal standard used to determine whether a defendant was incapable of understanding the nature of their actions due to a mental disorder.

- M

- Mens Rea: A legal term meaning "guilty mind," referring to the mental state of a person while committing a crime, crucial for determining criminal responsibility.

- Mitigation: The process of presenting evidence or arguments to reduce the severity of punishment in a legal case, often involving psychological assessments.

- N

- Not Guilty by Reason of Insanity (NGRI): A verdict where a defendant is found not guilty due to insanity, leading to mental health treatment rather than incarceration.

- Neuropsychological Assessment: An evaluation of cognitive, behavioral, and emotional functioning using standardized tests, often used in forensic contexts to assess brain injury or dysfunction.

- O

- Offender Profiling: The practice of identifying the characteristics of a criminal based on crime scene analysis and psychological insights, used in criminal investigations.

- Obsessive-Compulsive Disorder (OCD): A mental health disorder involving unwanted repetitive thoughts (obsessions) and actions (compulsions), sometimes relevant in legal cases involving compulsive behavior.

- P

- Psychopathy: A personality disorder marked by persistent antisocial behavior, lack of empathy, and egotistical traits, often studied in the context of criminal behavior.

- Paraphilia: A condition involving abnormal sexual desires that may involve extreme or dangerous activities, relevant in forensic cases involving sexual offenses.

- Q

- Qualified Immunity: A legal doctrine that protects government officials from liability for civil damages, provided their actions did not violate clearly established rights.

- Quantitative Analysis: The use of statistical methods to analyze data, commonly used in forensic psychology research to identify patterns in criminal behavior and assessments.

- R

- Recidivism: The tendency of a convicted criminal to reoffend, a key focus in forensic psychology for developing effective rehabilitation strategies.

- Risk Assessment: The evaluation of the potential risk an individual poses to themselves or others, often used to inform decisions in sentencing, parole, and treatment.

- S

- Sociopathy: A term often used interchangeably with psychopathy, though it generally emphasizes the role of environmental factors in antisocial behavior.

- Substance Abuse: The harmful use of substances like alcohol or drugs, often contributing to criminal behavior and relevant in forensic assessments.

- T

- Testimony: A formal statement given by a witness under oath in court, where forensic psychologists may serve as expert witnesses.

- Trauma-Informed Care: An approach that recognizes the impact of trauma on an individual's mental health, crucial in forensic settings for both victims and offenders.

- U

- Underreporting: The failure to report or the minimization of certain behaviors or symptoms, a common issue in forensic assessments where individuals may downplay their actions.
- Unfit to Plead: A legal determination that a defendant is not mentally capable of understanding court proceedings or assisting in their defense.

- V

- Victimology: The study of victims and their interactions with offenders and the legal system, including the psychological effects of being a crime victim.
- Voluntary Manslaughter: A legal term for a killing that occurs in the "heat of passion" due to provocation, often involving psychological evaluation of the defendant's state of mind.

- W

- Witness Credibility: The evaluation of a witness's reliability and trustworthiness, often assessed by forensic psychologists during legal proceedings.
- Weapons Effect: A psychological phenomenon where the presence of a weapon increases aggressive behavior, relevant in cases involving violent crimes.

- X

- XYY Syndrome: A genetic condition in which a male has an extra Y chromosome, historically (though controversially) linked to increased aggression, though not widely accepted as a cause of criminal behavior.

- Y

- Youth Offenders: Individuals under the age of 18 who commit crimes, often treated with a focus on rehabilitation rather than punishment in the legal system.

- Yerkes-Dodson Law: A psychological principle suggesting that performance increases with arousal to a point, but beyond that point, performance decreases, sometimes relevant in forensic assessments of stress-related behavior.

- Z

- Zero Tolerance: A policy that enforces strict punishment for infractions of a stated rule, often without consideration for individual circumstances, and occasionally relevant in discussions of juvenile justice and school policies.

Appendix B: Recommended Reading and Resources

This appendix offers a curated selection of books, articles, journals, and online resources to further enhance your understanding and expertise in forensic psychology. Whether you're a student, a practitioner, or simply interested in the field, these materials will provide valuable insights and keep you informed about the latest developments and best practices in forensic psychology.

1. Foundational Books

- Forensic Psychology: A Very Short Introduction by David Canter

- This concise introduction covers the essential concepts of forensic psychology, including its history, key principles, and applications within the legal system. It's an excellent starting point for those new to the field.

- Introduction to Forensic Psychology: Research and Application by Curt R. Bartol and Anne M. Bartol

- A comprehensive textbook that provides an in-depth look at the application of psychological principles in legal contexts. It includes topics such as criminal behavior, psychological assessment, and the role of forensic psychologists in court.

- The Psychology of Criminal Conduct by D.A. Andrews and James Bonta

  - This book explores the psychological factors that contribute to criminal behavior, offering a thorough analysis of the theories and research that inform forensic psychology practices.

2. *Specialized Topics*

- Criminal Profiling: An Introduction to Behavioral Evidence Analysis by Brent E. Turvey

  - A detailed guide to the techniques and methods used in criminal profiling, this book is particularly valuable for those interested in the investigative aspects of forensic psychology.

- The Psychopath Whisperer: The Science of Those Without Conscience by Kent A. Kiehl

  - An exploration of psychopathy, offering insights into the scientific understanding of this personality disorder and its implications in criminal behavior.

- Forensic Psychology and Law by Ronald Roesch, Stephen D. Hart, and James R.P. Ogloff

  - This resource bridges the gap between psychology and law, providing practical guidance on how psychological principles are applied in legal settings, including competency evaluations, insanity defenses, and risk assessment.

3. Key Journals

- Law and Human Behavior

- The official journal of the American Psychology-Law Society (AP-LS), featuring empirical studies, reviews, and theoretical articles on the intersection of psychology and law. A must-read for those engaged in forensic psychology research.

- Journal of Forensic Psychology Practice

- Focused on the practical application of forensic psychology, this journal provides articles on assessment techniques, intervention strategies, and the role of psychologists in legal contexts.

- Behavioral Sciences & the Law

- A multidisciplinary journal that publishes research and analysis on the intersection of behavioral sciences and the legal system, including topics related to forensic psychology, criminal justice, and legal decision-making.

4. Online Resources

- American Psychological Association (APA) Division 41: American Psychology-Law Society

- The APA's Division 41 offers a wide range of resources, including publications, conferences, and continuing education opportunities for those interested in the intersection of psychology and law. The website is a valuable hub for forensic psychology professionals.

- The Forensic Panel

- An expert organization providing resources on forensic psychology, psychiatry, and related fields. Their website includes case studies, expert opinions, and updates on the latest developments in forensic sciences.

- Psychology Today: Forensic Psychology Blog

- A blog offering articles and insights from experts in forensic psychology. It covers current issues, case studies, and practical advice for professionals in the field.

5. Continuing Education and Training

- Association for Psychological Science (APS) Forensic Psychology Workshops

- APS offers workshops and training sessions on various aspects of forensic psychology, providing opportunities for continuing education and professional development.

- National Register of Health Service Psychologists Continuing Education (CE) Programs

- The National Register offers CE programs specifically tailored for forensic psychologists, covering topics such as ethics, assessment, and courtroom testimony.

This recommended reading and resources list is designed to support your ongoing learning and professional development in forensic psychology. Whether you're looking to deepen your understanding of key concepts or stay updated on the latest research, these materials will serve as valuable tools in your educational and professional journey.

Appendix C: Professional Associations and Networks

Joining professional associations and networks is essential for staying connected with the latest developments in forensic psychology, expanding your professional network, and accessing valuable resources. This appendix lists key organizations and networks that offer opportunities for continuing education, professional development, and collaboration within the field of forensic psychology.

1. American Psychological Association (APA) - Division 41: American Psychology-Law Society (AP-LS)

- Overview: APA Division 41 is dedicated to the intersection of psychology and law. The AP-LS provides a platform for professionals interested in the study and application of psychology within the legal system.

- Benefits: Members gain access to a wealth of resources, including scholarly journals, newsletters, conferences, and continuing education opportunities. AP-LS also provides networking opportunities with other professionals in the field.

- Website: www.apadivisions.org/division-41

2. International Association for Correctional and Forensic Psychology (IACFP)

- Overview: IACFP is an organization that promotes the development of forensic psychology and correctional psychology through research, education, and practice.

- Benefits: Membership offers access to the *Journal of Forensic Psychology Practice*, educational webinars, conferences, and a global network of professionals in correctional and forensic psychology.

- Website: www.ia4cfp.org

3. Association for Psychological Science (APS) - Forensic Psychology Section

- Overview: APS is a leading international organization dedicated to advancing scientific psychology across various disciplines, including forensic psychology.

- Benefits: Members of the Forensic Psychology Section have access to cutting-edge research, annual conventions, workshops, and online resources tailored to forensic psychology professionals.

- Website: www.psychologicalscience.org

4. Society for Police and Criminal Psychology (SPCP)

- Overview: SPCP focuses on the application of psychological principles to law enforcement and criminal justice. It serves professionals in law enforcement, corrections, academia, and related fields.

- Benefits: Membership provides access to the *Journal of Police and Criminal Psychology*, annual conferences, and opportunities for collaboration with professionals in law enforcement and criminal justice.

- Website: www.policepsych.com

5. National Register of Health Service Psychologists

- Overview: The National Register is a nonprofit organization that credentials health service psychologists, including those specializing in forensic psychology, and provides resources for professional development.

- Benefits: Membership includes access to continuing education programs, a professional credentialing directory, and resources tailored to psychologists in clinical and forensic settings.

- Website: www.nationalregister.org

6. European Association of Psychology and Law (EAPL)

- Overview: EAPL is an organization that promotes the exchange of research and practice in the areas of psychology and law across Europe and beyond.

- Benefits: Members have access to conferences, publications, and networking opportunities with professionals across Europe interested in the interplay between psychology and law.

- Website: www.eapl.eu

7. British Psychological Society (BPS) - Division of Forensic Psychology (DFP)

- Overview: The DFP within the British Psychological Society is a leading organization for forensic psychologists in the UK, promoting excellence in practice, research, and education.

- Benefits: Membership offers access to the *Journal of Forensic Practice*, professional guidelines, conferences, and a network of forensic psychology professionals across the UK.

- Website: www.bps.org.uk/member-microsites/division-forensic-psychology

8. Australian Psychological Society (APS) - College of Forensic Psychologists

- Overview: The College of Forensic Psychologists is part of the APS, providing support and resources to forensic psychologists in Australia.

- Benefits: Membership includes access to professional development programs, a peer-reviewed journal, and opportunities to connect with forensic psychology professionals across Australia.

- Website: www.psychology.org.au

These professional associations and networks provide essential resources, support, and opportunities for forensic psychologists at all stages of their careers.

Whether you are seeking to enhance your expertise, engage with the latest research, or connect with peers, joining one or more of these organizations can significantly benefit your professional journey in forensic psychology.

Appendix D: Sample Tools and Assessment Forms

This appendix provides examples of essential tools and assessment forms commonly used in forensic psychology. These samples are designed to give you a practical understanding of the methodologies and instruments forensic psychologists use in various legal and clinical settings. The tools included here are valuable for conducting psychological assessments, evaluations, and forensic investigations.

1. Competency to Stand Trial Assessment Form

- Purpose: This form is used to evaluate whether a defendant has the mental capacity to understand the charges against them and assist in their defense.

- Components:

  - Mental State Evaluation: Includes questions to assess the defendant's current mental health status, including any signs of mental illness or cognitive impairment.

  - Understanding of Legal Proceedings: Evaluates the defendant's knowledge of the legal system, their role in the trial, and the potential consequences of the trial.

  - Ability to Communicate with Counsel: Assesses the defendant's capacity to effectively communicate with their attorney and participate in their defense strategy.

2. Risk Assessment Tool

- Purpose: This tool is used to evaluate the likelihood that an individual poses a risk of harm to themselves or others, which is crucial in sentencing, parole decisions, and treatment planning.

- Components:

  - Historical Factors: Includes a review of past behaviors, such as previous violent incidents, criminal history, and any history of substance abuse.

  - Clinical Factors: Evaluates current mental health status, including the presence of psychopathy, impulsivity, or other relevant psychological disorders.

  - Contextual Factors: Assesses the individual's environment, support systems, and any situational stressors that may influence their behavior.

3. Insanity Defense Evaluation Form

- Purpose: This form is used to determine whether a defendant was legally insane at the time of committing a crime, meaning they were unable to understand the nature or wrongfulness of their actions due to a severe mental disorder.

- Components:

  - Mental Health History: A detailed examination of the defendant's psychiatric history, including diagnoses, treatments, and any previous hospitalizations.

  - Mental State at the Time of the Offense: Questions designed to assess the defendant's mental state during the time of the crime, including their ability to distinguish right from wrong.

  - Collateral Information: Includes input from family members, medical records, and any eyewitness accounts that can provide insight into the defendant's mental condition at the time of the offense.

4. Juvenile Delinquency Assessment Form

- Purpose: This form is specifically designed for evaluating minors who have committed criminal offenses, focusing on their developmental stage and potential for rehabilitation.

- Components:

  - Developmental History: Includes questions about the juvenile's upbringing, family dynamics, educational background, and any history of trauma or abuse.

- Psychological Evaluation: Assesses the minor's mental health status, cognitive development, and any behavioral issues that may have contributed to delinquent behavior.

- Rehabilitation Potential: Evaluates the likelihood that the juvenile can be successfully rehabilitated through intervention programs, counseling, or other supportive measures.

5. *Victim Impact Statement Form*

- Purpose: This form is used to document the psychological and emotional effects of a crime on its victim(s), often presented during sentencing to inform the court of the crime's impact.

- Components:

- Emotional and Psychological Impact: Questions that assess the emotional and psychological toll the crime has taken on the victim, including symptoms of anxiety, depression, or PTSD.

- Physical and Financial Impact: Evaluates any physical injuries sustained and the financial burden resulting from the crime, such as medical bills or loss of income.

- Victim's Perspective: Provides space for the victim to express how the crime has affected their life and what they believe the appropriate legal outcome should be.

6. *Forensic Interview Checklist*

- Purpose: This checklist guides forensic psychologists through the process of conducting interviews with suspects, witnesses, or victims in a legal context.

- Components:

- Preparation: Steps to prepare for the interview, including reviewing case files, setting objectives, and establishing rapport with the interviewee.

- Interview Techniques: Tips on effective questioning strategies, managing interviewee stress, and ensuring that the interview remains unbiased and objective.

- Post-Interview Evaluation: Guidelines for evaluating the information gathered during the interview, including assessing the reliability and consistency of the interviewee's responses.

These sample tools and assessment forms are invaluable for forensic psychologists working in various legal contexts. They provide structured methods for conducting thorough and objective assessments, ensuring that psychological evaluations are accurate and legally sound. While these samples are illustrative, it is important to adapt them to specific cases and legal requirements, as well as to stay informed about best practices and updates in the field.

Appendix E: Additional Online Learning Resources

In the rapidly evolving field of forensic psychology, staying current with the latest research, methodologies, and legal practices is essential. This appendix provides a list of online resources that offer continuing education, professional development, and up-to-date information on various aspects of forensic psychology. These resources are ideal for students, practitioners, and anyone interested in deepening their understanding of the field.

1. Coursera - Forensic Psychology Courses

- Overview: Coursera offers a range of online courses from top universities and institutions on forensic psychology topics, including criminal behavior, psychological assessments, and the intersection of law and psychology.

- Key Features: Courses are typically self-paced, allowing you to learn at your own speed. Many courses offer certificates upon completion, which can enhance your professional credentials.

- Website: [Coursera Forensic Psychology Courses](https://www.coursera.org/courses?query=forensic%20psychology)

2. edX - Psychology and Law Courses

- Overview: edX provides access to courses from universities worldwide, covering various topics related to psychology and law, including forensic psychology, criminal justice, and ethics.

- Key Features: Courses are available for free with the option to purchase certificates. The platform offers a mix of beginner and advanced courses to suit different levels of expertise.

- Website: [edX Psychology and Law Courses](https://www.edx.org/learn/psychology)

3. American Psychological Association (APA) - Continuing Education

- Overview: The APA offers a wide range of online continuing education (CE) courses specifically tailored for psychologists, including topics in forensic psychology, ethics, and legal issues.

- Key Features: Courses are designed by experts in the field and are APA-approved for CE credits, making them ideal for licensed professionals seeking to maintain their credentials.

- Website: [APA Continuing Education](https://www.apa.org/ed/ce/online)

4. OpenLearn - Forensic Psychology Free Courses

- Overview: OpenLearn, provided by The Open University, offers free courses on forensic psychology. These courses cover topics such as criminal behavior, the role of forensic psychologists, and psychological assessments.

- Key Features: The courses are entirely free and accessible to anyone interested in learning about forensic psychology. They provide a solid introduction to key concepts and practices in the field.

- Website: [OpenLearn Forensic Psychology](https://www.open.edu/openlearn/society-politics-law/forensic-psychology/content-section-overview)

5. Psychology Tools - Forensic Psychology Resources

- Overview: Psychology Tools offers a variety of downloadable resources, including worksheets, assessment tools, and educational materials relevant to forensic psychology.

- Key Features: The resources are designed for use by practitioners in clinical and forensic settings. Many materials are available for free, while others require a subscription.

- Website: [Psychology Tools](https://www.psychologytools.com/forensic-psychology/)

6. The Forensic Examiner - Online Articles and Publications

- Overview: The Forensic Examiner is a publication of the American College of Forensic Examiners International (ACFEI). It offers articles, case studies, and research papers on forensic psychology and related disciplines.

- Key Features: The online platform provides access to a wealth of knowledge from experienced forensic professionals, offering insights into current trends and best practices in forensic psychology.

- Website: [The Forensic Examiner](https://www.acfei.com/forensic-examiner/)

7. YouTube - Forensic Psychology Channels

- Overview: YouTube hosts a variety of channels dedicated to forensic psychology, where experts share their knowledge through lectures, case studies, and educational videos.

- Key Features: Content is freely accessible and covers a broad spectrum of topics, from criminal profiling to courtroom psychology. Some popular channels include *Dr. Grande* and *Psychology In Seattle*.

- Website: [YouTube Forensic Psychology](https://www.youtube.com/results?search_query=forensic+psychology)

8. National Institute of Justice (NIJ) - Forensic Science Webinars

- Overview: The NIJ offers webinars and online training sessions on forensic science and forensic psychology topics, including the latest research and technological advancements in the field.

- Key Features: The webinars are designed for professionals working in forensic science and criminal justice, providing insights into contemporary challenges and innovations.

- Website: [NIJ Forensic Science Webinars](https://nij.ojp.gov/events/webinars)

These additional online learning resources provide a wealth of opportunities to enhance your knowledge and skills in forensic psychology. Whether you're looking for structured courses, practical tools, or the latest research, these resources will help you stay informed and advance your career in this dynamic field.

About the Author

HowExpert publishes how to guides on all topics from A to Z. Visit HowExpert.com to learn more.

About the Publisher

Byungjoon "BJ" Min is an author, publisher, entrepreneur, and the founder of HowExpert. He started off as a once broke convenience store clerk to eventually becoming a fulltime internet marketer and finding his niche in publishing. He is the founder and publisher of HowExpert where the mission is to discover, empower, and maximize everyday people's talents to ultimately make a positive impact in the world for all topics from A to Z. Visit BJMin.com and HowExpert.com to learn more. John 14:6

Recommended Resources

- HowExpert.com – How To Guides on All Topics from A to Z by Everyday Experts.
- HowExpert.com/free – Free HowExpert Email Newsletter.
- HowExpert.com/books – HowExpert Books
- HowExpert.com/courses – HowExpert Courses
- HowExpert.com/clothing – HowExpert Clothing
- HowExpert.com/membership – HowExpert Membership Site
- HowExpert.com/affiliates – HowExpert Affiliate Program
- HowExpert.com/jobs – HowExpert Jobs
- HowExpert.com/writers – Write About Your #1 Passion/Knowledge/Expertise & Become a HowExpert Author.
- HowExpert.com/resources – Additional HowExpert Recommended Resources
- YouTube.com/HowExpert – Subscribe to HowExpert YouTube.
- Instagram.com/HowExpert – Follow HowExpert on Instagram.
- Facebook.com/HowExpert – Follow HowExpert on Facebook.
- TikTok.com/@HowExpert – Follow HowExpert on TikTok.

Made in the USA
Monee, IL
17 November 2024